HOW TO

GO FROM BEING A

GOOD EVANGELICAL

TO A COMMITTED CATHOLIC

IN NINETY-FIVE

DIFFICULT STEPS

HOW TO
GO FROM BEING A
Good Evangelical
TO A Committed Catholic
IN NINETY-FIVE
DIFFICULT STEPS

CHRISTIAN **SMITH**

 CASCADE *Books* · Eugene, Oregon

How to Go From Being a Good Evangelical to a Committed Catholic in Ninety-Five Difficult Steps

Cascade Books
An Imprint of Wipf and Stock Publishers
199 W. 8th Ave., Suite 3
Eugene, OR 97401

www.wipfandstock.com

ISBN 13: 978-1-61097-033-4

Cataloging-in-Publication data:

Smith, Christian, 1960–

    How to go from being a good evangelical to a committed Catholic in ninety-five difficult steps / Christian Smith.

    viii + 206 p. ; 23 cm. — Includes bibliographical references and index.

    ISBN 13: 978-1-61097-033-4

    1. Catholic Church—Relations—Evangelicalism. 2. Evangelicalism—Relations—Catholic Church. I. Title.

BX4668 S55 2011

Manufactured in the U.S.A.

Contents

Acknowledgments

I am greatly indebted to Kari Christoffersen for her excellent research assistance digging up original versions of sixteenth-century Reformation texts through multiple library systems in the U.S. and Europe; and to Brad Gregory for his professional expertise in helping to translate those texts. I am grateful to Skip Smith, Andrew Casad, Jim Heft, Brad Gregory, Trish Herzog, Hilary Davidson, Katie Spencer, Nicole Garnett, Rick Garnett, Betsy Stokes, Emily Smith, Mark Regnerus, Dan Philpott, Todd Granger, Justin Farrell, John Barger, John Jones, Stan Gaede, Brandon and Claire Vaidyanathan, Will Gwaltney, Scott Hahn, Brian Brock, Jeremy Uecker, Lynn Baker, and Francis Beckwith for reading chapters of earlier versions of my manuscript and providing thoughtful and helpful feedback. I am thankful for the help they provided, though, as one must always say, none of them is responsible for any possible problems or errors in what follows. Thanks, finally, to Charlie Collier of Wipf and Stock/Cascade for his interest in and editorial help in publishing this book, which few Catholic presses would know how to market well and few evangelical presses would be interested in publishing.

Luther's emphasis is a corrective.
But, a corrective made into the normative, into the sum total,
is eo ispso [by that very fact] confusing in another generation
(when that for which it was a corrective does not exist).
And with every generation that goes by in this way, it must
become worse, until the end result is that this corrective,
which has independently established itself, produces characteristics
exactly the opposite of the original. And this has been the case.
Luther's corrective, when it independently is supposed to be
the sum total of Christianity, produces the most refined kind of
skepticism and paganism.

—Søren Kierkegaard, Danish Lutheran, 1854[1]

Catholicism is, at least in the West, the default position.
Rome has a better claim to historical continuity and institutional unity
than any Protestant denomination, let alone the strange hybrid
that is evangelicalism; in light of these facts, therefore, we need a good,
solid reason for not being Catholic; not being Catholic should,
in other words, be a positive act of will and commitment, something that
we need to get out of bed detemined to do each and every day.

—Carl Trueman, Westminster Theological Seminary[2]

Is the Reformation over?
—Mark Noll, University of Notre Dame[3]

1. Kierkegaard, "Luther's Emphasis," in *Søren Kierkegaard's Journals and Papers*, 333.
2. Trueman, *Minority Report*, 99.
3. Noll and Nystrom, *Is the Reformation Over?*

Introduction

Like many evangelicals of my generation, I was raised in a church environment that assumed Roman Catholics were not real Christians and so most likely were not going to heaven. That was because Catholics did not believe in the Bible, worshipped Mary, and believed in salvation by their own good works. Real Christians who were going to heaven were evangelical Protestants who believed the Bible, had the right theology, and trusted in Jesus alone for salvation. When Catholics died they would surely find out the hard way that their church was wrong and my kind of church was right. The truth of all of that was of course very clear in the Bible for anyone who would simply read it—but Catholics, apparently, did not or would not read the Bible. So a good part of our job was to stand firm against the errors of Catholicism (and, of course, liberal Protestantism).[1]

Two of my best neighborhood friends growing up—Steven and Nicky—were Italian Catholics. Their parents were first-generation emigrants into the suburbs from the crowded row houses of South Philadelphia. Years we spent together playing in the creek and swinging on the rope swing, building tree forts and riding bikes, playing tackle football and shooting BB guns. Their dads were blue collar workers, and their living-room couches had transparent vinyl slip-covers. My dad was a professional engineer, and our couch's slip covers were blue cloth. But that didn't matter. We grew up together in what was a wonderfully fun boyhood of freedom and adventure. The fact that my church said that Steven and Nicky were probably going to hell because they were Catholic was

1. Many evangelicals younger than I am, I realize, probably grew up in more accepting environments when it came to Catholicism; the evangelical subculture has been softening up since the 1960s and 70s.

1

never a problem for me. On Sunday mornings, they had their world and I had mine. The only other time their Catholicism crossed my path was when we spent all our saved-up allowance money at the annual carnival held on the parking lot of the Our Lady of Good Council Church. The rest of our time we were busy with rafts to build and dead squirrels to skin.

On April 24, 2010, my wife, Emily, and I were received into the full communion of the Catholic Church in the Log Chapel of the University of Notre Dame. It was a wonderful event for all who took part. We could not be happier to have joined the Church. Our final resolution to become Catholic, which had remained up in the air for years, was a great joy. After years of discernment, involving countless hours of reading, thinking, talking, listening, and praying, when we finally made the decision, everything became clear and confident. Although we had struggled for years for clarity on the matter, once we made up our minds, the idea of doing or being anything else made no sense. Catholicism was obvious.

Emily and I both hold only the deepest appreciation for the spiritual and faith formation and doctrinal training that we enjoyed growing up as evangelicals. None of our four parents were born into Christian homes. All four became Christians as children or young adults through the outreach efforts of evangelical Bible studies and Sunday schools in the 1940s and 50s—and to those who reached out to them we are eternally grateful. Most in our families remain evangelicals, and we love them all very much. Emily and I both grew up attending a Reformed evangelical Christian school and are the beneficiaries of fine educations received at Gordon College and Wheaton College, which formed us intellectually and relationally in some very positive and important ways, for which we are also thankful. We have many friends and acquaintances who are committed evangelicals who are among the finest people one might have the pleasure of knowing. We hold many evangelical churches, organizations, and parachurch ministries in very high regard. And we continue to believe that evangelicalism comprises certain powerful elements of truth and excellent proclivities of thought and life.

Nevertheless, despite our upbringing and many positive experiences in evangelicalism, we eventually both concluded that the evangelical tradition did not ultimately make sense, even on its own terms, that it could not live up to its own claim to truth, and was not a version of church in which we could continue. We became Catholic, then, by carefully considered conviction.

We are not alone in that. Many evangelicals have become Catholic and today continue to become Catholic. What is going on? What does it take for that to happen? How does a good evangelical become Catholic?

About This Book

I never thought I would write a "How To" book. I am a professional sociologist who writes scholarly books and articles. And yet here is a book with my name on the cover and "How To" in the title. And "How To" is really what this book is about. It is not a theological treatise, nor an apologetic argument for Catholicism. It is not an autobiography, although my own and my wife's experiences inform what follows. It is not primarily sociology, even though I am a sociologist. This book is not a systematic analysis of the biblical passages or doctrinal ideas relevant to evangelicalism and Catholicism. It is none of those things. Instead, this book simply offers some "How To"-do-something advice for those readers who may want to become Catholic.

That means that this book has a specific audience. It is written for American evangelical Protestants who for whatever reasons are intrigued enough to be open to the possibility or may be even actively contemplating the idea of becoming Catholic. That also means that this book is *not* particularly intended for other audiences. It is not written, for example, for people who are not committed to Christian faith. You have to be a serious Christian first for any of the following to make sense. Nor is this book written for those who are not open to doing what the "How To" of this book is written to help readers do. Evangelicals who cannot entertain the possibility that Catholicism has something good and true to offer might as well read something else more edifying to them. This book is for American evangelicals who find themselves somewhere between the sense that Catholicism is intriguing and those who are well on their way to reception into the Catholic Church. I hope it helps all of them to sort out their lives of faith and to move in good directions.

One more clarification about my intended audience. There are two kinds of "How To" books. One is for people who have already committed to doing something and simply need to be shown how to do it. *How to Build a Deck* might be an example. The second kind of "How To" book is for people who are *still trying to decide whether they even can and want to do* the thing that the book tells about. Part of the purpose of reading this second kind of book is precisely to help decide about doing it. An example of that kind of book might be *How to Get "Off the Grid" with Solar, Wind, and Other Alternative Energy Sources for Your House.* Doing what the book tells how to do would be a major project involving a lot of investment. So people read the book in part to learn what is involved, as part of the process of possibly committing to doing it.

The book in your hand is the second kind of "How To" book. I do not presume that the reader has already committed to becoming Catholic. I only assume that he or she is somewhere between curious-about and very-interested-in becoming Catholic. The reader may want to become Catholic, but is not yet sure about it. Part of the function of this book, then, is to lay out what for many are the typical issues, reasons, and steps involved in becoming Catholic—precisely in order to help readers discern whether they are really ready to make that change in their lives.

Despite that, at times the book may read like the first kind of "How To" book, as if the reader has already decided to become Catholic and simply needs to be told how. But many of the 95 steps prescribed below turn out to be not as simple as digging postholes and sawing lumber to build a deck. Evangelicals becoming Catholic involves a personal discernment process. And that means that each person involved might decide in the end to become or not to become Catholic. Furthermore, different readers will come to this book at different stages of their discernment processes. I have written it as if all readers are starting from the beginning, although I know they are not. But I am confident that all readers will be able to see how the book fits their own personal situation and so will know where and how to engage in the steps below.

Unlike many "How To" books, this one does not promise that the recommended steps will be easy or simple. In fact, many will be difficult. Shifting from being evangelical to Catholic is no small thing. Most people starting off as good evangelical Protestants find the road to Catholicism—for all of its rewards and sense of rightness—to be long, laborious, and often fraught with troubles. Among other problems involved, one usually encounters any number of friends, family members, and acquaintances who simply cannot begin to understand why one would become Catholic. Not having undergone their own "paradigm shift" on the matter, which I describe below, the very idea seems insane, not much different from becoming Mormon or a Jehovah's Witness. And that can be an unpleasant situation with which to have to deal. The book's title therefore is frank in its full disclosure: going from evangelical to Catholic is probably not going to be easy, but rather difficult. (Then again, whoever said Christian life lived as faithfully as one knows how would be easy?)

I have attached numbers to my "How To" instructions below because there are many of them and "How To" books often number their steps. The numbered steps in this book tend to progress in clusters, in the experience of many who have trod this path, in rough chronological order as proposed. Certain typical concerns and understandings do tend to come before others in this process for a lot of people. But obviously the numbered steps need not be followed in a sequential, linear order. Readers are free to rearrange the order or skip steps as it happens to work for them. The paths through which we understand God moving in people's lives can vary greatly. While there is often a broad typical pattern, there clearly is no formula. Some evangelicals come into Catholicism through paths quite different from the kind I outline below.[2] So, while I offer the following in hope that it will help many, I do not pretend to claim that it is the main or only way for evangelicals to become Catholic.

Paradigm Revolution as this Book's Organizing Framework

Most evangelicals who become Catholic do not simply find out some new information, change their minds as a consequence, and then join the Catholic Church. The change is usually more complex and profound than that. It is more like what I am calling here a "paradigm revolution." Perhaps you have heard that term before. It means a basic reorientation of assumptions, perceptions, and concerns that changes the way one views and lives life. For you to become Catholic will likely require a revolution in your Christian paradigm, not simply a change of affiliation. It will mean a big shift from your current evangelical paradigm to a new Catholic paradigm.

The best way to understand the kind of change I am talking about here is to refer to the model of how science develops that was proposed by an historian of science named Thomas Kuhn. I spell out Kuhn's theory in more detail in the appendix, but for readers less interested in such theory I summarize the essential points here. In his famous 1962 book,

---

2. Some, for example, "feel" their way into the Church through intuition, aesthetics, and ineffable experience, rather than taking the more reasoned, ideas-centered path I describe in this book.

The Structure of Scientific Revolutions, Kuhn observed that scientific development and change often does not actually take place in a gradual, incremental, and continuous way. Big scientific advances often do not happen by adding more bits of research findings to established bodies of scientific knowledge.

Instead, Kuhn says, scientific development and change happens dramatically, through revolutions. In those scientific revolutions, entire established research programs are overturned and replaced by upstart programs that seem to explain the observed world better. Kuhn calls those research programs "paradigms." When scientific paradigms go about their normal business of conducting scientific research, Kuhn calls that "normal science." But one established scientific paradigm being overturned by a rival paradigm is a "paradigm revolution." Your becoming Catholic will be something like that—your "normal-science" evangelical paradigm will be challenged and overturned by the alternative Catholic paradigm.

But how and why do paradigm revolutions occur? Kuhn says this happens when established paradigms become increasingly unable to explain new observations. Kuhn calls these observed facts for which an established paradigm cannot account "anomalies." Sometimes then a different paradigm comes along which does a better job of both explaining the anomalies and conducting the science in which the original paradigm was engaged. That leads to paradigm shifts.

Established paradigms of course do their best to ignore and explain away anomalies. But sometimes the anomalies become too many to handle. When too many anomalies accumulate, some of the adherents of an established paradigm begin to doubt its validity and so may be thrown into a "paradigm crisis." Those are the people who are primed for a paradigm revolution. All they need is to encounter an alternative paradigm that promises to do the work of science better than the previous paradigm does. Then the "ah-ha" light goes on and the paradigm revolution is underway.

In a paradigm revolution, the old paradigm is displaced, scientists increasingly embrace the better-explaining paradigm, and a new program of scientific research that is governed by different assumptions and concerns is set into motion. Scientists then go to work to develop and consolidate the new paradigm and explore all the new scientific knowledge it can help to generate.

Kuhn points to a number of historical cases in order to illustrate this model of scientific change. One is the sixteenth and seventeenth century shift away from an earth-centered ("geocentric" or Ptolemaic) paradigm of astronomy and to the sun-centered ("heliocentric" or Copernican) paradigm championed by Galileo. That shift—which told scientists to assume that the sun, not the earth, is the center of our planetary system—required a veritable *revolution* in outlook, evidence, and explanation—an often mind-blowing reorientation to thinking and seeing. Your becoming Catholic will likely involve something like that.

There are many strong parallels between Thomas Kuhn's theory about scientific change through paradigm revolutions and your possible shift from evangelicalism to Catholicism. I therefore use Kuhn's theory as the organizing framework for the ideas of this book. So, to understand what comes in the following chapters, you'll need to be somewhat familiar with Kuhn's basic concepts and arguments.

The appendix describes Kuhn's approach in greater depth, for those who want to go there. I recommend it. Meanwhile, at the very least, what all readers need to make sense of the following chapters is a basic grasp of the meaning of the terms "paradigm," "normal science," "anomalies," "paradigm crisis," and "paradigm revolution." Again, to summarize, "paradigms" tell people what matters, what to look for, and how to explain things in life. "Normal science" is the routine activity that people conduct within the logic and outlook of a given paradigm. "Anomalies" are facts or observations that do not fit into paradigms, that a paradigm cannot explain. A "crisis" happens when people who have taken an established paradigm for granted begin to doubt it and look for a better alternative paradigm. And a "paradigm revolution" is the fundamental shift in presuppositions, interests, and explanations that takes place when people move out of an old paradigm and into a new one.

And If the "How To" Doesn't Work?

What about evangelicals who read this book and decide that they should not or cannot become Catholic? That, of course, is their just prerogative by virtue of—from the Catholic point of view—their God-given birth-right of individual conscience[3] and of the American political system's

---

3. The Catholic *Catechism*, for instance, teaches this: "2106. Nobody may be forced to act against his convictions, nor is anyone to be restrained from acting in accordance with

guarantee of religious freedom. God bless them. Nobody should become Catholic who is not persuaded by Catholicism. In fact, Catholicism will not *allow* anyone to become Catholic who is not persuaded by its truth and does not affirm those beliefs proclaimed to be divinely revealed.

(Of course, persuasiveness itself does not make anything true. Not becoming Catholic could be the wrong thing to do. Becoming Catholic could also be wrong. If everyone absolutely knew and agreed about one or the other of these possibilities, then there would be no need for this book. But all people do not know and agree. Many hold different beliefs. Hence, searching people should try to discern as best as they can. And, in that, in the end persuasion is all that any of us ever has to go by, thankfully. When all is said and done, we all need to trust that God's grace is bigger than our puny capacity to discern and know what is true—which it surely is.)

Evangelicals who remain unpersuaded about becoming Catholic shouldn't become Catholic. And then? They will remain—from the Catholic perspective—as "separated brothers and sisters," to be treated "with respect and affection as brothers [and sisters]" and as "brothers [and sisters] in the Lord." They will be viewed as not guilty of the sins of schism and disunity committed by past generations of both Catholic and Protestant Christians. They will be seen as living as fellow Christian believers in a state of "real" though "imperfect" communion with the Catholic Church, which recognizes many elements of truth and sanctification in non-Catholic churches, brought about by the genuine working of the Holy Spirit in them, which lead to the salvation of many people through them.[4]

---

his conscience in religious matters in private or in public, alone or in association with others, within due limits. This right is based on the very nature of the human person, whose dignity enables him freely to assent to the divine truth which transcends the temporal order. For this reason it continues to exist even in those who do not live up to their obligation of seeking the truth and adhering to it. 2107. If because of the circumstances of a particular people special civil recognition is given to one religious community in the constitutional organization of a state, the right of all citizens and religious communities to religious freedom must be recognized and respected as well. 2108. The right to religious liberty is . . . a natural right of the human person to civil liberty . . . . This natural right ought to be acknowledged in the juridical order of society in such a way that it constitutes a civil right." Also see the Second Vatican Council's (Vatican II) "Decree on Religious Liberty," *Dignitas Humanae*.

4. See point #86 for the full text.

Not bad treatment—coming from a faith tradition that claims to be the Church in which the fullness of Christian truth subsists. Considering that not too many centuries ago Catholics and Protestants were killing and being killed by each other, things have happily come a long way. Even so, the question of truth remains.

A Note on Terminology

Two phrases commonly used to designate becoming Catholic are "swimming the Tiber" and "returning to Rome."[5] These are fine, but not my preferred way of describing the matter in question. I have zero problems with Rome, the pope, or the Vatican per se. But for present purposes it is important to realize that Catholicism is an immense, global church with varying expressions in every country it inhabits. What will matter most in the routine lives of evangelicals who become Catholic will not be the waters of the Tiber or the grandeur of Rome but ordinary life in their local parishes and dioceses. One's priest and bishop will be as or more important than the pope when it comes to most practical matters of faith and life in the Church.

Descriptors that focus on Rome and the Tiber I think also needlessly play into the hands of Catholicism's ill-informed antagonists, in ways that may distort, in the minds of those discerning these issues, the nature of what they are doing. Catholicism's Protestant adversaries, I have observed, tend to harp on the matter of *Rome*. They rarely say or write simply "Catholic" or "Catholicism." It is always *Roman* Catholic and *Roman* Catholicism—even though Catholicism does not routinely use that language of itself. I suspect they think that by shoving *Rome* in people's faces they will both highlight the obvious deplorability of papal primacy and rescue themselves as legitimate, (small-"o") orthodox, (small-"c") catholics, among all professed Christians, in their own right.

Let them. Arguing such terminology will never change their minds. And thankfully there are fewer such Protestant antagonists around these days. What matters more for present purposes is that evangelical converts to Catholicism should not, as a result of that kind of rhetorical behavior,

---

5. Many speak of the matter as a "conversion." But, to be precise, the Catholic Church does not consider Protestants becoming Catholic to be a matter of conversion, but rather of "being received into the full communion of the Church." When it comes to conversion, Catholicism rightly speaks of conversion *to Christ*, not the Church.

accept the premise that what matters most about Catholicism is that it is *Roman*. Again, Rome, the pope, and the Vatican have their essential and important place. But that is not as "corporate headquarters" of a "Catholic denomination," but rather to unify and serve the Church Catholic, the reality lived out around the world. That is worth keeping in perspective.

I also worry a bit in all of this that, for all of the standard associations of apostasy and error that "Rome" evokes for some Protestants, the same "Rome" may stir up unduly romanticized visions among evangelicals who are contemplating "swimming the Tiber." Becoming Catholic, we must remember, is not primarily a matter of venturing off "to Rome" to soak up the splendor of Saint Peter's Basilica, the wonder of the ancient Catacombs, the endless memorials to Christian martyrs, and the like. All of that is good and fine, as long as it is not turned into some kind of "Catholic Disneyland." But Rome is not ultimately what Catholicism is about.

Becoming Catholic is primarily a matter of learning to live out from and carry on the daily life of the Church, as received from the apostles, in one's own local context—in different parts of the world, in various and sundry circumstances, in the hum-drum of ordinary life, and faithfully, in whatever culture and society is one's own. Rome is certainly an indispensible, authoritative sign of Christian communion, a testimony and instrument of the authentic catholicity of the believers and churches which stand in full communion with her. But Rome is not everything. Rome is one thing in one place—as central, indispensible, and valuable as it is. The Catholic Church, by contrast, is nearly everywhere, doing lots of things, in various ways.[6]

It is upon the Catholic Church in the places where "converts to Rome" will actually live their daily lives as Christians that I think those discerning becoming Catholic ought to be primarily focused. It is from that perspective that the true meaning and importance of Rome can be properly understood and not unduly romanticized.

---

6. The Catholic Church is typically viewed by outsiders as a single, hierarchical body radiating throughout the world from its center in Rome. That view is not incorrect. But it is also truth that the Catholic Church is an assembly of thousands of distinct dioceses spread throughout the world that are united through the bonds of mutual communion, especially as embodied through their full communion with the bishop of Rome and all bishops throughout the world. It is the latter view, which sees one diocese and parish as one's true local home, which I wish to emphasize to evangelicals considering any "return to Rome."

What Follows

The next chapter briefly describes the typical starting point of American evangelicalism, from which many readers will be working. This, following Kuhn's terminology, is the "normal science" mode of assuming, seeing, thinking, and explaining that takes place in the standard evangelical paradigm. Although the details will vary with each reader, what I describe will be for many readers the baseline position from which possible moves toward Catholicism will take place.

Chapter 2 begins to lay out some specific initial steps recommended to American evangelicals who might consider or perhaps are considering becoming Catholic. Those steps consist of taking note of a number of "anomalies," to use Kuhn's terms, which do not seem to fit into or be explained well by the established evangelical paradigm. Simply following the steps proposed in chapter 2 will do nothing itself to make anyone Catholic. Lots of evangelicals are "on to" the kinds of anomalies suggested there and figure out various ways to deal with them. But it's a start. To keep moving forward, chapter 3 proposes even more—and more serious—anomalies that evangelicalism has greater difficulty explaining away. By the time readers have experienced the anomalies offered in these chapters, evangelicalism will have begun to look more tenuous and the Catholic alternative might start to begin to make sense.

Chapters 4 and 5 then shifts to the level of "revolutionary science," to use Kuhn's phrase again. Readers who get to that stage should start to feel the old paradigm falling apart and an alternative paradigm beginning to seem plausible, if not sensible. Here is where the focus starts to shift away from problems within evangelicalism and toward the compelling and sense-making nature of Catholicism. Once the vision of revolutionary science is grasped, it is often difficult to revert to and remain satisfied with the old paradigm.

Finally, chapter 6 proposes the kind of last steps needed to solidify the move from evangelicalism to Catholicism. Once one has worked through the "revolutionary science" of the matter, described in chapters 4 and 5, one still needs to consolidate the new presuppositions, questions, outlook, understandings, beliefs, and explanations in the Catholic paradigm that one has embraced—or, perhaps more accurately, by which one has been embraced. Chapter 6 proposes the kinds of steps needed to accomplish that solidification and consolidation.

In the end, readers who have completed the proposed 95 difficult steps will have undergone a process that leads many evangelicals who have done so, perhaps even you, to become Catholic. Nothing is guaranteed, of course, despite what some "How To" books claim, and I cannot offer your money back. But following the 95 steps proposed below is something like what very many American evangelicals have done to become Catholic. So it is a pretty good way to get the goal of this book accomplished, if that is what by reading it you discern that you should do.

Two Last Words

First, nothing in what follows suggests or should be interpreted to be saying that evangelicals are bad, dumb, or insincere people. Very much the contrary is true. American evangelicals are, on the whole, very impressive and likable people. Evangelicals are among some of the most serious, committed, sincere Christians I know. Some evangelicals with whom I have the privilege to be friends and acquaintances are incredibly smart and insightful people who do good things for God's kingdom. And I remain very impressed with the excellent work in which some evangelical para-church ministries, such as World Vision, are engaged.

Furthermore, nothing in what follows suggests or should be interpreted to be claiming that evangelicalism as a religious tradition is worthless, bankrupt, or not to be taken seriously. I do not think that at all. The following chapters do imply and state various criticisms of evangelicalism, offered in the service of those who want to consider becoming Catholic. But, even so, I think it is important to recognize the crucial role that evangelicalism has rendered American Protestantism in struggling to keep something like a doctrinally orthodox faith alive in face of the threats of Enlightenment skepticism and theological modernism during the late nineteenth and the twentieth century. I, for one, am deeply impressed, when I study the history, by the immense difficulty of that challenge and the sincere efforts made by the countless evangelicals (and, we must admit, fundamentalists) to address it faithfully (as they understood that) and sometimes smartly.

Any informed observer must also acknowledge that much of American Protestantism, especially evangelicalism, is particularly strong in many areas where American Catholicism is often comparatively weak. For example, significant sectors of Protestantism, particularly evangeli-

calism, enjoy relatively stronger participation of laity in church, knowledge of the Bible and sometimes even theology by church members, lay
hospitality, strong practices of financial giving, and relatively effective
church and parachurch ministries to children and youth. Protestantism
has also historically been and remains an important force in the world
for religious freedom and modern democracy. All of that is to be com-
mended (even if it does not justify Protestant evangelicalism per se),
and needs to be brought into the Catholic Church for Christian unity to
be made more perfect.

So, the criticisms in what follows are not directed at evangelical
people. Nor are they meant to dishonor the good that evangelicalism as
a movement has accomplished in the past. Rather, the criticisms in what
follows concern many of the deep presuppositions and current practices
of evangelicalism as a subculture. Despite all that is also good in evangelicalism, some of its presuppositions and practices are problematic. And
they cannot be evaded. Simply being in the evangelical subculture means
one has to deal with their influence. If we grant evangelicalism's presuppositions and beliefs as true, then there is not a lot to argue about. My
contentions below instead concern some of evangelicalism's very prem-
ises, and the problematic ways that they play out in evangelical belief and
practice. But in the end, in any case, there is no need for anyone to take
this personally. Again, what matters is not what we are attached to or the
particulars of our biographies, but what is good, right, and true.

Second, although I reiterate this point about process later in this
book, it is well worth stating now, up front, as well: as you focus on your
discernment of the possibility of becoming Catholic, be patient. Give
yourself time. Try to restrain yourself from making premature, seemingly-self-assuring declarations either for or against Catholicism. See how it
turns out in the end. Eventually, you will be in a position to make definitive statements. But don't rush them in the meantime.

one

Normal Evangelicalism

What does normal American evangelicalism look like? What are the baseline assumptions, questions, and concerns of evangelicals? What are the identities, activities, artifacts, and associations that comprise the subcultural starting point for many of the readers of this book—perhaps including you? Many evangelicals are familiar enough with their own subculture. But a few pages describing it will help to set the stage for the transitions that follow.

American evangelicalism is a complicated thing. If you are an evangelical, you are a child of the sixteenth century Reformation, European pietism movements of the seventeenth and eighteenth centuries, American Puritanism of the seventeenth and eighteenth centuries, the First Great Awakening of the eighteenth century, the Second Great Awakening of the nineteenth century, the missionary movements of the nineteenth and twentieth centuries, and the fundamentalist-modernist controversy (on the fundamentalist side) of the twentieth century. You may also be an heir of the charismatic movement of the late-twentieth century or the Pentecostal movement of the same century.

Denominationally, you may be Baptist, Presbyterian, Wesleyan, Pentecostal, Holiness, Christian Reformed, Free Church, Brethren, Missionary, Mennonite, or from one of a host of other denominational types. You may belong to a pocket of evangelicals found among United Methodists, Episcopalians, or other mainline Protestant churches. Or you belong to an independent, non-denominational, community, or Bible church.

Theologically, as an evangelical you believe in the Bible as God's only revelation of truth. You probably believe the Bible to be "inerrant." You believe all Christians should read the Bible regularly and obey its teachings. You haven't thought much about where the Bible actually came from historically—it's just always been there. You also believe a gospel message teaching that only those who choose a personal faith in Jesus Christ can be saved from their sins and go to heaven. Faith in Christ is a personal matter that must be embraced, sustained, and made subjectively meaningful through various practices, such as prayer, devotional readings, and "quiet time."

Everyone needs a "personal relationship with Jesus Christ." That means "accepting Jesus Christ as Lord and Savior." Nobody is born into faith or inherits salvation. Each individual must consciously and willfully choose to believe in Jesus (though Calvinist evangelicals who believe in a certain version of predestination would modify this language). Therefore, you believe in—or at least know that you are supposed to believe in—working for the faith conversion of other people who do not yet believe, so that they too can go to heaven. That includes children raised by evangelicals, who need in due time to make their own personal profession of faith. You also believe that Christians should be active in the world, persistently mobilizing resources, movements, and activities to carry out works of ministry, service, and evangelism. Being a Christian means bringing light to spiritual darkness, resisting evil social trends, relieving suffering, and caring for the needy.

Normal-science evangelicalism means you go to your local church every week and attend a Sunday school class. You are also likely involved in a "small group," which meets regularly for fellowship, prayer, and support. You may be in a Bible study or other prayer group. And you are probably involved in some other ministry or activity connected to your church, such as teaching Sunday school, volunteering for nursery, helping with vacation Bible school, or attending a men's prayer breakfast or missions support group. You do your part to sing well in church, and perhaps even occasionally take notes on sermons or Christian education lessons.

Institutionally, you are connected in some ways to at least a few of the institutions that knit together the evangelical world. In high school, you may have been part of Fellowship of Christian Athletes, Youth for Christ, or Young Life. You were probably also in your church's youth group. In college, it might have been Campus Crusade for Christ,

InterVarsity Christian Fellowship, Reformed University Fellowship, or the Navigators—especially if you went to a secular college or state university. Colleges and universities directly connected to your evangelical world include Wheaton, Calvin, Gordon, Westmont, Bethel, Houghton, Asbury, Messiah, Taylor, Greenville, Trinity, Covenant, Eastern, Dordt, Malone, Seattle Pacific, Azusa-Pacific, the various Nazarene and Wesleyan colleges, and any number of other schools in the Council for Christian Colleges and Universities. You also likely have some connection to one or more other parachurch organizations, such as Athletes in Action, Back to the Bible, Ligonier Ministries, Focus on the Family, Promise Keepers, or Teen Mania Ministries. You may send money to support the good work of World Vision, Compassion International, World Relief, or the Mennonite Central Committee.

You know what L'Abri and Urbana mean. You know who John Stott, Chuck Swindoll, Chuck Colson, and Francis Schaeffer are. You have at least heard of Gordon-Conwell Seminary, Fuller Seminary, and Trinity Evangelical Divinity School. You have books on your shelves published by Zondervan, Baker, InterVarsity Press, Eerdmans, Moody, Thomas Nelson, or Crossway. You know that "The Vineyard" is not something about grape arbors. You know that YWAM is not a word in Arabic or Nepalese. You know something about the "church growth movement." You have an opinion about the "emergent church" movement. You are amused but also curious when you hear about a "Toronto Blessing" and its reported "holy laughter." You have read *Christianity Today* and maybe *Charisma, Moody Monthly*, or *World* magazines. You may also subscribe to *Books & Culture, Men of Integrity*, or *Today's Christian Woman*.

As a good evangelical, you know a lot of hymns to sing in church, but you also know at least some "praise and worship" songs. You can carry your own on "How Great Thou Art" as well as "Shout to the Lord" and "Better is One Day." If you're the kind of person who pays attention, you know the names Chris Tomlin, Stuart Townend, and Keith Getty. If you dislike praise choruses, you at least try to tolerate them. If you like praise and worship songs, you probably have a CD or two of them to listen to in the car or the kitchen. You also likely have CDs by musicians like Jars of Clay, Casting Crowns, Michael W. Smith, Jeremy Camp, Michael Card, and Third Day. If you're cool, you have Switchfoot, Skillet, Tobymac, or Relient K. If you're not, you have The Gaithers. If you're old enough, you might have vinyl records of Keith Green, Randy Stonehill,

Second Chapter of Acts, and late-1970s Bob Dylan collecting dust in your closet. If you are younger or have kids of your own, you or they have watched a bunch of *Veggie Tales* videos or DVDs and listened to hours of "Adventures in Odyssey."

The homes of other evangelicals you visit for dinner, small group, or Bible study have religious items on display. One near the front entry says, "As for Me and My House, We Will Serve the Lord." On the kitchen counter sits a "Names of Jesus Stones" plaque, in which "Bread of Life," "I Am," "Emmanuel" and other named stones are set around the "Jesus" stone at the center. A "Trust in the Lord" magnet holds up coupons on the fridge. Or hanging nearby may be an "Amazing Grace" hand towel. In the family room you may find a "Lion and Lamb" tapestry, or a three piece carved teak saying, "Love," "Hope," and "Pray." A "God's Love" candle orb sits on the coffee table, alongside a copy of John Eldredge's *Wild at Heart* or maybe Bruce Wilkinson's *The Prayer of Jabez*. A "Footprints" throw might be tossed across the couch. "Love Never Fails" may be calligraphied on the dining room wall clock face. In the living room, a plaque declares, "I Know the Plans," "God Answers Prayer," "Trust in the Lord," "God Keeps His Promises," "Sing Unto the Lord," or "Great is Thy Faithfulness." The artwork may include baby footprints, butterflies, Celtic crosses, a trio of running horses, Washington's prayer at Valley Forge, or soft lithographs of pastoral scenes or lighthouses overlooking beaches. Out in the garage, above the work bench, you may find a "Serve the Lord" tire clock. In the guest bathroom, you might spot "The Serenity Prayer" or a "Friends in Christ" angel. Inside the kids' bedrooms "God Created Everything" and "Jesus Loves Me" nightlights glow. Curious, you poke your head into the master bedroom. "A Woman Who Fears the Lord" music box may sit on the dresser, next to a pewter "As You Live on in Heaven" framing the photo of a smiling, deceased parent.[1]

When running errands at the area mall or shopping center, you stop into the Christian bookstore. You purposefully ignore the large section across from the cash register displaying the kind of plaques, figurines, needlepoint, graduation gifts, garden stepping-stones, wind chimes, jewelry, ball ornaments, magnets, tea sets, Bible covers, Holy Land gifts, home accents, and other collectables and kitsch that you saw at the house

---

1. Of course Catholics have plenty of kitsch too, but, as we will see below, they at least have an explicit theological rationale for how and why visible "sacramentals" strengthen faith.

you visited. You probably have a particular interest in theology, biblical studies, or ethics, so you head there. You wonder why those sections are so small and why some books have been put there. Is Lee Strobel's *The Case for Christ* really theology? Or John MacArthur's *Terrorism, Jihad, and the Bible* really Christian ethics? You browse. The music section has a Christian/secular music-comparisons display. If you like Goo Goo Dolls, consider Newsboys. If you like Counting Crows, consider Jennifer Knapp.[2] And so on. You don't like the idea of Christian music simply replicating secular equivalents and markets.

The Bibles section is huge—there is a Bible packaged for every evangelical demographic type imaginable. You didn't know there was an NIV compact Thinline bride's Bible in bonded white imitation leather, or a NKJV Life Principles Daily Bible for Working Women. You notice that *Every Man's Battle* has spun-off versions for *Every Single Man's Battle, Every Young Man's Battle, Every Man's Marriage, Every Man's Challenge, Preparing Your Son For Every Man's Battle, Every Woman's Battle, Every Single Woman's Battle, Every Young Woman's Battle, Every Woman's Marriage,* and *Preparing Your Daughter for Every Woman's Battle*—in paperback, audio CD, and downloads, with related workbooks, accompanying versions of the Bible, "Promise Books," and Bible studies, to help with *Discovering God's Plan for Sexual and Emotional Fulfillment* and *Igniting the Joy and Passion You Both Desire*. You start to feel overwhelmed. The young-Amish-women romance novel series, Resurrection Easter Egg sets, "Guitar Praise: Solid Rock" on CD-ROM software, I-Can-Do-All-Things canvas tote bags, and the rest are starting to get to you. You head out and catch lunch at Chick-fil-A.

When it comes to your broad religious identity, whether you think about it much or not, as an evangelical you have been defined by your subculture as being *not* Catholic, in fact, as being against Catholicism. Catholics are off-base on lots of issues and not very serious about their faith. You are also against Protestant liberalism. That is what took over most mainline denominations decades ago, corrupted doctrine and churches, and pushed evangelicals out into their own smaller denominations and independent churches. They've got it really screwed up. Your evangelical identity has also been defined since the 1970s as against "secular humanism." These are the people who don't believe in God, who

2. This one will quickly be changed, however, as Knapp recently came out as a lesbian.

have lots of power in American institutions and culture, and who are trying to purge religious influences from America.

Finally, you are against Christian fundamentalists. These are your crazy faith-cousins who are well meaning but who wear crew cuts, are afraid of teens holding hands, insist on the King James Bible, won't touch a drop of beer, and think everyone but their own kind are going to hell. Fundamentalists embarrass you, partly because they are such close "relatives" in the Christian family, too close for comfort. Their strident narrowness also spoils evangelicalism's public image, which seeks to make being a Christian look appealing and relevant to unbelievers. Plus, fundamentalist separatism does not know how to enjoy the good things in life, like nice furniture, prestigious college degrees, a glass of wine, and the occasional R-rated movie at the theater. These, then, are your out-groups: Catholics, liberal Protestants, secular humanists, and fundamentalists. You, by comparison, live your life on the more reasonable and faithful grounds of evangelicalism.

You find yourself negotiating a middle position between Christians who are either too conservative or too loosey-goosy for you. Bob Jones University is always fun to dump on. So are formerly Protestant colleges that have been secularized. People who believe in gay rights and abortion rights you cannot agree with, but Christians who picket abortion clinics make you uncomfortable. Christians who are into "Meet Me at the Flagpole" and "True Love Waits" may be too zealous for your taste. But single Christians you may know who are sleeping together are self-centered and hypocritical. Leaders like Jerry Falwell and Pat Robertson are not your cup of tea. But you are probably not ready to jump on board with Ron Sider or Jim Wallis either. By your lights, some dispensationalist or hyper-Calvinist authors and seminaries are too narrow or extreme. But rumors you heard about postmodernist funny business at places like Regent College in Vancouver or the Institute for Christian Studies in Toronto make you wonder as well.

Christians who write books about the next military-political crisis in the Middle East being foretold by the Book of Revelation and signaling the end of the world you think are ridiculous. But you also question scholars who seem to suggest that not everything the Bible describes necessarily really happened in history as possibly soft on inerrancy. You are annoyed by patriotic Christians who mindlessly wrap the Bible in the American flag. You also think the absolute separation of church and state is probably a bad idea. You wish that most televangelists would just get off of TV. Some of the shows on secular cable television, however, you suspect would be worth censoring. You have heard of some hip evangelical churches that turn their services into rock concerts or whose sermons contain blunt talk about hot-button issues—they make you worry the church is accommodating to culture. But you also want church services and programs to be vibrant, alive, and "relevant" to the culture. You are not confused or duplicitous in any of this. You are simply trying to strike a smart middle ground between the extremes that is reasonable, balanced, and attractive to outsiders.

And what is church? Church is any local community of Christians who share the same beliefs in Jesus and who get together to worship, fellowship, and learn. Where two or three are gathered, Jesus is with them. Churches are formed by people who agree to become churches and to meet together. They are collections of individuals who have chosen the same path of faith. They raise their own money, hire their own pastors, decide on their own building campaigns, and choose their own missionaries and ministries to support.

You may believe that individual congregations can stand on their own, independently, as self-contained churches. Or you may believe that individual churches should band together into like-minded denominations, associations, or conventions by state or regionally or nationally. But you tolerate people who "feel differently" about such matters. Different Christians, after all, have lots of different views of very many such issues. What matters is that evangelicals hold together on the core essentials of faith and work, despite their other differences, in effective coalitions of witness, ministry, and mission.

You have done some church shopping. Having looked around at different churches to see which one best fits your needs, interests, and tastes, you have ended up at one with which you are fairly happy. It is not perfect. But you like the music well enough and the preaching is pretty good. It helps too that you have friends there. It is a good community. If you ever move away from your current home, you will take a good while to check out all of the church possibilities in your new area. It is important to find the right one. And if too much were to change at your current church, you might start looking elsewhere again.

People around you and maybe you yourself pray with a lot of particular, but by now so-familiar-that-they-usually-go-unnoticed, phrases, such as, "Father God," "we would lift up," "I just have a heart for," "as unto the Lord," "knit our hearts together," "we are convicted," "if it be your will," "pray a 'hedge' around," and "in Jesus' name." About 10–20 percent of the words used in the informal prayers of more than a few of the people around you consist of the one word "just"—as in, "Lord, we just ask that you just give us the eyes just to see you, Lord." Your community believes in praying authentic, spontaneous, personal prayers—not rote, ritualistic, formal, dusty, traditional prayers. It once occurred to you, however, that most people's spontaneous, personal prayers sound an awful lot alike. They actually seem to follow standard formats. You yourself wish you could be a better pray-er—and might have some books on your shelf about improving your prayer life—but you usually fall back into your old habits and familiar prayer wordings.

As to the teachings of Scripture, when Jesus in the Bible says that the apostle Peter is the rock upon which he will build his church, you know perfectly well that what he meant by "rock" was only Peter's *confession* of Christ as the Messiah, not Peter as an apostolic leader. When Jesus says, "This is my body, this is my blood," you know he is only using a figure of speech. When the Bible hails Jesus' mother, Mary, as "full of grace" and says that "all generations will count [her] blessed," you know, without even having to think, to not pay much attention.

When you confess that you believe in "one, holy, catholic, and apostolic church" (if you are into such creedal statements), you know that "catholic" there only means "universal," that is, all true Christians from all times and places. You also know that "apostolic" means nothing more than faithful to the teachings of the apostles as recorded in the New Testament. When Paul's second letter to the Thessalonians instructs believers to "hold firm to the traditions which you were taught . . . by word of mouth," you know that that could not mean that Christians today should pay attention to church traditions, since traditions are human and prone to error and even Jesus condemned them.

You have learned all of this instinctive knowledge about correct Bible interpretation from teachers, preachers, parents, and books you've read. It all makes sense. The Bible is pretty clear to those who read it with good intentions. Those who disagree, like Catholics, are simply not interpreting the Bible correctly. They probably have too much at stake in defending their long-held beliefs.

Not only are you against the alleged authority of tradition, for the reasons just noted, you in fact are also suspicious of any Christian leader or institution which claims to have authority. Authority means power, and power means power-*over*. And that means abusive constraints on free, individual conscience and judgment. Christ has authority. The Bible is an authority. Other than that, the rest of us are simply followers. And Christians have been set free by Christ, we are free from human rules and authorities. Legalism of any kind is a real problem.

Every Christian is a saint, nobody is special, not even clergy. Church authority and saints and priests and the like, you semi-consciously associate with the Dark Ages, a time of religious oppression and human misery. How the true gospel survived such a bleak epoch is hardly imaginable, not that you think about it much. You get a better feeling when you think about the Enlightenment brought by the Reformation, the reestablishment of the true church, and perhaps the rise of modern democracy and capitalist prosperity that somehow seems to be associated with that. You are not big into the "Christian America" mantra, but you certainly appreciate the individual religious liberties that America guarantees.

So, what then are your tasks in life? What is your mission? Well, lots of things. Live a clean life. Get married and have a nice family. Don't have marital problems or get divorced. Don't curse or smoke. Pay your taxes. You might drink alcohol, but not too much. Be loving and forgiving. Live with the kind of visible integrity that will be a good "witness" to those around you. Try to be as successful in society as you can—Jesus, after all, has nothing against success, and Christians need to get into more positions of social influence where they can be "salt and light." The suburbs are a good place to live. Look for opportunities to share your faith, maybe invite someone to church, serve perhaps on a short-term missions trip or evangelism project. Get involved in your church. Volunteer, support the programs, get to know people, maybe give money. If the occasion arises and you "feel called," maybe become part of a "church plant" team in a new neighborhood.

Read Christian books, enough at least to maintain your spiritual health and to not get out of touch with what's happening. Go to an occasional conference or seminar on worship or missions or how to have a good Christian family. Make sure your kids turn out good—no drugs, no drinking, no sex, no rebellion. Don't refuse any of life's blessings. God created the material world as good and wants us to enjoy it. Ideally you should tithe your money, though that's pretty hard to do. But as long as you give your part (more or less) back to God, and as long as you can afford it, it's also fine to enjoy nice homes, cars, clothes, vacations, whatever. In and through all that, though, you need to read your Bible, pray, perhaps have a regular "quiet time," get "plugged into" a "church body" or other fellowship group, have some kind of ministry you do or support, and generally let your light shine as a good witness to others. Maybe you have had a bumper sticker or Sign-of-the-Fish on your car, but maybe too you've decided you don't like that anymore.

In any case, all of this is not just about your little individual life. You are part of the kingdom of God. You belong to a larger movement of truth and right that is spreading the good news around the world and ministering to people's needs. Your life is connected to the historical and contemporary life and work of Bible translators laboring in foreign tribes, Christian ministers working in inner cities, faithful seminaries training the next generation of pastors, youth ministers working with troubled teens, Christ-based orphanages taking care of poor children, and advocates for religious freedom, the right to life, and development projects in poor countries around the world. Those are your kind of people.

You are in it together with the likes of Billy Graham, Rick Warren, Ravi Zacharias, Chuck Colson, maybe Josh McDowell, maybe James Dobson, and other important leaders who are doing the work of Christ in the world. Your life has historic and cosmic significance in the evangelical movement—made possible by evangelicalism's church and parachurch networks, ministries, campaigns, mobilizations, crusades, and media production capacities. In short, faith matters, church matters, life matters, you matter. Or at least you know they are supposed to matter.

This, or something like it, is your starting point. It is what Thomas Kuhn would call "normal science" in the established American evangelical Protestant paradigm.[3] It offers a fairly coherent outlook on faith and life that makes a lot of sense, when viewed from and lived within the paradigm. Most of the pieces hang together. The paradigm provides adequately compelling answers to critics. And it offers a vision for life and history that is compelling for many who live it.

---

3. I have played the description here straight. For a more humorous, satirical look at American evangelical subculture, written by an insider, see Kilpatrick, *Field Guide to Evangelicals.*

This paradigm fits well enough into mainstream American society, but not too, too comfortably. That would be a problem. It is important to "get out of your comfort zone" every now and then. This paradigm works particularly for people wanting to live a good life—in more than one sense of the word "good"—and especially those who want to have successful families.

So, once one has "bought into" this paradigm, whether through childhood socialization or a later conversion, there is not a lot that challenges or overturns it from the inside or the outside. Some sad cases crash on the rocks of disbelieving in Biblical inerrancy, going liberal, or perhaps going all the way into religious skepticism. Some others get badly burned in personal ways associated with faith or church that causes them to bail out of evangelicalism. A few others just don't care that much. But, overall, evangelicalism is pretty good at keeping its faithful and supporting a reasonably happy life.

How is it, then, that some evangelicals, perhaps even you, could end up becoming Catholic? What could possibly bring that about?

two

Accumulating Anomalies in Evangelicalism

If you, a good evangelical, want to become Catholic, you need first to start accumulating anomalies that do not fit your established evangelical paradigm. There are lots of them. Most likely the fact that you are even considering Catholicism enough to read this book means that you have noticed some or many of these anomalies already. But in what follows I assume the baseline of pure "normal science" evangelicalism described in the previous chapter. From there we begin to surface some of the anomalies that typically start evangelicals on the road to Catholicism.

Remember that the surfacing of anomalies is *not* about making *arguments* for and against. Anomalies are merely observations that somehow do not fit an established paradigm. They need not suggest any possible changes and are not decisive when it comes to any issue. Anomalies are usually readily dismissed, rationalized, or explained away by adherents of the reigning paradigm. The first steps toward becoming Catholic are therefore not posed as direct critiques or arguments against evangelicalism. They are literally only the sorts of observations and experiences that many evangelicals who may be on the road to Catholicism often seem to have. Here we go.

1. Begin to feel rootless. For most of your life, the evangelical world has felt a comfortable and secure place to you. You feel connected to a bigger truth and cause. You have God-inspired answers to life's questions in the Bible. You have some acquaintance with apologetics, so you can answer the typical questions thrown at Christianity by skeptics. You know about the Reformation and have been told that the Reformers reconnected the church to the true, faithful heritage of the early church.

For reasons that you cannot explain, however, you find yourself feeling a lack of roots. At first, this is not a conscious idea to be examined, but an intuitive sense that you can hardly name, much less explain. At times it strikes you out of the blue that something about your life in society and history feels increasingly shallow, somehow vulnerable. Some days you feel like an ant clinging to a leaf on the surface of a lake that is churning in a storm. The next day all is well. Sometime later you feel like a tree without a taproot that will shrivel up in a drought or be blown over by a storm. Much of the time, however, you don't feel that way and life goes on. But the feeling of rootlessness continues to come back and bother, maybe even haunt you.

The sensation is hard to describe, but somehow it feels like living on the edge, carrying a low balance in life's checking account, being stuck in the present. You find yourself vaguely longing for crazy things, like knowing your family history back into the Middle Ages or having a "people" of whom you are a real descendent. You might catch yourself somewhat admiring observant Jews or other people with strong ethnic heritages. The sensation, however, does not fit the evangelical paradigm, in which your faith is founded on the Bible and you are connected to the "true vine."

Do not run away from this nagging sense. Pursue it. Attend to it. Allow yourself to own it, to examine it. It is not crazy. There are good reasons for your feeling this way. This intuition is telling you something important. Something is missing. You need to find out what it is.

2. Start to notice church fragmentation and disunity. Until now you've never really noticed the extent to which the Christian church is divided or paid it much concern. God knows who his faithful are—and whoever they are comprise the true church. The unity of the church is in "the invisible church," all of the saints in all places and times, not the visible church. Either that or the unity the Bible talks about merely concerns members of specific congregations not fighting too much. Christians disagree about lots of things, but that is no big deal. Evangelicals, at least, pretty much all get along. Look at how well they cooperate in ministry and missions.

At some point, that view begins to fail you. Something or other hits you that makes you notice in a new way how thoroughly and deeply the visible Christian church is divided. And that starts to bother you. Scores of Bible passages calling for Christian unity and harmony and condemning church division and schism start coming to mind (e.g., Rom 15:5–6, 16:17; 1 Cor 1:10–13, 3:3–4, 11:18–19, 12:12–26; Eph 4:2; Phil 2:2,14, 4:1; 1Pet 3:8; 2 Tim 2:23–24). Think, for a most compelling example, of Christ's final prayer for unity among believers in John 17, just before he headed to Gethsemane. "May they be brought to complete unity, to let the world know that you sent me and have loved them even as you have loved me."

You know that many evangelicals who actually agree on most things theological seem content to remain separated in different denominations and independent churches. Why? The Reformers separating from a corrupt medieval Catholicism was one thing, you think, but literally thousands of different denominations is something else altogether. The uncomfortable idea arises that maybe the entire system of endless denominational and non-denominational churches is wrong, perhaps even sinful.[1] Maybe you are part of a sectarian order. Whatever happened to "one Lord, one faith, one baptism?"

You try to explain to yourself again why the fragmentation and disunity of the visible church is not a problem. That helps for a while. But you keep asking questions, and your explanations to yourself over time and those that others give you become less plausible. They begin to sound like special pleading and rationalizing. Still, you realize that they *have* to be true if the Protestant status quo is justifiable. But increasingly you wonder if the long section of "Churches" listed in the Yellow Pages is a real problem, if that somehow isn't a terrible witness against unity in Christ. Why should anyone believe the gospel of justification, reconciliation, and peace if the people who already believe and profess it can't get their act together enough to stop arguing and splitting off from each

---

1. There is much truth in Flannery O'Connor's satirization of the evangelical tendency toward private interpretation of Scripture in her novel, *Wise Blood*, in which the con-man street preacher, Onnie Jay, proclaims, "Now friends . . . I want to tell you a second reason why you can absolutely trust this church—it's based on the Bible. Yes, sir! It's based on your own personal interpitation of the Bible, friends. You can sit at home and interpit your own Bible however you feel in your heart it ought to be interpited. That's right . . . just the way Jesus would have done it" (152–53).

other? How could all of this division and disunity be honoring to God? And why does everyone else seem so complacent about it?

Those are great questions. Stop taking easy answers that letting divided Christianity off the hook. The more you tune into this problem, the more you'll notice it, and the more that you notice it, the more it will bother you. That's a good thing.

3. Notice the Bible's inability to settle matters in dispute. Once the previous anomaly lodges itself in your consciousness, this next one follows immediately. You, a good evangelical, believe that the Bible is a divinely-inspired and infallible authority for the faith and practice of the church. You surely believe in the Protestant idea of *sola Scriptura*—the Bible alone as the only authority. You also believe (whether you know the technical terminology or not) in the "perspicuity" of Scripture—namely, that the Bible is clear in its teachings so that even ordinary people can understand it well. No pope or other authorized teaching office of the church is needed to tell you what Scripture says. You know that when you want the final word of God on anything, you go to the Bible.

The obvious anomaly you run up against here is that lots of Christians believe the same as you about the Bible but, lo and behold, end up claiming that the Bible teaches very different and sometimes incompatible things on a host of primary matters. Though they all appeal to the same clear, lone authority, they come away from reading the apparently authorized Scripture believing it teaches a panoply of quite different things. The Bible, in fact, when you are honest, seems to give rise to a variety of different views on a host of different issues.[2] What's up with that?

This problem may strike you first about "the women's issue." Can women hold authority in church or not? Or it may hit you on other issues, like war and pacifism, predestination and free will, or church polity. In any case, the more you think about it, and the more you search for issues where Christians do *not* disagree on biblical grounds, the longer the list of biblical *dis*agreements grows. Let's see: views of baptism, the atonement, divorce and remarriage, the work of Christ, eternal security, the Lord's Supper, divine foreknowledge, the nature of revelation, charismatic gifts, the millennium, creationism and evolution, the rapture, church and state, the eternal fate of the unevangelized, divine providence, sanctification, hell, proper worship protocols, the role of "good works" in salvation, the fate of the Jews, the "headship" of husbands, Old Testament

2. See Smith, *Bible Made Impossible*.

law, the ethics of wealth, depravity and original sin, church discipline, birth control, tithing, alcohol, swearing oaths, and on and on. With each of these issues you know that there is an arguably good "biblical" basis for two or three positions. That is why sincere Christians believe them. These differences also seem to have a lot to do with the church conflicts and disunity noted above.

How can all this be, given your assumptions about the sufficiency, authority, and perspicuity of Scripture? Something must be wrong. But it is not clear what. You can't say that all but one of the parties on every issue in these disagreements reads the Bible in bad faith, or wants to believe falsehoods, or is just ignorant about biblical studies. Why then do so many people read the Bible in so many different ways?

Note that this problem of evangelical disunity started with the first generation of Protestant Reformers. They saw disagreements emerging quickly and tried, unsuccessfully, to contain them.[3] The Swiss Reformer, John Calvin, for example, wrote in a letter in 1552 to the Lutheran reformer, Philip Melanchthon, warning that:

> The eyes of many are turned upon us, so that the wicked take occasion from our dissensions to speak evil, and the weak are only perplexed by our unintelligible disputations. Nor, in truth, is it of little importance to prevent the suspicion of any difference having arisen between us from being handed down in any way to posterity; for it is worse than absurd that parties should be found disagreeing on the very principles, after we have been compelled to make our departure from the world. I know and confess, moreover, that we occupy widely different positions; still, because I am not ignorant of the place in his theatre to which God has elevated me, there is no reason for my concealing that our friendship could not be interrupted without great injury to the Church.[4]

Melanchthon's own concerns about such matters he expressed in a 1548 letter to the English reformer Thomas Cranmer. Referring to divisive disagreements among Reformation leaders over controversial issues, especially the Lord's Supper, Melanchthon confided, "There is nothing in this letter that I desire to make known except my grief, which is so great that it could not be drained even by a shedding of tears as abundant as

---

3. See Payton, *Getting the Reformation Wrong*, 98–115.
4. November 28, 1552. Quoted in Bonnet, *Letters of John Calvin*.

the water borne in the currents of our Elbe or those of your Thames."[5] Calvin's successor, Theodore Beza, later wrote: "On what point of religion do the churches which have declared war against the Roman Pontiff agree among themselves? If you run through them all, from head to foot, you will hardly find anything affirmed by one which is not immediately rejected as ungodly by the other."[6] Luther himself, looking back at the consequences of the Reformation one year before his death, observed with exasperation in a 1525 letter to fellow reformer Heinrich Zwingli:

> The tiresome devil begins to rage among the ungodly and to belch forth many wild and crazy beliefs and doctrines. This man will have nothing of baptism, that one denies the Sacrament, a third awaits another world between this and the Last Day; some teach that Christ is not God; some say this, some that, and there are as many sects and beliefs as there are heads; no peasant is so rude but that if he dreams or fancies something, it must in truth be the Holy Spirit which inspires him, and he himself must be a prophet.[7]

Indeed. The more things change . . .

Until now, you've looked at the different "biblical" views that Christians hold as an interesting study in theology, a natural part of church history that illuminates different understandings of doctrine. Perhaps you have read and enjoyed some of the many "Four Views of _____" books. But now the multiplicity of biblical views is starting to feel like a problem. You can't see how it does not contradict your basic assumptions about the Bible. If the Bible is such a sufficient, clear, single, and ultimate authority given by God to Christians, then why does it seem unable to settle so many matters of dispute that so divide Christians, including evangelicals?

5. Melanchthon, *Episolarum*. Lib. XI. No. 4142. Some translate this passage as follows: "The Elbe with all its waters could not furnish tears enough to weep over the miseries of the distracted reformation."

6. "*In quo tandem religionis capite congruunt inter se Ecclesiae quae Romano Pontifici bellum indixerunt? A capite ad calcem si percurras omnia, nihil propemodum reperias ab uno affirmari, quod alter statim non impium esse clamitet*" (Bèze, *Epistola I*).

7. Luther, "Letter to the Christians of Antwerp," in *Werke*, 547, Lines 26–34. Nor did Luther note the Reformation producing an increase of spiritual and social order: "Unfortunately, it is our daily experience that now under the [Protestant] Gospel the people entertain greater and bitterer hatred and envy and are worse with their avarice and money-grabbing than before under the Papacy"—quoted in Peters, *Scripture Alone?* 30–31.

Again, a very good question. You have noticed a huge vulnerability in an important part of the world that you have until now taken for granted as being solid. Do not sweep your questions under a rug. You are not crazy. These are real issues and major problems. You are not going to resolve them anytime soon. So get used to feeling uncomfortable for a while.

4. Start to grow weary of "meaningful" worship services. You've been to a lot of good church services with moving and powerful worship experiences. You know good worship from dragging or schmaltzy worship. You can tell talented worship leaders and musicians from those who lack talent. You're not into being "slain in the Spirit" by any means, but you know what it is like in worship to feel refreshed, blessed, spoken to, or moved. Those experiences have been very meaningful to you at times. So much so that you have sought them out. You have tried repeatedly to "enter into" worship in ways that will again evoke that kind of amazing meaning and power.

The problem is, sometimes you've felt some disquiet about it. You've worried at points that that kind of worship experience might be more a matter of you "whomphing" yourself up for it, than of God himself speaking or moving in it. At times you've felt self-conscious about your worship, as if somehow it is your job to generate some kind of special worshipful inner state. Sometimes it feels like you are trying too hard, or that the worship leader is trying too hard. On occasion, you've looked around and wondered whether the whole congregation is trying too hard.

Thinking that, you've felt like a sacrilegious cynic. But the thought has come back to you. Maybe some of this "meaningful" worship is really more about the subjective affective states of the worshippers than about their objective act of offering praise and reverence to God. Could this just be a lot of people blowing off emotional catharsis or just feeling good together?

You put that thought away. Then sometime later you realize that some people you know seem nearly addicted to finding out the next hot worship chorus so they can really get into it. Or they always seek to discover new contemporary music settings to the words of old hymns. Or perhaps it is only certain, recurrently emotionally moving hymns that you or others want to sing, not the full range of truth-packed possibilities. Then you start to wonder, what *is* worship anyway? What is this all about? And what do worship leaders, guitars, pianos, microphones, worship songs, praise choruses, ear monitors, and the subjective affective feelings that they can arouse in the worshippers have to do with worship at all? What does it mean when a powerful song that has in the past transported you to great heights of praise now feels routine and empty? Are you going nuts?

You're not going nuts. You're raising questions well worth asking. They may seem unbelieving, sacrilegious, or debunking. Sometimes that is exactly what's needed. God can handle it. Keep asking.

5. Get annoyed and stay annoyed at embarrassing evangelical spokespeople. This one is very simple. You spend your life learning, thinking, speaking, and living in ways that are thoughtful, reasonable, balanced, and acceptable. People need to know that Christians don't have to be loonies. Christians can be relevant and respectable. "Friendship evangelism" depends upon that. So does the larger influence Christians have in the culture.

Then you turn on the TV, open the newspaper, or click on the radio and what do you hear? Some loudmouth leader, speaking in the name of Christ or even evangelicals, saying crazy things. It may be the self-appointed President of an upstart Christian college talking about God taking his life if they don't raise more money. It may be some high-profile pastor or book author shooting his mouth off about feminists and gays and abortionists and the end of the world. It might be the head of some right-wing Christian think-tank or political lobbying group talking about "family values" in a way that is rigid and self-righteous. It might be some faith healer acting ridiculously on stage. It doesn't matter. What matters is that these lunatics are irresponsible, embarrassing, and impossible to shut up—all of which only hurts the gospel. Reasonable Christians like you work hard for years to create a thoughtful and respectable atmosphere in which the Christian message might be heard. Then these idiotic talking heads ruin it all in one sound bite.

Who died and made them king? You well know the usual-suspect list of names of such "leaders," on whom you wish you could just pull the plug. You cringe anytime you find out they are about to speak. But you can't pull the plug. It's a free country with free speech. Evangelicalism itself has no organized way to constrain or regulate the worst types—it's a diffuse and decentralized movement full of self-appointed entrepreneurs, populists, and media personalities. If they can form a constituency that provides enough money to get on the radio or television, they can say almost anything they wish, unfortunately. And the secular media itself is always looking for extreme religious perspectives to spotlight—it boosts their ratings and keeps the news interesting. It also helps keep the culture wars going. So, crazy people for whom you never voted somehow get to represent you in public in ways that makes you and your people look like asses. You're infuriated.

You're not wrong. There is not much good about these embarrassing evangelical spokespeople. Keep your annoyance going. In due time you'll need to develop it into a deeper analysis of why evangelicalism inevitably generates such problems. But for now, simple annoyance will do.

6. Grow tired of church shopping and start to wonder whether church is something that is even supposed to be shopped for. You've hit a new problem. It's your church. The new pastor is a bomb. Or most of your friends have left. Or the hip worship music has gotten stale. Or the traditional worship service is being replaced by a contemporary style. Or the Sunday school or youth group programming isn't right for your kids. Or you've got a new romantic interest who's not interested in your church. Or the elders have made a really stupid decision, like taking out a huge mortgage to finance a risky new building campaign. That recent conflict or embarrassing situation with those other people in church doesn't help you to feel very good about things either.

Whatever. You're dissatisfied. The idea of staying grows bleaker by the week. You start looking around. At first, you simply check out a promising new church or two. Next thing you know you're systematically asking around and planning which week to visit where. You are working out in your mind the comparisons between the various churches you're looking at.

At some point, however, you get tired. You feel homeless. You wonder how it could be that even though you're surrounded by multiple church options, none of them seems quite right for you. You hope to find the right one, a church that meets your needs. But sometimes you just despair of the state of the church in general. Why can't they be more together, more alive, more interesting, more satisfying? People at your "former" church are asking about your whereabouts. What do you tell them? You keep looking. But once a week turns out to burn up a lot of time in order to visit enough of the options to really know which church is right for you.

Then you start to wonder. Is this really what church is supposed to be about, anyway? How in the world have we gotten to the point that church is something people have to *shop* for, like a new car or vacation condo? Is church and the experience of church just a commodity? Why do so many people bounce around among churches so much? The poor pastors! They must feel like car salesmen. What is going on here? How and why are *my* "needs" and preferences driving the church I end up in?

Again, great questions. Keep asking. Something about church shopping is indeed alien to the New Testament picture of church, to the very idea of church itself. Let the thought sink in that church shopping is itself indicative of a deep difficulty, is part of the problem itself.

7. Start wondering where the mystery of faith and life are. You've been pretty comfortable as a Christian in the modern world. You like living in an enlightened era that has dispelled the ignorance, superstition, idolatries, and magic of corrupt pre-modern popular religion. You know the truth about God, revelation, the atonement, the Lord's Supper, and other points of doctrine. The Bible and Protestant theologies have answers to those questions. You're also pretty happy to live in the age of science, capitalism, and democracy. Modernity's mastery of the material and social world makes living a lot more enjoyable than in the old days

But now, if you are curious about becoming Catholic, start paying attention to that weak but insistent voice inside of you that keeps asking, "But where's the mystery?" Sure, it's nice to have answers and creaturely comforts. But some days you wonder if there's also not something flat, even empty, about supposedly having it all figured out, about modern knowledge and mastery.

In reality, the mental world you inhabit as a Protestant is powerfully shaped by a disenchanting modernity. The monasteries have been dissolved and plundered, the saints have been driven away, and prayers with the dead are abolished. All of the embodied mumbo-jumbo of the medieval sacramental world has been stripped away. The statues have been smashed, the faces of holy images scraped away. The material world is now emptied of spiritual occupation and meaning. Material substances no longer offer ties to the "great cloud of witnesses," to celestial realities, to worlds unknown. Your beliefs reside in your head. Your prayers are made to God alone. Mary is dead, or at least cut off from you, along with the souls of all of the faithful of millennia past.

You stand as a solitary soul before God, prayed for by your family and perhaps by your small group, but otherwise on your own as an individual—fortified only by the knowledge that you indeed have chosen a "personal faith," you have decided to trust Jesus, maybe even have experienced a personal conversion. But something about ultimately being a solitary individual is odd to you. It feels naked or disconnected.

Attend to that. Start to wonder whether the bare bones, the stripped altars, the austere white walls of Protestantism are all there is. Ponder the question: is knowing God the Holy Trinity really as straightforward as the theology books suggest? Do the pat answers—such as the "penal satisfaction" theory—really capture the fullness of the reality of what salvation is all about? Is the Lord's Supper really only a "memorial" in the sense of merely *reminding* us of the cross? Is the Church triumphant really absolutely sealed off from the church still on earth? Why should that be?

For most of Christian history, the material and spiritual world was much more enchanted, thicker with spiritual meaning, and full of greater mystery than modern evangelicalism knows. Modernity suffers a "mystery deficit"—an inability to even conceive of unknowns and realities beyond those accessible to rational understanding. Indeed, that mystery deficit is central to the corrosions of secularization. Evangelicalism participates in that mystery deficit.

Start feeling the deficit of mystery—the mystery of the Trinity, of being "*in*" Christ," of the cosmic meaning of the atonement, of the Eucharist, of the sacraments that laden the material with the spiritual. Start suspecting that reality is much richer, more unknown, more strange than you ever imagined. Then start to want to get in touch with that reality more fully.

8. Hear about someone you respect becoming Catholic. In the old days, Catholics stayed Catholic and evangelicals stayed evangelical. No longer. More than a few evangelicals today were raised Catholic. And more than a few evangelicals are also converting *to* Catholicism. Why Catholics might become evangelical is clear to you. But evangelicals becoming Catholic is weird. Isn't that a step backward, a kind of willful betrayal of truth? Still, you know that some high-profile evangelicals have gone off on the Canterbury Trail (to Anglicanism) and others have "converted to Rome." Francis Beckwith, John Michael Talbot, Scott Hahn, and Joshua Hochschild are some of the names you might have heard. Interesting, from a distance, you think.

Then you hear that someone you actually personally know and re-spect has become Catholic (or discover that someone you have known for a while and respect is Catholic). (For me, this happened when a beloved Gordon College professor, Tom Howard, from whom I learned Tolkien and Williams and Lewis in his class on "Modern Myth," who helped draw me out of the depressing emptiness of modern rationalism and secularity, and who volunteered his time and attention in an inde-pendent study to teach me how to write better prose, became Catholic in 1984, one year after I graduated.) Huh. What's up with that? Why did he or she do it? The fact of their conversion itself hardly makes a personal claim or demand on your life. Still, it is not nothing. It opens up an initial crack, perhaps imperceptible at first, to a reality into which the more you peer, the more it opens up and the more you may be drawn.

9. Begin wondering if being "relevant" is simply irrelevant. American evangelicalism is obsessed with being *relevant*. Evangelicalism wants to be culturally and intellectually hip, really engaged with The Big Boys, respectable to outsiders—all in the name of Jesus.

That's the understandable result of evangelical history. Once upon a time, in the early and mid-nineteenth century, evangelicals were the proprietary custodian of American culture. Then they lost that influ-ence and respect in the late nineteenth-century with the rise of secular modernism. The new elites and their liberal lapdogs then kicked evan-gelicals when they were down, scornfully mocking and tossing them aside as rednecks and yokels after the loss of the fundamentalist battles in the 1920s.[8] Evangelicals licked their wounds in the shadows, but then launched a counter-offensive in the 1940s and after. By the 1970s and 80s, evangelicals were back on the public stage, throwing weight around in culture and even national politics. 1976 was declared by *Newsweek* the "Year of the Evangelical." That was more like it.

Still, the insecure fixation with relevance won't go away. It shapes church growth strategies, rock bands, tee shirts, media productions, evangelism campaigns. "Christians Don't Have to be Losers," evangeli-cals always want to say. So you need to be sharp and to look good. You need a worship team that is impressive. You need the latest technology. You need to have Christ-centered answers for all of the social and po-litical problems of the world. You need to place believers in positions of status and influence. You need celebrities and pro sports stars who point

8. See Marsden, *Fundamentalism and American Culture.*

a finger to heaven or thank the Lord on camera. You need to show good numbers. You need to *not* commit the ultimate sin of being out of touch, behind the times, extraneous. That is mortifying.

At some point along the way, however, start asking: isn't this obsession with being "relevant" rather obsequious? Why let the world set the standards for Christians to follow? Do we really think we will ever impress the world into the kingdom? Isn't Christ actually a stumbling block to all human pride? Might there not be more integrity in owning up to the foolishness of the gospel than in doing everything possible to make it relevant? Again, good questions. Keep asking.

10. Notice American evangelicalism's cultural accommodations. Evangelicalism talks a lot about being "salt and light" in the world, about not being conformed to the world, and having the answer (Jesus) for the world's problems and questions. But you are already likely tuned into the fact that, rather than presenting much of an alternative or counter-cultural witness informed by the gospel, contemporary American evangelicalism seems to have significantly accommodated itself to the dominant culture in a variety of ways. A lot of this results from the effort to be "relevant," just described; and to be not-fundamentalist, by living in a way that is palatable and hopefully attractive to mainstream America.

Whatever the reason, however, you detect various forms of cultural accommodation, some subtle, some obvious. You notice, for example, that much of evangelicalism has bought deeply into the self-fulfillment ethos of therapeutic culture. Way too much of the faith is about coping with life, managing emotions and problems, and feeling better about oneself. You also see that a huge amount of popular evangelical book publishing—evident when you browse the Internet websites of any major evangelical bookstore chain—cranks out all sorts of fluffy, feel-good, biblically-thin, theologically-vacuous, human-interest and how-to books that spray a thin "Christian" coating on top of the regular secular fare. It might be *Losing Weight with the Holy Spirit, How to Protect Yourself against the Coming Economic Crisis, Be the Best You that You Were Created to Be, God's Way to Reignite the Passion in Your Marriage,* or whatever—the underlying cultural accommodation is the same.

Politically, you also note, much of evangelicalism can hardly distinguish between its own religious faith and that of the Republican Party. Economically, lots of evangelicals adopt the same material lifestyle aspirations and consumerist mentality as every other American. In worship styles, too many evangelical churches seem prepared to chase after any latest trend or fad in order not to seem "old fashioned." Militarily, evangelicalism seems unable to muster much critical distance from whatever war a President wants to fight or even the ability to criticize whatever forms of torture of enemies in which the national security regime insists we must engage. Too many evangelicals seem all too happy to simply watch TV, see all the movies, and shop at the mall on Sunday afternoons. Keep all of this in mind, too.

11. Read some church history. A famous nineteenth-century British convert from Anglicanism to Catholicism, John Henry Cardinal Newman, once wrote very perceptively that, "To be deep in history is to cease to be a Protestant."[9] The more you learn about the long term of Christian history, the less Protestantism makes sense. Your next step, therefore, is to read more Christian history, going all the way back to the beginning.

Try to avoid the many confessional histories written by Protestants that embody strong Reformation biases. Far too much church history on which evangelicals have been raised reads the Church Fathers highly selectively, framing history in a highly self-congratulatory, "whiggish" way, wrongly assuming an *inevitable* progression toward the outcome that so happened to transpire. That tends to embody an unjustified and distorted triumphalism about the Reformation. This can be corrected by reading a combination of original sources, the best of Christian history written by non-Christians, and some good church history written by some of the right Catholics.

For example, do not read books *about* St. Augustine of Hippo or about the Reformers' claims to be the true heirs or interpreters of Augustine. Instead, read Augustine himself, his original works. You will discover in so doing that Augustine is in fact a thoroughly Catholic thinker and bishop, utterly dedicated to the Catholic Church, and a forceful advocate of a host of Catholic doctrines that contemporary evangelicals reject. Likewise, read the original works of Ignatius of Antioch, Athanasius, Origen, Clement, Irenaeus, Tertullian, Justin Martyr, Polycarp, Ambrose, Cyril, and John Chrysostom—that is, central figures who established the foundations of Christian truth against heresy—and you will discover the same: they are utterly and devotedly Catholic.

9. Newman, *An Essay on the Development of Christian Doctrine*, 8.

In the abstract, of course, we all know that these church luminaries were part of the early Catholic Church, since that was the only Christian church existing at the time. But directly reading their very own words somehow drives this point home in a way that makes perfectly clear with great existential force that the separatist movement that was to erupt 1,000-1,200 years later, known as the Reformation, actually feels highly alien to the writings of the Church Fathers.

Keep reading. Like most evangelicals, you were probably raised to believe that the Christian church was rescued from the darkness of a disastrous medieval Catholicism by a coherent, smooth, stable, and glorious Reformation. So, read *The Reformation*, by Diarmaid MacCulloch, a balanced, world-class historian of the Reformation. You will discover there depressing heaps of misunderstanding, conflicts, disasters, violence, bad faith, and lost opportunities both within the Reformation movement itself and set into motion socially by the Reformation.[10] While you're at it, read *Getting the Reformation Wrong: Correcting Some Misunderstandings*, by James Payton.

You may also assume that the Reformation was happily welcomed with open arms by the mass of Christians who were suffering under a decaying Catholicism. If so, then read *The Stripping of the Altars: English Traditional Religion c1400-c1700*. This highly-acclaimed, discipline-reorienting history of the English Reformation was penned by Eamon Duffy, an eminent Cambridge University professor and historian. You will discover there mounds of evidence suggesting that the late-medieval English Catholicism that Henry VIII dissolved and plundered in fact enjoyed the widespread devotion of the people, was institutionally vibrant, and was only abandoned by most with immense reluctance and sorrow, under pain of punishment by law. Very many of them, in fact, welcomed the brief Catholic restoration during Queen Mary's subsequent reign—after the young King Edward's untimely death—with rejoicing.

In short, a great deal of Christian church history—especially that to which most evangelicals are usually exposed—has been more or less biased by partisan Protestant authors in a way that validates, valorizes,

---

10. Evangelicals also reflect far too little on the fact that the success of the Protestant Reformation depended primarily not upon the inherently superior logic of Reformation ideas, but primarily upon early modern state rulers wanting to flex their political muscles autonomously, without interference from the Vatican. Their motive was largely political and only secondarily theological. This too provides another tie-in of the Reformation to modernity.

and makes "obvious" and inevitable the Protestant Reformation. But reading history not written in that partial, self-congratulating Protestant mode provides a more accurate and illuminating perspective on the reality. Doing so helps to paint a truer picture of the fullness and complexity of Christian church history. And the more one gains such a picture, the more Christian history itself becomes an uncomfortable anomaly within the evangelical paradigm.

12. Start to wonder where the New Testament came from. As an evangelical, the Bible is the foundation of all of your beliefs. At least that is what evangelicals say. You've always taken the Bible for granted. It's always been there. For all you've known, the apostles wrote the Bible after Christ's ascension and the early church bound it together in book form soon after their death. You might even come from among the kind of evangelicals who assume or suppose that God dictated the words of the Bible to its various human authors. But for the most part, evangelicals simply don't think much about where the Bible came from.

Here is your next step: begin wondering how we got the New Testament, start asking questions about it, and do some reading on the matter.[11] What you'll learn will be enlightening. The contents of the New Testament as we know it, the authorized Christian scriptural canon (literally: rule, measure), were not finally decided upon and pulled together until the *end of the fourth century*. For the first *three hundred years* of church history, in other words, Christians did not possess the New Testament as we know it. That is much longer than the United States has existed as a country. During that time, different churches possessed and read as Scripture copies of different written documents, many of which ended up in our New Testament.[12] But few churches had the entire contents of the New Testament as we know it. And different leaders and congregations held somewhat differing views about what was even scriptural.

11. For starters, I recommend Allert's *High View of Scripture?*

12. Not all biblical scholars agree on all of the details but here is what most say. The three synoptic Gospels were not written down by the apostles soon after Christ's ascension but existed in content as an oral tradition for roughly twenty-five to eighty years (depending on exact dates of writing). It was not until the second century—between 60 and 115 CE—that the synoptic Gospels were put into writing. The gospel of John was written at the end of the first century. The apostle Paul's epistles were written by Paul himself or one of his scribes during his ministry, and copies of many of them were circulated among many of the churches around the Roman Empire and beyond. Some other New Testament epistles, however, perhaps especially the so-called "pastoral epistles," appear to have been written or compiled by their authors sometime in the second century.

The drive even to define a Christian scriptural canon was set into motion by the heretic Marcion of Sinope (85–160 CE), who wanted to disregard the Old Testament and exclude as non-authoritative what eventually became certain New Testament books. The threat of Gnosticism contributed too. Responding to Marcion's challenge and sorting out what deserved to be canonized took about three centuries. Eventually, leaders from the many churches—Catholic bishops, to be specific—came together in synods to define exactly what should constitute Christian Scriptures. It was not until the synods at Hippo in 393 and Carthage in 397 and 419 that Western Catholic bishops and theologians representing the various churches finally agreed to the authorized content of the Christian Bible, that is, the canonical New Testament that we possess. In the East, that process continued still longer.[13]

In the end, some of the written texts that some churches had believed *were* scriptural (e.g., *The Shepherd of Hermas, Book of Baruch, Letter of Jeremiah, 1 Clement, 2 Clement*) were later *excluded* from that canonical list. Other written texts that some churches believed were *not* scriptural (Hebrews, James, 2 Peter, Jude, 2 John, 3 John, Revelation) ended up being *included* in the final New Testament list. And some texts that various churches had never possessed copies of were also incorporated in the final New Testament canon.

These historical facts raise some troubling questions for Bible-only Protestants. For example, with what scriptural authority did the Christian churches operate for their first 350 years, during which time they did not commonly possess the complete New Testament that Protestants today now claim is (along with the Old Testament) the necessary and only authority for Christian faith and practice? Was it whichever texts they happened to possess, even if some of them later turned out *not* to be included in the New Testament? Did different churches that possessed different documents have different authoritative scriptures? How could what eventually turned out to be the contents of the New Testament have possibly functioned (along with the Old Testament) during this time as the sole and sufficient authority in and for the Christian church, when

---

13. The working canon defined by the end of the fourth century was, to be precise, decided not by ecumenical councils but regional synods. Full dogmatic articulations of the canons were not made until the Council of Trent of 1546 for Roman Catholicism, the Thirty-Nine Articles of 1563 for the Church of England, the Westminster Confession of Faith of 1647 for British Calvinism, and the Synod of Jerusalem of 1672 for the Greek Orthodox.

it took bishops and theologians of the Church to decide, after several centuries lacking a consensus on the matter, the very content of the New Testament canon itself?

And who or what actually authorized those bishops and theologians to even make those monumental decisions? How can evangelicals trust the New Testament itself—which exists in its received canonical form only and precisely because Catholic bishops and theologians met to define them—since evangelicals, who insist on *sola Scriptura*, do not even believe in the legitimacy or authority of Catholic bishops? Hmm.

Start to realize that the evangelical paradigm cannot have it both ways. Evangelicals cannot both deny that bishops of the Catholic Church possess the legitimate authority to collegially decide on binding teachings concerning faith and life *and* simultaneously insist that the Bible as received is the only and sufficient authority for Christian faith and life. That is a self-contradicting and therefore self-defeating position. The canonical existence of the New Testament as we know it is dependent for its very being on the authoritative decisions of Catholic bishops meeting in synods to define it. To take the New Testament as authoritative therefore presupposes the authority of bishops to define the content of the New Testament—even if they themselves did not create the content.

Some evangelicals will at this point shine the spotlight away from the Catholic bishops and theologians and instead toward the Holy Spirit: "It was the Holy Spirit who led the church to define the right documents as scriptural canon." Of course. Catholics believe that. But note the method. The Holy Spirit did not drop the Bible out of the sky. Nor did the New Testament canon somehow mysteriously form itself under the Spirit's guidance apart from the work of the Church. "Led the Church to define" is a crucial part of the statement above. So why do these evangelicals assume we are dealing with a zero-sum game? The Holy Spirit's crucial role does not make the bishops role irrelevant. If anything, it shows the true legitimacy of the authority of the Church to define matters as important as the contents of Scripture—God, apparently, was pleased to use the Church in this way.

In case my overall argument here has not been clear, let me put it another way. Either the Catholic Church's episcopate had a legitimate authority to define the content of the New Testament Scriptures, or it did not have the authority. If the latter is correct, then the status of the canon of New Testament Scriptures itself is called into question, and what is scriptural is an open-ended question. If the former is true, then we have a defensible account explaining the composition and authority of the New Testament. But we must then also accept the legitimate authority of the Catholic episcopate for defining matters as serious as the content of the canon of Christian Scripture. We cannot turn around and deny the authority of Catholic bishops—now that they have helped provide us the authorized New Testament canon—and say that the *only* authority is the Bible which the Church helped to constitute.

13. Read J. R. R. Tolkien. You've seen Peter Jackson's *Lord of the Rings* and have probably read *The Hobbit*. Good. Now sit down, read, and soak in the original *Lord of the Rings* trilogy in its full splendor. Wait a year, then read it again. Let the power and pathos of the epic seep into your spirit. Soak up the mystery, the songs, the prophesies, the enchanted power of speech and spells. Hear in Middle Earth's nature a living protest against a dead, industrial, Saruman-esque world, mirroring the modernity of our world. Feel its thickly significant life mock the thinness of our contemporary existence. Wonder who or what is the "Secret Fire" of which Gandalf is a servant. What is the "flame of Anor" which he wields against the Balrog on the Bridge of Khazad Dhum in the Mines of Moria? Contemplate the light providential hand that seems to guide epic events to their rightful end, beyond the capacity of any actor to control and often beyond all reasonable hope. Consider what it means that Gandalf the Grey returns from death in white.

Having soaked in the depths of the horrors and glory of Tolkien's epic, then ask yourself: what connection might there be between his fictional imagination and Tolkien's real, traditional, committed Catholic faith? Why does this kind of literature come from the hands of Catholics, like Tolkien, or at times from the almost-Catholic, high-Anglican hands of C. S. Lewis and Charles Williams?[14] Why don't or can't American evangelical authors write like this? Why instead are the evangelical equivalents that make for its bestsellers more like Frank Peretti's *This Present Darkness*, Tim LaHaye's *Left Behind*, or the scads of cleaned-up, Christian romance novels published as counterparts of their secular Harlequin Romance equivalents? Pathetic. Something more than sheer coincidence is going on here. What is it?

14. Some who knew Lewis believed that he became Catholic in all but name at the end of his life.

14. Start asking why evangelical churches are so segregated by race and social class. The old saw says, "Sunday morning is the most segregated time of the week." We've heard it many times. But it is true. Protestant churches, including most evangelical churches, are highly segregated by race and social class. That's a sociological fact[15]— despite the many (inerrant) Bible verses about Christian brotherhood, unity, and preference for the poor. Many evangelicals are concerned about the racial division, at least, and have worked hard on efforts at "racial reconciliation." But those have typically been conceived in personal, relational terms. The real racial problems, however, are often complex and structural.[16] So personal "racial reconciliation" has been limited in its effectiveness.

Add to your to-do list: starting thinking about the way churches and the larger religious system are structured that encourages racial and social-class segregation. Focus on the American religious economy, built on free congregational choice, not designated parish location. In it congregations operate like firms, religious believers are consumers, and the choice of church-product depends entirely on the wants, "needs," and preferences of each individual and family (again, think church shopping). Anybody can change their congregation anytime, at will.

Then add the idea of "homophily," that people usually like and want to be around other people who are like them. Presto! You have churches that are highly segregated by race and social class. Birds of a feather flock together, etc.—all made possible by the free-market, choose-your-own-church, Protestant, congregational system.

What might it take to overcome this unbiblical, racial, and social-class system of church segregation? Well, in most places residential neighborhoods are themselves segregated by race and social class, so a simple change to a geographical parish-based system will not automatically solve the problem (besides, a lot of American Catholics have become influenced by the Protestant church-shop mentality, significantly eroding the geographically-based parish system, an erosion you could help work against). But a functioning Catholic parish system, defining which local church one ought to attend based on one's residence (again, something you could help to strengthen), would go a long way toward breaking down the segregation. It already does. It could do even more.

15. Smith and Faris, "Socioeconomic Inequality," 95–104.
16. Emerson and Smith, *Divided by Faith*.

For one thing, the common Catholic faith would dissolve the zillions of denominational barriers to common Christian identity and fellowship. For another, many Catholic parishes even in our segregated American society comprise people from varying races and social classes. The most consistently diverse type of churches that I, as a professional observer of American religion, have visited in my life have been Catholic parishes—whites and blacks and Hispanics and Asians are often commonly seen worshipping together without tension or rancor. Social science studies support this observation to be empirically true.[17] Is that not a better foretaste of the kingdom coming?

15. Feel some dismay about evangelical social ethics. Evangelicalism is big on individual salvation and personal ethics. It is less impressive when it comes to social ethics. This has probably already bothered you. Let it. Pay attention to the fact. Consider the full extent of the problem. When it comes to social ethics, evangelicalism is beset by one of two problems. Either it has few social teachings to offer at all (go save souls, obey the government, etc.). Or else it has a social-ethics position for every political ideology on the spectrum—from "biblically supported" libertarian Republicanism to middle-of-the-road Americanism to liberal do-goodism to gospel-inspired socialism. Take your pick: Rousas Rushdooney, Pat Robertson, James Skillen, Stephen Mott, Tony Campolo, Jim Wallis, Ronald Sider, or Brian Moore. With of course no authoritative evangelical-church teaching on social doctrine, every individual evangelical simply ends up picking their personal favorite approach (often driven by their own social class interests), and the larger disagreement and disunity of Protestantism continues.

Further down the road in this process, you will learn that the Catholic Church possesses a rich, intelligent, coherent, balanced, compelling body of social doctrines. But hold off on that for now. For the moment, simply take note of the neglect and disarray when it comes to American evangelical social ethics.

16. Begin noticing how allergic evangelicals are to Mary. With the exception of some high-church Anglicans, Protestants, we all know, reject the Catholic view of Mary. She is the mother of Jesus, remember? The first generation of Reformers—particularly Luther—continued to believe some of Catholicism's Marian doctrines, such as her perpetual

17. Emerson and Woo, *People of the Dream,* 28–46.

virginity. But in due time, the bitter anti-Catholic struggles of history stripped Mary out of the picture.

Mary became a kind of noxious allergen against which Protestants, maybe especially evangelicals, have automatic allergic reactions. A lot of work goes into inoculating the Protestant faithful against Mary, filtering her out of the air in the religious atmosphere. Normally that work is highly successful, so that few Protestants are even aware of Mary's virtual absence—the matter in the end is simply invisible.

It is of course impossible for evangelicals to eliminate Mary entirely, especially at Christmas time. But that can be managed. Mary is made a mere necessary biological conduit for the Incarnation to happen, who, after the stable and the manger, can be set aside as irrelevant if not potentially dangerous—like Baal or Asherah or Moloch in her threat to become a corrupting idol of worship. Ancient historical Christian theological understandings of Mary as the "Second Eve" and a stunning exemplar of obedient faith in the face of confusion and fear, proclaimed by Church Fathers and Catholic (and Orthodox) believers thereafter, are jettisoned.

In all of this, however, there is a certain over-exertion that would be pathetically amusing were the subject matter not so consequential and, well, biblical.

I still remember my sixth-grade school class singing "Faith of Our Fathers"—#487 in the (Presbyterian) *Trinity Hymnal*—at the start of school days. Our earnest Dutch Calvinist teacher (first name: Calvin) pounded away stirringly at the piano, as we voice-cracking twerps belted out:

> Faith of our fathers, living still, In spite of dungeon, fire and sword;
> O how our hearts beat high with joy, Whenever we hear that glorious Word!

> *Faith of our fathers, holy faith! We will be true to thee till death.*

What a glorious tribute to our valiant and heroic Protestant forebears who for the sake of the Reformation suffered persecution and death at the hands of Catholic tyrants! Could *I* be faithful enough to endure dungeon, fire, and sword?

Thirty-five years later, I learned that this is actually a Catholic hymn, written by the mid-nineteenth-century British Catholic, Frederick William Faber, whose originally-penned last verse declared:

> Faith of our fathers, Mary's prayers, Shall win our country back
> to Thee;

And through the truth that comes from God, England shall then
indeed be free.

Faith of our fathers, holy faith! We will be true to thee till death.

Oh, my. Well, we certainly cannot have talk of a divinely-true Catholic
faith freeing England from Protestant oppression! The hymn had to be
confiscated and Mary deleted. (Alas for Faber that England has not been
won back to the true faith—at best the papists are merely tolerated as the
dominant Protestant culture becomes ever more secularized.)

What is the anomaly here? Evangelicals trust in the Bible, on which
they say they base their beliefs. But, when it comes to things even only
remotely and by association "too Catholic," like Mary, the verses are read
over and past and ignored. It is like Mary hardly matters, as if the verses
were not in the Bible, as if Mary deserves no theological reflection. That
is no huge crime in and of itself—at least from a Protestant perspective.
But it *is* revealing. All is not confident, healthy, balanced, or settled on
the matter. "The lady doth protest too much, methinks," one might observe, with a Shakespearean flair. Keep that in mind too.

**17. Start to grow bored with white bread and vanilla flavored
evangelicalism.** One of the hallmarks of early Reformation churches
was their whitewashing of church walls. All of the idolatrous Catholic
paintings and images of the Patriarchs, the prophets, the suffering Christ,
Mary, and the saints had to be covered over. Whitewash was the main
means to get that done. Bare, stark white walls—that was the Protestant
way. Many Protestant churches even today continue that stark, white-
wall tradition. You have probably already noticed that many aspects of
American evangelicalism also have, speaking broadly and metaphori-
cally, a "white" or "bare" tone to them. A lot of evangelicalism tastes like
white bread and vanilla ice cream. Both of those can taste good. But when
they're all one eats, it starts to get old and bland. There are a lot more
interesting kinds of bread and flavors of ice cream. Think about the verse,
"Everything God created is good, and nothing is to be rejected if it is
received with thanksgiving, because it is consecrated by the word of God
and prayer" (1 Tim 4:4-5). And allow yourself to admit your boredom
with evangelicalism's bare, stark, white, vanilla approach to faith.

**18. Note your dissatisfaction with the heavily cognitive, often
rationalist, nature of much of Protestantism.** There is no denying it:
Protestantism is a religion of the head. What matters most are holding the

right beliefs. And right beliefs are things that reside between one's ears. Having the right cognitions is the essence of Protestantism. So is possessing, professing, and defending the right *words*. And those words come from and enter into the head as well. True, evangelicalism includes strains of pietism, charismatic tendencies, revivalist emotion, and a love of practical activism that can help counter-balance the heavily cognitive leanings of Protestantism. But in the end, as you well know, what is ultimately important is having the right beliefs, the right ideas, the right words (even if that is in some ways contradicted among the laity by a simultaneous cultural emphasis on the subjectivistic opinions and feelings of individuals when interpreting the Bible, as discussed below in point 25).

Sometimes, this cognitive bias even takes on a strongly rationalist feel in evangelical apologetics and theology. And even the standard way that ordinary Protestants obey the scriptural teaching to "confess your sins to one another" is to have repentant private mental conversations with God in the head. Very strange.

So, your next step: start feeling your discontent with this religion of the head. Allow yourself to recognize that there is something constricted, even emaciated and distorted, about such a heavily cognitive, mentalist, rationalist sort of faith. Start asking yourself: if God created the material world and our bodies as good, and if God himself took on human flesh amid this world of matter in the Incarnation, then why are flesh and materiality so minimized, even shunted aside, in so many evangelical churches and forms of spirituality? Is the heart of Christianity really about believing correct *ideas*? What about the movement of the body in communal liturgy? What about kneeling and standing in reverence? What about ingesting the Body and Blood of Christ? What about water and oil and incense and color in abundance as part of worship and spiritual life? Why should confessions of sin not be spoken out loud, by real mouths, to real people, through sound waves in the air, who tell us vocally in reply that our sins are indeed forgiven through Christ? Why shouldn't visual images of saints—of the "great cloud of witnesses"—help to inspire us to holy living? Why shouldn't God's grace be mediated through a variety of material and bodily sacraments, including anointing of the sick and holy marriage? What is it about bodies and materiality, when it comes to Christian faith, that Protestantism, that American evangelicalism, is so afraid of?

19. Start noticing that evangelicalism seems to thrive on external threats and alarmist claims. What is the "juice" on which American evangelicalism thrives? What fuels its engine? Well, lots of things, of course, including some good things. But among them all, a very important source of evangelical thriving is not so good: a continual perception of internal crises and external threats which require a reaffirmation of committed identity and renewed mobilizations of resources. In short, evangelicalism thrives on being embattled—of seeing itself as continually "fighting the good fight" against those who are out to wreck the true faith. Evangelicalism sustains its energy and perpetual self-mobilization in significant part by continually feeling threats to the gospel and to Christianity's influence, whether through laxity and accommodation on the inside or from hostile forces menacing from the outside.[18] All social groups engage in this kind of behavior more or less intensely and in different ways—evangelicalism just happens to be particularly incessant and alarmist about it.

This embattled-and-thriving dynamic, once started, is addictive and relentless. It requires constantly having an enemy, a peril, or a threat to meet, to overcome, and defeat. If real threats do not naturally present themselves, it is all too easy for leaders to invent them. For not to have a threatening "other" with which evangelicalism can do battle means a drying up of its very life, its vitality, its turbo-charging fueling system. Sometimes, once you tune into all of this, you can witness in real time evangelical leaders inventing a new or pumping up an old threat against which they then sound the "gospel" alarm and volunteer to lead the faithful into battle in order to overcome. The tail is wagging the dog.

You will not at this point need me to tell you what step to take here. You'll already know the right questions to ask: Isn't something wrong with a Christian enterprise that requires some threat, inside or outside, real or imagined, to sustain its vitality? Shouldn't it be the love of Christ, and not ever-menacing threats in the world, that is our source of life? Does not the evangelical reliance on being embattled for its thriving build into its identity a permanent culture of insecurity, alarmism, and sectarian defensiveness? Doesn't it all lead to the continual drawing and

---

18. Which I have written an entire book describing: Smith et al, *American Evangelicalism*. I have also written elsewhere about how this feeding-on-threat dynamic tends to distort evangelicals' public use of statistics, even to the point of being scandalously idiotic and dishonest. Smith, "Evangelicals Behaving Badly," 11.

policing of symbolic boundaries, rather than a confident and open entering into the life of the world for the sake of the gospel? Once this dynamic is recognized, such questions become obvious and troubling. Keep asking them.

20. Begin to see how very thin the "biblical basis" of many evangelical beliefs are. American evangelicals make no secret of their conviction that their beliefs are "based on the Bible." And when you're inside that world, it sure seems that way. By comparison, evangelicals also often criticize Catholics for having little biblical basis for some of their beliefs.[19] What is interesting, however, (in addition to learning about the actual biblical basis of so many allegedly "unbiblical" Catholic teachings) is pushing against the claims about how solidly biblical evangelical beliefs are. In more than a few cases, one starts to notice that the biblical bases for such claims are actually quite thin.

Take, for example, the obvious need for churches to have paid, ordained clergy. That's pretty central in evangelical life, but in fact only weakly supported by the Bible. Yes, there are some New Testament verses about "double honor" (not that any good teacher in church ever gets paid double salary) and "do not muzzle the ox while it is threshing." But both of those are somewhat cryptic in meaning. In any case, you'll have to look long and hard, maybe forever, to find scriptural support for the kind of professional clergy role that is ubiquitous in evangelical churches today.

Or take the belief common among some evangelicals that every individual needs an identifiable point of personal faith conversion to create a "personal relationship with Jesus." That's certainly a key to evangelical revivalism, and one can definitely find various Bible verses that seem to buttress such a claim. But, altogether, the direct biblical evidence for that theology and rhetoric is in fact pretty thin.

The same is true about husbands being the "spiritual heads" of their households (not one verse says that), about Sunday and not Saturday being Christians' set-apart day of rest and worship (just ask Seventh Day Adventists), about the church's essential need for theological seminaries and divinity schools (did Barnabas and Silas get MDiv degrees?), among a variety of other similarly biblically thin beliefs. It's just not there.

Looked at from a different perspective, if evangelicals really wanted to be truly biblical about church, and not simply follow traditions developed over church history, they would, for example, not meet in church

19. See, however, Armstrong, *Catholic Verses.*

buildings but rather in the homes of believers (e.g. Rom 16:5; 1 Cor 16:19; Col 4:15) and would greet each other with holy kisses (literally) (Rom 16:16; 1 Cor 16:20; 2 Cor 16:12; 1 Thess 5:26). Scriptural support for such practices is a lot more solid than some of the items mentioned above. But not many evangelicals are going to be "biblical" in those ways.

The point is this: more than a little of what evangelicals take to be obviously and solidly biblical about their beliefs and practices are, upon closer inspection, actually not obviously so. Oftentimes lame proof-texting and unjustified leaps of interpretive logic are required to make it work. That itself is not damning. It need not be fatal that evangelicals are not as scripturally consistent as they think they are. Still, it does raise questions about crucial issues of authority and consistency related to the smooth operation of normal science in the evangelical paradigm. If you suspect that you should keep contemplating become Catholic, pay attention to this too.

21. Start wondering why authors and publishers of evangelical prophesy books are never held accountable for their failed predictions. It happens every time. Whenever there is some significant political or military event in the Middle East, a new crop of books from various evangelical presses is published warning readers about the specific events and their historical actors being foretold in the Bible, to declare that the end of the world is coming, and explain how it will climax in an apocalyptic battle involving Israel and many other armies on the Plain of Megiddo. It might have been triggered by the OPEC Oil Embargo of 1973, the Soviet invasion of Afghanistan in 1979–80, the Gulf War of 1990–91, or some other such event. Russia and Egypt are always involved, as are ominous politicians or military leaders, like Saddam Hussein or Leonid Brezhnev. One way or another, however, this predictable evangelical publishing exercise never fails.

What *does* fail, however, are *all* of the books' predicted scenarios (at least to date). OPEC did not turn out to be the anti-Christ. The Soviet Union was not the third horn of the Beast. Saddam Hussein was not one of the four horsemen poised to pour fire onto the earth.

Curiously, however, neither the book authors nor their publishers are *ever* held accountable for their failed predictions. Never mind that their warnings and forecasts were "biblical." Never mind that they made public claims that have turned out time and again to be wrong. The unsold copies are simply put out on the $1 table. And when the next political-military event happens, the next round of books is published, and the ridiculous mess is repeated.

Now ask yourself: what is wrong with this picture?

22. Think about why American evangelicalism continually spins off a never-ending supply of problematic preachers, like Robert Schuller, Jimmy Swaggart, Jim and Tammy Bakker, Pat Robertson, and Joel Osteen, to name a few. Little explanation or commentary is needed here. It's a simple, historical fact. Every religious tradition—including Catholicism, God knows—has its share of problematic clergy. But American evangelicalism seems particularly adept as generating a constant flow of high-profile, lone-ranger preachers and televangelists who, by nearly everyone's account, are real problems.

With a bit of thought, you realize it is no accident. It has something to do with evangelicalism's free-wheeling, individualistic, market-driven, populist, entrepreneurial culture and structure, which lack any system or norm of collegial accountability. That's part of where evangelicalism's vitality comes from. Unfortunately, it's also the source of the recurrent lunacy. Any hack or smooth talker can simply grab a microphone, raise an audience, and—if they can collect the dough—"be someone" who gets to say whatever cockamamie hoo-ha they want, in the name of Jesus. The problem is systemic. And nobody else in evangelicaldom can do any-thing about it (until the "someone" breaks the law or gets caught with a prostitute). *Is everyone okay with this?*

23. Notice that too many evangelical pastors and other leaders seem to thrive and perhaps even entertain themselves and others by disputing minor doctrinal issues. Again, little commentary is needed here. You already know that more than a few evangelicals are great at majoring in the minors, making mountains out of molehills, splitting doctrinal hairs. This is especially, though not exclusively, true of those who lean in fundamentalist directions, whether it be a Reformed fundamentalism that specializes in doctrinal legalism, or the garden variety fundamentalism that is adept at all legalisms.

What's going on here is not an aberration. It is the Protestant separatist tradition on American evangelical steroids. It is the inevitable result of life in a fractured church run by too many autonomous leaders who are hyper about "biblical" precision, super-vigilant about creeping liberalism, and over-invested in their particular version of reality.

I suspect it is also a perverse form of self-entertainment, misrecognized as serious business. When clergy and seminary professors and denominational bureaucrats are not sufficiently engaged directly with real issues and real people in the real challenges of the real big world beyond their own limited and safe subcultures, it is easy to major in the doctrinal minors. It is easy to make livings off of trivialities—whether or not it actually honors God or serves his kingdom. This, too, is anomalous to the evangelical paradigm when it is at its best.

24. Pay closer attention to any of your own or others' primordial, emotional reactions against Catholicism. Evangelicals usually focus their opposition to Catholicism on doctrinal issues, such as the papacy, Mary, infallibility, the necessity of good works, and so on. In many cases, however, I strongly suspect that those are not the real issues why many evangelicals resist Catholicism.

For one thing, a lot of evangelical beliefs about Catholicism are, as we will see below, just plain wrong. Yet most evangelicals seem to want to resist correcting their beliefs with the facts. For another thing, when one gets into conversations with evangelicals about Catholicism, what often comes out are visceral anti-Catholic *emotions* that actually have little to do with theology. Those gut emotions are well worth paying attention to.

One anti-Catholic evangelical I know is primordially reactive against all authority and power, mostly due, from what I can tell, to a bad childhood relationship with her father. She associates Catholicism with abuses of power and so automatically rejects it. Protestantism, by contrast, grants total individual freedom. At first, discussions with this person focus on doctrinal objections. It turns out, however, that she actually knows very little about theology beyond certain slogans. But very soon the discussion shifts to the emotionally-laden matter of power and individual freedom. At bottom, the problem with Catholicism has little to do with the Immaculate Conception. It is really about symbolic religious representations of her problematic father and her ongoing emotional wresting into middle age with his abusive authority. I am sorry to know that this person's father was authoritarian. But that is not itself a good reason to reject Catholicism.

Another anti-Catholic evangelical I know similarly throws up initial theological concerns in conversations. But eventually it comes out that the deepest source of his hostility to Catholicism is actually the experience sixty years earlier of having been socially excluded and teased in elementary school for not being Catholic by his Catholic classmates in his Catholic-dominated public school. Shame on those Catholic kids. But again, this is not a good reason to remain separated from the Church today.

Yet another anti-Catholic evangelical I know was raised Catholic by parents who did not take their faith seriously. He loves his parents but associates Catholicism with heavy drinking, swearing, and materialistic Christmases and so cannot imagine being Catholic. Needless to say, the "Catholicism" this person rejected is not authentic Catholicism. Others I know have emotional reactions to "Vatican bureaucracy" and "all the men who are in charge." I could multiply such stories, but the point is clear: all too often theological arguments seem to be smokescreens that obscure the strongest reasons why many evangelicals oppose Catholicism, which often turn out to be viscerally emotional, having little to do with doctrine. Psychologists call this kind of emotional behavior "transference"— something I think is all too common in this area of life, even though it often poses itself simply as theological concern.

In some cases, emotionally-driven anti-Catholicism may have less to do with autobiographies and more with broad cultural associations. For some anglophile American Protestants, for example, Catholicism can feel so . . . well, "immigrant"—so Polish, Hispanic, Irish, Italian, Portuguese, etcetera. Deep down, to many WASProtestants, Catholicism "smells" by cultural association of olive oil, tamales, kielbasa, and beer and wine aplenty. As part of this, Catholicism in America was historically associated with urban ghettos, bars and pubs, brawling Irish, dirty working classes, and (supposedly) un-American, anti-democratic loyalties to Vatican tyranny. American Protestantism has a long, ugly history of disdain for and violence toward Catholics and Catholicism. But all of that has in fact been mostly about ethnic superiority, social-class control, and nationalistic individualism, not about authentic Christian faith and practice.[20]

Now ask yourself: should such residual cultural prejudices and stereotypes, however emotionally powerful they may be, have anything to do with understanding where the "one, holy, catholic, and apostolic church" in history rightly subsists?

At an even broader and deeper level, I am certain that some evangelicals hold unconscious, primordial cultural associations that again have little to do with theology but which tacitly mark Catholicism as bad

20. See Jenkins, *New Anti-Catholicism*.

and evangelicalism as good. Catholicism easily associates with the Dark Ages, whereas evangelicalism associates with modernity and democracy. Catholicism associates culturally with the Old World of Europe, while evangelicalism associates with the New World of America. People feel such associations often below the level of consciousness, in their bones, so to speak. For much of my own life, I did. That makes such emotion-driving associations both more powerful in their effects and harder to even identify and evaluate.

Another possible factor in possible affective reactions against Catholicism might be personal likes and dislikes in art styles. Speaking for myself, I like most early Christian, Byzantine, Orthodox, Medieval, Romanesque, Gothic, and some Renaissance Catholic art. But I quite dislike some other Renaissance, most Baroque, Rococo, and nineteenth century, and some twentieth century Catholic art. When I simply lay eyes on Baroque or Rococo Catholic paintings, I typically have an automatic negative reaction that easily associates for me with Catholicism generally. When I think rationally about the issue, however, I realize that this is merely a matter of my autobiography and personal taste, not doctrinal truth.

So, again, ask yourself: are such culturally-constructed, historically contingent emotional associations really the thing that should determine one's beliefs and commitments about Christianity and the church? And prepare yourself: it may be that your change from evangelicalism to Catholicism will require you getting over a certain subconscious anglophile Americanism that you did not even know was there.

25. Attend one too many Bible studies that turns out not to be about the Bible, actually, but instead about the largely-uninformed "opinions" and "feelings" of the participants. It sounds like this: "Well, I'm not really sure what this passage is saying, but what it means *to me* is that . . ." and "You know, this verse really 'speaks to me,' because the other day, when I was . . ." In such cases, the Bible study as a context does not actually study the text as a text in order to understand and obey it. Rather, it uses the biblical text as a *pretext* to enable the opinions and ideas and feelings of the people sitting in a circle—the real focus of the group discussion—to be voiced, explored, and mutually affirmed. "Well, what *I* feel that this text is probably saying, based on my experience, is . . ." and "The thing about this verse that I really connect with is my thought that . . . ." Blah, blah, blah.

For all of evangelicalism's belief about the authority of the Bible (not to mention the emphasis from pulpits and books on holding the right beliefs, noted in point 18 above), a lot of evangelical laity are actually really good at superficially skipping past what the Bible says and focusing instead on their own views, experiences, and affective states *related* to "what it seems to say." Too often it degenerates into a lot of mutual sharing of ignorance, all in the name of good Christian fellowship and Bible learning. Having attended one too many of these, ask yourself: where can I actually find some authoritative teaching about Christian faith?[21]

26. Ask yourself why we need a "new monasticism" when Catholicism still has Christianity's old monasticism. Evangelicals love to re-invent the wheel time and again. First, they cut themselves off from historical tradition. Then they face the same basic issues and problems that have formed Christian historical tradition for two millennia. But rather than learning from the past, they simply invent their own versions of new solutions. And what they make up on the spot usually proves less grounded, satisfying, and sustainable than what historical tradition offers.

Examples are myriad. One of my favorites is evangelical parachurch organizations incessantly writing their own "statements of faith," to be approved by their boards of trustees, which are often composed primarily of successful evangelical business people with little theological training.

Another example is the so-called evangelical "new monasticism" movement.[22] What that movement is trying to do I think is mostly admirable. But why do we need a *new* monasticism? Christian monasticism has been around for nearly 2000 years. And a lot has been learned about monasticism in the meantime. The "new monasticism" is, I am afraid, yet another instance of a presumptuous American evangelical hubris, which is particularly ironic when it comes to monasticism, of all things. That hubris automatically assumes that all that has gone before is contaminated and so evangelicals can and must invent everything anew to be right, unsullied, and relevant.

21. Catholicism admittedly has its share if this kind of individual subjectivism in Bible studies, though it at least possesses an authoritative Church teaching against which such claims and practices can be weighed and judged.

22. See, as descriptions of this movement, for example, Wilson-Hartgrove, *New Monasticism*; Rutba House, *School(s) for Conversion*; Bessenecker, *New Friars*; also see online: http://www.newmonasticism.org/.

News flash: the Catholic Church in the United States includes thousands of monastic religious orders and communities that have been living and continue to live the kinds of values, commitments, and practices that the "new monasticism" teaches. Isn't it funny that evangelicals feel the need to invent their own, new brand of it?

27. Start wondering whether "getting into heaven" is the core of what Christianity is about. American evangelicalism's strong populist and pragmatic evangelistic streak has over time packaged "the gospel" into a few tightly bundled sound-bites and slogans. The Four Spiritual Laws is one example. "Accepting Jesus Christ as your personal Lord and Savior so that your sins can be forgiven and you can go to heaven" is another. Evangelicalism's interest in communicating with ordinary people at the grassroots is admirable. But you rightly find yourself wondering now and again if the message has not gotten squashed in the package.

When a lot of evangelical-speak about the gospel comes down to it, especially at a popular level, it often seems to boil down to *getting a ticket to get into heaven*. The old "fire insurance" image is often not far off. "If you were to die tonight, do you know for sure that you would go to heaven?" is a standard evangelical pitch (for those who still engage in overt evangelism). Perhaps particularly in the South, where I have lived for years, one will often hear in conversation, "Sure, I believe in Jesus, so my soul's goin' to heaven." But I don't think this soul-going-to-heaven mentality is limited to the South.

Ask yourself: is having your "soul go to heaven" really what Christianity is *about*? It seems like an emaciated version of the long work of God in history. And meanwhile it seems to leave a pretty narrow job for Christians and the church here on earth, before we die—to not lose one's ticket to heaven and to help get even more other souls into heaven, it would seem. If it were all that simple, then why is the Bible so elaborate and complex? And why do so many different churches have so many different ideas about what is true and right in the Christian faith and life? Keep wondering.

Okay, so you have started accumulating anomalies and have gotten through step #27. Even if you have gotten this far, you are still nowhere close to becoming Catholic. This is only the beginning of the road to your new identity. Remember that very little of the observations and ideas in the steps so far are, in and of themselves, arguments against evangelicalism or for Catholicism. We have not yet gotten to explicitly arguing for or against. The matters so far concern merely anomalies, things that do not fit the evangelical paradigm very well, that are hard to explain, from an evangelical normal-science paradigm. If you have gotten to this point, you are ready to move on to the next steps: seeing and accumulating even bigger anomalies.

three

Accumulating More Anomalies

You've accumulated a lot of anomalies. Time to accumulate some more, some that are more troublesome than those of the previous chapter.

28. Start wondering when the supposed "great apostasy" happened and where the true Christian church was for the 1,000–1,400 years between then and the Reformation. American evangelicals operate with a background belief that, sometime after "the early church," which was the ideal model for subsequent church history, Christianity suffered a great apostasy. And whatever the evangelical Protestant group in question is, *it* so happens to provide the restoration of Christian truth that undoes this apostasy.

Start asking yourself: When exactly *was* this great apostasy? Was it after the death of the apostles? Maybe after the Christian conversion of the Roman Emperor Constantine? Or when? The New Testament canon, we have already seen, was not firmly defined and established until the end of the fourth century. That is more years after Christ's ascension than we today have lived since, say, Oliver Cromwell's death in the mid-1600s. So was the Christian church already fallen into error by then, when it was defining the New Testament canon?

Or if we suppose the alleged great apostasy was after the conversion of the Emperor Constantine, then we have to reckon with this fact: it was Constantine who summoned the Council of Nicaea in 325 in which orthodox Christology was defined. If Nicaea was part of what was already an essentially unfaithful church, then the basis of all of orthodox Christology starts to fall apart.

If the Christian church was not in error by these times, then when *did* the supposed great apostasy happen? And when you've figured that out, ask yourself: why then is the experience of the Catholic Church in the centuries before that time not normative? And, having established when the supposed great apostasy did take place, start thinking hard about what we ought to make of the apparent "black hole" of the 500 or 1000 or 1400 years before the Reformation, during which time the Church was allegedly fundamentally in error and unfaithful. What was that about? Had the Holy Spirit fallen asleep on the job? Had the gospel gone into hibernation?

Then start pondering this kind of possibility instead: along with its strengths and achievements, the Church has always also suffered sin and failures along the way, as do all churches today. But the "great apostasy" narrative as a general background assumption legitimating Protestant restorationism really doesn't work. Or, rather, it only works when one does not think very carefully about the actual history. Once you've grasped and assimilated that anomaly, you've made a major step in the right direction.

29. Take note that even evangelical churches that are opposed to "human traditions" and "rituals" turn out to have an awful lot of their own human traditions and rituals. Evangelicalism is about having a direct, personal, vibrant faith in Jesus Christ that makes one spiritually alive and produces continual spiritual growth. When you have that kind of experience and life of faith, human institutions and routines are normally viewed as a threat. In fact, anything involving repetition— except regular prayer and Bible reading—is a problem. Human traditions and rituals are certainly a problem, because they make faith grow stale, routine, dull.

Most evangelicals are thus raised to assume that traditions and rituals are bad. Those are associated with theologically wrong and/or spiritually dead groups, like Catholics and moribund liberal Protestants. Adjectives that instead capture the true heart of an evangelical spirituality are things like Fresh!, Renewed!, Alive!, Refreshing!, and Vibrant! But most of the assumptions behind this outlook are untenable, if not exhausting—it's the evangelical spiritual equivalent of secular radio's laughably impossible amorous refrain, "All Night Long! Making Love All Night Long!"

But that is not our present concern. The observation that matters to us here, rather, is the fact that human traditions and rituals are simply unavoidable. People can deny and denounce human traditions and rituals till the cows come home. But they always still have their own. For such people, in fact, the insistent repudiation of all human traditions turns out to be one of their own most cherished human traditions. But they also have many others.

A bit of thought turns up an initial list: the particular order of worship services, the consistent forms of "informal, spontaneous" prayers, everyone closing their eyes and bowing their heads (and maybe folding their hands) in prayer, the expected dress of the preacher, one hymn book instead of another, the American and Christian flags at the front of the sanctuary, the pastor walking down the aisle after the benediction to greet everyone exiting the front doorway, vacation Bible school programs, the peculiar ways that Scripture passages are always read in public, the Sunday school curricular material, and on and on. So, you have churches that decry other churches for treating faith as if it were an automatic family inheritance or a taken-for-granted ethnic heritage to simply absorb, and then they turn around and, lo and behold, have their own regular processions of twelve-year-old children standing up to give their own (very similar sounding) personal testimonies about their coming to personal faith, of being converted, of "becoming Christians," which conveniently fits them for baptism, church membership, and quarterly communion.[1]

Again, the contradictions and blind-spots would all be rather amusing if the larger issues of tradition and ritual didn't matter so much and if it were not such a point of contention and division among Christians. But they do and it is. Happily, simply realizing that human traditions and rituals are inevitable itself frees one up from the futile attempt to escape them. The question is no longer human traditions and rituals versus none. The question is: *which* human traditions and rituals are worth

---

1. Thanks to John Wilson for pointing out this parallel to me. Analogously, it is well worth noting that everybody—including Protestant denominations—has a functional Magisterium, which is treated as de facto infallible in its judgments. Sociologically, it is impossible for organizations such as churches to function without a functionally authorized teaching office. They are simply required. Catholics are merely honest and explicit about that. Evangelicals instead rely on denominational leaders, seminary teachers, popular book authors, or charismatic figures to function as their magisteria. Evangelical popes, rather than being elected through due process, instead rise and fall according to mass popularity—they are functionally "popes of the market."

building into Christian life and the life of the church and why those particular ones?

30. Start asking where the theologically orthodox doctrines of the Trinity and Christology came from. This anomaly is obvious, when you think about it. Evangelicals rightly believe in God as Trinity, Father, Son, and Holy Spirit. Concerning the Son, they also believe in the two united natures of Jesus Christ, that he is both fully God and fully human in the same person. These doctrines evangelicals receive from the first ecumenical councils of the Christian Church—Nicaea (325 CE), Constantinople (381 CE), Ephesus (431 CE), and Chalcedon (451 CE).

But wait a minute! Those were councils of the Catholic Church, held when the bishop of Rome was increasingly understood as primary among dioceses with bishops. The councils consisted of Catholic bishops and theologians meeting to decide upon authoritative and binding doctrinal truths and to reject heresy. In short, the most important doctrinal core of the Christian faith that evangelicals today champion is the product of five hundred years of discernment and authorized creedal definition by leaders of the Catholic Church.

Now, ask yourself this question: how can evangelicals *both* deny the legitimacy of an authoritative teaching office of the Catholic Church functioning many centuries after the death of the original apostles *and* take as non-negotiable truths the doctrines of the Trinity and Nicene Christology, which were established as orthodoxy against the pressing claims of many heresies by the same authoritative teaching office of the Catholic Church? You can't do both. If someone tries to tell you that the Catholic teaching office was merely incidental in the process, that the conclusions of those ecumenical councils were actually over-determined by a straight reading of the Bible, don't buy it for a second. For one thing, as we have already seen, although the different churches of this era possessed various of the gospels and epistles that eventually became the content of the New Testament canon (and others that did not), that scriptural canon as such had not yet itself been authoritatively defined.

Second, most of the heresies rejected by these councils could and did appeal to very many scriptural passages to justify their errors—the eventual orthodox conclusions were actually not so obviously the only plausible reading of what were taken to be scriptural texts. The Arianism that the Council of Nicaea rejected, for instance, enjoyed all kinds of apparent biblical support. In fact, Arianism for a period of time in this era actually won the doctrinal struggle and was only eventually repudiated by bishops meeting in council because of the relentless championing of orthodoxy by Catholic theologians like Athanasius of Alexandria and others like him. Believing that the orthodox doctrines concluded by these councils simply flowed out of the pages of Scripture requires a blissful ignorance of history and of the scriptural and doctrinal complexities involved. But since you're on the road to Catholicism, you are learning to know better.

31. Read Martin Luther's 95 theses supposedly "nailed to the door in protest" at Wittenberg. Protestants are raised on folk legends about Luther's famous 95 theses. Since few Protestants have actually read the 95 theses themselves, they have reason for not knowing better about their true nature. But you need to know better. So go and search "Luther 95 theses" on the Internet and read them closely.

The first thing you will learn is that Luther's 95 theses were hardly a radical protest. In posting them, Luther was not somehow nailing an unusual "This Church is Toast!" message of early Protestant revolt against Rome. He was rather doing what university professors of theology, of which he was one, regularly did in his day. That was to propose theses for academic debate on the equivalent of a public bulletin board used for such purposes in order to invite participation in a standard theological disputation. Thus, Luther's theses open with this preamble: "The following propositions will be discussed, under the presidency of the Reverend Martin Luther, Master of Arts and of Sacred Theology, and Lecturer in Oratory on the same at that place. Wherefore he requests that those who are unable to be present and debate orally with us, may do so by letter." That this reads more like a departmental email announcement than the bold manifesto of a radical, world-transforming protest is no accident. That's essentially what it was.

The second thing you will learn by reading the 95 theses for yourself is that, at the time that Luther posted them, he was very much a late medieval Catholic theologian—and Augustinian monk, no less—who presupposed the authority of the Church and the pope and the truth of Catholic teachings. All of the leverage in his theses' arguments depends upon Catholicism's legitimacy, truth, and authority. In all of them, in fact, he only once (thesis 78) referenced a Bible passage (1 Corinthians 12). Luther was not against what the Catholic Church taught. He only wanted it practiced well, to not see it abused. So his theses proposed to debate certain questions concerning "the power and efficacy of indulgences." Luther saw that some instances of selling indulgences in parts of Europe for the remission of penalties for those in purgatory were abusing the correct doctrine of purgatory, indulgences, and the reduction of penalties for sin. But Luther was not at all contesting a proper understanding of those doctrines themselves.

The 95 theses assumed the reality of purgatory, the need to rectify sins after death, and the legitimacy of penance, indulgences, canonical church law, intercessory prayers for the dead, the pardoning power of the Church, the treasury of merit, the growth of love by works of love, and the inviolability of Mary as the "Mother of God." Luther clearly believed in and honored the authority of God's "vicar, the priest" (7), the oversight role of bishops (11), "the reverence due to the pope" (81), and the need to defend the Bishop of Rome against the "enemies of Christ and of the pope" (53). Note particularly these distinctly non-Protestant theses:

25. "The power which the pope has, in a general way, over purgatory, is just like the power which any bishop or curate has, in a special way, within his own diocese or parish."

38. "The remission [of penalties for sin] and participation [in the blessings of the Church] which are granted by the pope are in no way to be despised, for they are, as I have said, the declaration of divine remission."

69. "Bishops and curates are bound to admit the commissaries of apostolic pardons, with all reverence."

71. "He who speaks against the truth of apostolic pardons, let him be anathema and accursed!"

73. "The pope justly thunders against those who, by any art, contrive the injury of the traffic in pardons."

91. "If . . . pardons were preached according to the spirit and mind of the pope, all these doubts [voiced by critical lay people against indulgences] would be resolved; nay, they would not exist."

94-95. "Christians are to be exhorted that they be diligent in following Christ, their Head, through penalties, deaths, and hell; and thus be confident of entering into heaven rather through many tribulations, than through the assurance of peace."

What Luther wanted at the end of the day was for the sale of indulgences not to allow a neglect of "outwardly . . . diverse mortifications of the flesh" (3) by the repentant (i.e., cheap grace), since "true contrition seeks and loves penalties" (40). He wanted those buying indulgences to be "truly penitent" (31), to express "contrition" (35), and to realize that indulgences only promise the remission of some (instead of all) penalties—except perhaps in the case of "the most perfect" believers, for whom all penalties might be remitted (23). Luther also wanted canonical penances to be imposed after, not before, absolution for sin was given (12). He was concerned that the sale of penances was exploiting the poor (45–46, 50–51). And he wanted Christians to be taught that the power of indulgences ultimately came from God, not an autonomous authority of the Church (6, 26, 62, 68); and that letters of pardon were not necessary for eternal salvation (36). Far from a radical reformation are *those* claims.

Of course we know that the Catholic Church did not respond to Luther's ideas with the kind of openness with which it might and should have responded. Had it done so, the entire divisive Reformation might have been averted. Matters quickly "went south" from there. Both sides got increasingly upset and inflexible, Luther became radicalized, and the rest is history.

But what might have been is not our main point here. What matters for present purposes is realizing that what later became called "The Reformation" started out not as a major schism but as a genuine effort at reformation focused on a very particular area of abuse in Church life, and that the Catholic Church blew its chance to respond well to the constructive criticism. The 95 theses asked for a reconsideration of some of the practices around standard Church views, not an overturning of those views per se.

Note that, for American Catholics today, purgatory and indulgences are nearly irrelevant matters.[2] Looking back, Catholics now should be able to see that Luther was essentially right on these points and should have been taken seriously. It would have saved a whole lot of trouble and curbed some bad practices in the Church.

At the same time, the Church failing to respond well to constructive criticisms in a timely manner does not itself justify Luther's reactive radicalization, nor legitimate the theological content of his increasingly

2. They would, however, be more relevant for some Catholics in Latin America and parts of Africa.

historically-novel claims that followed. Where the radicalized Luther went in his thinking after the Wittenberg disputation is another matter altogether. In any case, you now know that the common Protestant idea that Luther's nailing his theses to the door at Wittenberg launched the Reformation protest is erroneous.[3] And that might make you wonder what other common Protestant ideas and historical accounts are also mistaken.

32. Begin to realize how very modern evangelicalism is. Protestantism and evangelicalism were integral to the birth and development of modernity and continue to be profoundly modern realities.[4] Both are a mere 300 or 500 years old, depending on how you count such matters. Protestantism itself was a crucial force setting modernity into motion. The birth of Protestantism marks the onset of the early modern period in history. And Protestantism in all of its forms has grown up entirely within the developing modern world. There is no such thing as pre-modern Protestantism. Protestantism has no authentically Protestant references, resources, or formations that predate modernity.

Now, start to suspect that a Christian church tradition that is *of* modernity will eventually be consumed *by* modernity and postmodernity. The signs of that are already evident, for those who have the eyes to see them. Begin to wrap your mind around the idea that if the Christian church is to survive modernity it very likely needs to have spiritual, intellectual, theological roots that predate modernity. To be *of* modernity is to be captive to modernity, not just its ways of life but its basic presuppositions and instinctive outlooks. By this I mean things like autonomous individualism, Enlightenment skepticism, distrust of tradition, moral relativism, consumerist materialism, knee-jerk hostility toward authority, the market's colonization of non-economic spheres of life (such as church), and the domination of mass media, advertising, scientism, and rationalism.

---

3. See Payton, *Getting the Reformation Wrong.*

4. By modernity here I mean the process of social and cultural change proceeding from and relating to economic growth, usually dated as beginning in the sixteenth century and rapidly accelerating in the eighteenth and nineteenth centuries with the onset of the Industrial revolution in the West. The social science and historical literatures on modernity are bigger than massive, but for present purposes, begin with Hunter, *American Evangelicalism*; Berger, Berger, and Kellner, *Homeless Mind*; Chadwick, *Secularization of the European Mind*; and Heelas, Lash, and Morris, *Detraditionalization*.

In contrast to Protestantism's position, Catholicism goes back to the very beginning with deep roots in the ancient world. That provides references and resources that enable modern Christians to potentially transcend modernity and so perhaps to resist its corrosive effects.

33. Consider the historic sociological connection between the Reformation and secularization. Think about these correlations. Liberal Protestantism was originally invented and spread from Lutheran Germany—the heartland of the Protestant Reformation—and Anglican England. Those are theological liberalism's epicenters. The modern European countries that have most thoroughly become secularized, and did so earliest in history, are all Protestant: Lutheran Germany, Sweden, Denmark, and Norway; Calvinist Scotland, the Netherlands, and German-Speaking Switzerland; and Anglican England. By contrast, the Catholic nations of Poland, Italy, Spain, Portugal, and Ireland were much delayed in and, until quite recently, remained more moderate in their levels of secularization. (The one exception to the otherwise strong correlation is Catholic France, the secularization of which was enforced by government law, constitution, and policy, which since the French Revolution has been actively hostile to the Church—a cultural orientation, not incidentally, that was strongly promoted by the French Protestant Huguenots.)

What about elsewhere? Among Canadian provinces, Catholic Quebec resisted secularization the longest. Anglo Protestant New Zealand and Australia have become highly secularized. The United States appears to be an exception to the secularization process. But even here, Protestantism is shrinking in numbers and the more obvious forms of external secularization (e.g., declining church membership) have been resisted in part through a devil's bargain with "internal" forms of secularization (e.g., cultural accommodation).

The point is this: a strong empirical, historical correlation exists between the spread of Protestantism, theological liberalism, and societal secularization.[5] That much is historically clear. The chance that this correlation is a random occurrence is extremely unlikely. Rather, it appears that something about Protestantism per se contains the seeds of and fertilizer for secularization. Those include Protestantism's demystification of the world (e.g., banishing saints and prayers for the dead), its tendencies toward rationalism, inherent individualism, anti-traditionalism, skepticism of institutional authority, and stripping down of a rich sacramental

5. See Gregory, *Unintended Reformation*.

imagination. That Catholic cultures have also secularized—which they clearly have—reflects a growing influence by what were already more secular surrounding Protestant cultures.

The empirical cases of historic, confessional Protestant churches sustaining theological orthodoxy in face of the secularizing forces of modernity are few indeed. Can you think of any? In the United States, mainline Protestantism has embraced theological modernism with open arms. Consequently, evangelicalism has been forced to break away from historic denominations and start their own (usually small) denominations, conventions, and non-denominational churches. Yet observation suggests that, even so, significant sectors of evangelicalism are becoming increasingly culturally accommodated and so internally secularized. It is not at all clear that American evangelicalism will be able to survive its own success achieved during the mid- and late-twentieth century.

In short, the historical track record of Protestantism seems to be one of recurrent inability to resist the forces of secularization. Not one obvious case to the contrary in the West presents itself. In fact, Protestantism seems to itself embody elements that spawn and promote secularization, its own destruction, and then later to "infect" Catholic countries and cultures. Might not this suggest something important?

34. Get to know personally some Catholics who believe in Jesus and are impressive in their faith. Most evangelicals are exposed to few Catholics in their lives. Even fewer are exposed to faithful, practicing Catholics who love Jesus and are serious about their faith. And even fewer build real friendships with them. Yet sociologists have long known that meaningful social relationships and affectively-significant social-network ties are a crucial part of religious change and conversion. That certainly holds true for evangelicals becoming Catholic. You need to get to know some Catholics who are committed, practicing, and thoughtful. There are actually a lot of them out there—your evangelical social networks have simply tended to insulate you from them. But getting to know some good Catholics is critical.

That will add to your growing pile of anomalies, because you will learn through those relationships just how "off" some of what you have been taught about Catholicism actually is. Building such relationships will provide a context to see a good version of Catholicism modeled and to get some of your questions answered. Simply to realize at an existential and not simply intellectual level that many Catholics truly love God, know what they believe, practice their faith, and do not have horns sticking out of their heads is a major accomplishment. In short, let Catholicism become humanized for you. You need this human connection for this process to work. In due time you will need such Catholic friends to be your "sponsors" into the Church (but more on that below).

35. Take note of sub-standard preaching. Protestants, especially evangelicals, pride themselves on being "churches of the Word." They place the pulpit, not the altar, at the center of church platforms and sermons, not the Eucharist, in the center of church services. By reputation, Catholic homilies are notoriously weak—not, admittedly, without some reason.

In my experience, however, and perhaps yours, if you pay more attention, many Protestants grossly overestimate the quality and value of their preaching. Over the years, I have visited many different churches and heard many sermons. Some Protestant preachers are terrific and some of their sermons are excellent—but those, I think, are the minority. Very many Protestant, including evangelical, sermons I have heard are mediocre if not simply awful. They are sprawling, unfocused, interminable, moralistic, not Christocentric, and theologically thin, if not in outright theological error.

At the same time, I have also heard some truly fantastic Catholic homilies. In my experience, contemporary American Protestantism enjoys no comparative advantages in preaching over the Catholic Church. Strong, Christocentric preaching can be found in pockets in both, and mediocre and even terrible preaching can also be found in both. In my observation Catholic homilies nearly always focus on the specific scriptural texts of the day's lectionary (the commonly designated Scripture passages for the day), whereas Protestant sermons often wander off into pastors' personal ideas.

Furthermore, bad Protestant sermons invariably drag on for seeming eternities, there being always just one more point to add, and reflecting little self-awareness of how bad they truly are. At least bad Catholic homilies, when they must be endured, are almost always short, like 10–15 minutes long, and are *always* immediately followed by the congregation reciting the Nicene Creed.

In short: if great preaching ever was a hallmark of American Protestantism, it no longer is, from all I have seen, and no longer stands as a particularly compelling appeal of evangelicalism. Pay closer attention to these matters and you might come to see the same.

36. Entertain the question whether the kingdom of God really stands and falls on the doctrine of biblical inerrancy. Evangelicalism in the twentieth century backed itself into the epistemological corner of having to stake the truthfulness of Christianity on the doctrine of biblical inerrancy. Epistemology, again, has to do with how we know what we reliably know. The Catholic and Orthodox belief that sacred Christian tradition serves a necessary authoritative function in understanding Christian truth was officially (wrongly) eliminated by Protestantism. And the liberal Protestant idea that enlightened modern human *experience* should serve a governing role in knowing Christian truth was officially (rightly) also rejected by evangelicalism.[6]

All that was then left to evangelicals, officially, at least, was the Bible. In that context, Christian truth was believed to have to be indubitable, certain, and authoritative. This was necessary in order to defend against the epistemological challenges of modernity, the terms of which evangelicals allowed to be set by modern secular epistemology. So it became necessary to place all of the theological eggs into the biblical-inerrancy basket.

You do not need to reject inerrancy to become Catholic. In fact, the Catholic Church teaches a very strong, high view of the authority of the Bible. But one step toward your becoming Catholic is beginning to doubt whether evangelical inerrancy is or ever could or should be the litmus test and keystone of all Christian truth. At least some definitions of inerrancy definitely seem problematic, when we are honest about the biblical text. In the end, it proves difficult to defend the position that the entirety of the truth and power of the Christian gospel and life of the church depend on an absolute defense of the theory of inerrancy—that it all falls apart if the bulwark of inerrancy is breached.

Why and how, ask yourself, should or must that be so? Doesn't the fact that evangelicalism has gotten itself painted into the difficult corner of inerrancy itself suggest that something more basic about its larger approach to knowledge and authority is off? As you think about these issues, pray and ask God to guide you into the truth.

6. I refer here to the approach classically advocated by the liberal Protestant German thinker Friedrich Schleiermacher. As it turned out, however, personal experience came increasingly to pay a large epistemological role in evangelicalism in the latter decades of the twentieth century—such that one might have reason to think of contemporary evangelicals as latter-day liberals, in their own particular way.

37. Start wondering what it means to profess "one holy, catholic, and apostolic church." These are the four marks of the authentic Christian church first articulated in the first century by Ignatius of Antioch, spelled out explicitly at the Council of Nicaea in 325 CE, and often repeated in Protestant creedal recitations today. Of course some American evangelicals—mostly "primitivists" and "restorationists"—do not believe in any creeds, and so do not adhere to this creedal language. But most evangelicals affirm the church as one, holy, catholic, and apostolic.

The question to next ponder is: what exactly do these terms mean? Visibly, the Christian church is hardly *one*. Protestantism especially comes in a vast assortment of kinds, types, and flavors. Protestantism is not one, but many, myriad. One census counts more than 23,000 different Protestant sects and schisms in the world today; another evangelical scholar counts more than 30,000.[7] Historically, Protestants have skirted this problem by making the oneness of the church a spiritual abstraction. The church is "one" not in a substantively visible sense, but simply in sharing a common, true faith in Christ. Conceptually, that definition of oneness is said not to be violated by the fragmentation of the visible church on earth.

Likewise, Protestantism reinterpreted what it means to be "catholic" to denote, essentially, the aggregate collection of all of those true believers across space and time. John Calvin greatly developed and extended the theological language of an "invisible church" (not a biblical term) to try to give expression to the oneness and catholicity of the real church, in contrast to the divisions, conflicts, and partitioning of the visible church on earth.

Protestantism also redefined "apostolic" not to mean handed down directly from the apostles from bishop to bishop through orderly teaching and ordination. That would be too Catholic, and the Reformation had already broken from Catholic bishops. Rather, "apostolic" was redefined to refer to faithfulness to the apostle's *cognitive teachings* as recorded in the New Testament. One was "apostolic" merely if one taught the same *ideas* that the apostles taught. The relational aspect of standing in full communion with recognized church leaders around the world who were ordained from generation to generation by those whom the actual apostles ordained was irrelevant. It had to be.

7. *World Census of Religious Activities*; See also Barrett, Kurian and Johnson, *World Christian Encyclopedia*.

In short, when Protestantism violated the historic creedal marks of the Christian Church, they got around that problem by redefining it away. What the Church had always taught and believed those four marks meant were not *really* what they meant. Really they meant something else that, if believed, made Protestantism valid, despite the multiplicity and divisions the Reformation had created. Your next step, then, is to question whether the Protestant accounts of "one," "catholic," and "apostolic" are credible.

38. Begin wondering what the difference is between evangelical museum pieces, memorials, and kitsch and Catholic icons, statues, and other sacramentals. Evangelicals dismiss and sometimes make fun of Catholic statues and images and other material trappings. It seems idolatrous. Why would anyone have a statue of Mary, for instance, if one wasn't worshipping her?

The basic problem with this kind of outlook is that evangelicals often have their own versions of such images and statues. But they are so "obvious" to evangelicals that they cannot recognize them as such. Still, just as Catholics take their images and statues as normal, evangelicals take their own for granted. In many ways, they are not that different. To perceive that, you simply have to be able to see things the right way.

Consider, for example, the idea of a religious tradition naming and honoring saints. On the surface, it seems that Catholics do and evangelicals don't. The truth, however, is that evangelicals have their own saints. They just don't call them that. But the functional effect is the same.

Wheaton College, for example, is an archtypically evangelical institution. Yet it possesses the relics of evangelical saints which it preserves in material form for veneration by the faithful. If you do not believe this, then visit the Marion E. Wade Center museum. Therein is kept "The Wardrobe" of C. S. Lewis, in which he and his brother, Warnie, played as children. This is the wardrobe which, legend has it, inspired Lewis' imagined portal to Narnia in his book, *The Lion, the Witch, and the Wardrobe*. Evangelicals take pilgrimages to pay homage to it like Catholics visit Lourdes. The Wade Center also houses a bust statue of Lewis and relics of other literary saints venerated by evangelicals, including Charles Williams, George McDonald, and Dorothy Sayers.

Close by, in Wheaton's Billy Graham Center, you can also visit with relics of Billy Graham himself. These include some of his grade school papers, classroom notes from his Florida Bible Institute days, medals and keys to cities, and even his very own traveling pulpit with sermon notes and Bible, behind which visitors are allowed physically to stand.

Material images venerating other Wheaton saints elsewhere on campus include a highly poignant one in Beamer Student Center. This memorializes a Wheaton graduate, Todd Beamer, who acted heroically on September 11, 2001 to help prevent Flight 93 from being used by the al-Qaeda hijackers as a weapon of terror. Beamer helped to bring the plane down in a field in rural Pennsylvania rather than have it crashed into a building in Washington, D.C. The memorial is quite moving.

Keep looking around. One of the walls of Blanchard Hall, the main icon of Wheaton, has the names and years displayed of all alumni who, time out of mind, had graduated and gone to serve on the foreign mission field. These graduates were of course being honored and revered for what in that subculture is essentially held to qualify one for sainthood: becoming a foreign missionary.[8]

In short, Wheaton College has plenty of its own saints and displays their images, statues, memorials, and relics in material form for believers to visit, honor, even venerate. To be clear, I am not belittling or criticizing any of this. It is all highly appropriate. The point here, rather, is simply to notice the *functional* similarity between such things and the images and statues in Catholicism. Viewed sociologically, the actual differences are slight, perhaps nil.[9]

It is not just Wheaton. I recently visited a different evangelical liberal arts college, a good school doing impressive things (though I'll leave it unnamed). I noticed during my campus tour that this college had built a "Hall of World Changers." It was a handsome two-story rotunda dedicated solely to the honoring of evangelicals who had "changed the world." The circumference of the hall was lined with bronze busts of inductees, including James Dobson, Bill and Gloria Gaither, Tony Dungy, Frank Peretti, and Joni Earekson Tada. The obvious purpose was to connect current students, parents, and visitors in a reverential atmosphere to this "great cloud of evangelical witnesses" who have led saintly lives in

8. The embarrassing thing, when I was a student at Wheaton in the late 1970s, was that over the previous decades the number of Wheaton alumni becoming missionaries had significantly dropped. A sense was in the air, sometimes spoken in chapel, that something had gone wrong, that contemporary students had lost much of the vision of these former students who stood as a great cloud of witnesses.

9. That is, at a human level. Catholics, however, rightly believe that there are major differences at a spiritual level.

"impacting the world for Christ." There were of course no kneelers or candles to burn. But the material representations in statues, the veneration, the intent to encourage and inspire were all there.

I have focused here on the matter of material representations of saints. With a bit of thought one could ponder similar parallels between Catholic visual paraphernalia and the great jolly gobs of evangelical material kitsch sold in Christian bookstores and displayed with spiritual seriousness in many evangelical homes. The pieties and practices involved in these are not strictly identical to that involved in Catholic material religion. But the parallels are more functionally similar than evangelicals normally ever imagine.

Could it simply be that the banishing of saints is a futile and misguided Protestant project? Might it be that the Protestant proclivity to move all things spiritual out of the material world and either into the human head or heart or into heaven is sadly misguided? Think about it.

39. Ask yourself why and how what began as a reform and renewal movement became entrenched as yet another established religious institution. Evangelicalism is at heart a reform and renewal movement. Its impulses of spiritual awakening, reformation, pietism, and revivalism have always sought to purify and renew the church and Christian living. There is much good in that, particularly in its intentions.

But evangelicalism, like everything else human, inescapably encounters what the sociologist Max Weber calls the "routinization of charisma." Entrepreneurial movements of the Spirit become denominations. Inspirations are institutionalized. The oppositional church becomes the organized church and sometimes the ossified church. Entropy happens.

From a Catholic perspective, accepting much about the stable, routinized, institutional aspect of the Church is fine. That is not the only important aspect of the Church, but it is part of the things that are important. Of course the Church continually prays for renewal, rejuvenation, appropriate reforms, and deeper spiritual insight. But it is in and through the one, holy, catholic, and apostolic Church—and not endless splinter groups and movements—that such renewal and reform takes place. The one Church is the object of loyal renewal, not the enemy against which renewal must continually rebel.

American evangelicals, however, are caught between the horns of a dilemma on this matter. They cannot abide the kind of institutionally envisioned and committed view of church that is embraced by Catholicism.

Yet their own churches inevitably do, have, and always will become settled, routine, established, bureaucratic institutions—like it or not. That tension then sets into motion an incessant subcultural drive. The drive is to worry, to defend, to accuse, and to be ever ready to break, leave, and start something again that is more pure, more vibrant, more faithful. That is the Puritan way. In its worst forms, revival and renewal become a kind of addiction that is satisfied for a while but then needs again and again to be sated by new breaks and initiatives.

To be a Protestant is to be a *protester*, one who protests, ultimately, against Catholicism, against Rome. Now ask yourself: Do you really want your Christian identity, doctrine, and life to be defined primarily as a protest *against*? Is that really right? In the long run, is faithful Christianity actually about standing on the outside of the center and perpetually protesting in opposition to it?

40. Start doubting that the next evangelical renewal movement will really renew the church. The latest renewal movement among some evangelicals is the so-called emerging or emergent church movement. It has generated a lot of controversy among and (for some) hope for evangelicalism. Your next step on the road to Catholicism: start to doubt it. Begin to realize that all kinds of renewal movements have come and gone in Protestantism, some making a mark, others not. More than a few have been fads. Notice how renewal movements today that are arising out of discontent with established evangelicalism seem, if anything, to base their promised renewal on "action" and "practice" at the expense of thought and doctrine. "Forget theology, let's just *live* faithfully," is the idea. Warning signal: Dead End Ahead.

41. Read G. K. Chesterton. Begin with his book, *Orthodoxy*. Enjoy the wit, bemusement, criticism, and insight. Keep in mind that Chesterton became a converted, committed traditional Catholic. If that is not enough for you, then also try out the Victorian poet, Gerard Manley Hopkins, who also converted from High Church Anglicanism to Catholicism.

42. Take notice of John Paul II. Pope John Paul II was simply incredible. His integrity, outreach, teachings, and courage in so many things, from defending life from beginning to end to confronting and helping to bring down Soviet communism are amazing. Learn about John Paul II and look to him as a shining example of what impressive Catholic leadership and living can be.[10]

10. See Weigel, *Witness to Hope*.

43. Start to wonder if American evangelicalism, not to mention Protestantism, actually ever really reforms itself. Protestants like to think that they are continually reforming themselves. They habitually reiterate the Reformation slogan, "Reformed and ever reforming!" They also assume that Catholicism is stuck forever in error.

The historical track record of the twentieth century, however, in fact, shows the opposite. Recent history shows the Catholic Church reforming itself in good ways more than Protestant denominations doing so. A fair-minded observation discovers a highly self-reflective, self-adjusting, self-reforming Catholic Church that has—even with difficulty—sustained continuity with tradition while re-reading and reforming itself in important and in some cases dramatic ways. The Second Vatican Council and much else are clear evidence of this, when taken seriously.

Meanwhile, Protestantism, including evangelicalism, hardly ever actually reforms itself. That is because anytime things get too bad, the disaffected people simply leave and start their own new group, and the old stay in place. Reform is thus neutralized by the joint dynamics of resistance and exit. In my experience, in fact, some evangelical churches—being so sure that they have the truth—can be among the *most* resistant of all to internal change and reform. If anything, in terms of change more broadly, when it does happen, Protestantism in the long run tends either toward theological liberalism and cultural accommodation or toward defensive sectarianism. A stable middle ground seems nearly impossible to sustain in Protestantism over time. And that is a big anomaly for the evangelical paradigm.

44. Start to wonder where all the evangelical intellectuals are. Okay, there are some greats. Alvin Plantinga, George Marsden, Mark Noll, Nick Wolterstorff, and some others. But not too many. Furthermore, the first three I just mentioned gravitated not to an evangelical research university (there isn't one) but to the Catholic University of Notre Dame. Moreover, most of these were not formed intellectually by vanilla American evangelicalism but by Dutch Calvinism, a particular European-rooted confessional Protestantism. Beyond these observations, I need write nothing more on this point, since Mark Noll already summarized it himself in his book, *The Scandal of the Evangelical Mind*—the scandal of the evangelical mind is that there is no such thing.

By contrast, consider the list of major Catholic intellectuals: Alasdair MacIntyre, Charles Taylor, Elizabeth Anscombe, Jacques Maritain, Mary

Douglas, Robert P. George, Mary Ann Glendon, Michael Dummett, René Girard, John Finnis, Jean-Luc Marion, Peter Geach, Etiene Gilson, John Rist, Christopher Dawson, Edith Stein, Louis Dupre, Gabriel Marcel, John Haldane, William F. Buckley Jr., Russel Kirk, Immanuel Mornier, Max Scheler, Josef Pieper, Gustavo Gutierrez, Karol Wojtyla, Bernard Longeran, John Henry Cardinal Newman, Ralph McInerny, Germain Grisez, Romano Guardini, and so on. Think too about the list of Catholic writers: J. R. R. Tolkien, G. K. Chesterton, Walker Percy, Flannery O'Connor, Graham Greene, Evelyn Waugh, Hillaire Belloc, Gerard Manley Hopkins, Orestes Brownson, Henri Nouwen, Shusaku Endo, Ronald Knox, Paul Johnson, Léon Bloy, Victor Hugo, Malcolm Muggeridge, Robert Hugh Benson, Charles Péguy, Paul Claudel, Tony Hillerman, Georges Bernanos, Francois Mauriac, Marshall McLuhan, Rumer Godden, Muriel Spark, John Lukacs, and Thomas Merton (besides these there are many others writing in other languages with whom American evangelicals are not likely to be familiar). And, for that matter, what's up with the fact that six of the nine Supreme Court justices (as of the time of this writing) are Catholic, while there has never been one modern evangelical serving on the Court?

Who among evangelicals compares to these intellectuals and writers and jurists? Of course, such observations are not decisive in matters of faith. But the dearth of major American evangelical intellectuals tells us something significant about the depth and generativity of its religious tradition. Ponder that too.

Okay, if you are still with me, then you have accumulated more anomalies. The weight of observed evidence that is not fitting the evangelical paradigm has grown heavy. Increasingly, if all has gone well, you are realizing that something has to give. Either you need to find some major new answers to deal with all of these anomalies and so salvage the evangelical paradigm. Or else you need a new, quite different, more convincing approach that explains things better. You are on the cusp of a possible paradigm shift, a revolution in basic outlook. You still may not become Catholic. It is still possible to pull back, to find ways to account for the anomalies, and to remain evangelical. In order to become Catholic, you need to start seriously entertaining the possibility of "revolutionary science." That's what comes next.

four

Catholic Revolutionary Science

This is the stage in your transformation process that gets really interesting, if you keep moving forward. What was previously secure starts to feel uncertain. What you have always relied upon, you start to have doubts about. You begin to catch glimpses of very different possibilities, alternative outlooks that can feel quite radical. You for the first time begin to entertain the idea that something big might have to change. You start to suspect that the fixes to the problems you have discovered cannot be merely piecemeal. Band-aids won't do it, nor will theological gymnastics. You begin to suspect that the fixes needed are systemic. You start to allow yourself at times to envision yourself not as an evangelical but as something else, maybe Episcopalian, maybe Catholic, maybe Eastern Orthodox.

Just as often, you find yourself telling yourself that this whole thing is crazy, that you are probably over-blowing issues and making big problems where there really are none. That works for a while. A lot about what is familiar to you is comforting. But then the weight of all of the already-accumulated anomalies returns, and you start to face the fact that, no, you have actually stumbled upon some real problems that won't go away. It is probably too late to turn back or pretend they do not exist. You need to do something about them if you are to maintain your spiritual and intellectual integrity. You are reaching the point of no return—time to bail quickly or get ready to go all the way.

If you are ready to go all the way, then start working through the next seventeen steps laid out in this chapter. They should throw you into what Kuhn calls a "paradigm crisis." Your old evangelical paradigm is about to break down and hit a real crisis of inability to make the best sense of Christian faith and life. That does not sound fun. But it is exactly what you want, if you intend to continue on the path toward becoming Catholic. In that crisis, and partly as a cause of it, what you need to see is that a revolutionary different paradigm—the Catholic faith—offers an account that makes better sense of Christianity than your old, disintegrating paradigm. Here goes.

45. Try not to make definitive proclamations to yourself or others during this discernment process about whether Catholicism is possible for you or not. This is in anticipation of all of the points that follow. If your experience is like that of others, including my own, you will be tempted during this perhaps long and challenging process to make definitive statements about what you can and cannot believe, what is possible and impossible for you to accept or embrace, when it comes to Catholicism. That is understandable, but usually not helpful. Until you come to the true end of your discernment process and make a commitment one way or another, what you may declare along the way may very well prove incorrect. And then you'll have to eat crow.

I have known people who have "prematurely" decided to become Catholic, and then changed their minds at the last second, when the reality of joining the Church was immediately upon them. I have also known people who have publicly declared certain beliefs and possibilities concerning Catholicism to be absolutely impossible, but who have later, with more time and learning, come around with very good reasons to believing and pursuing those very possibilities. In my own case, I can remember more than once, during my long process of learning about and considering the Catholic Church, when I declared to other people, "Well, this is not an option, I simply can't become Catholic. No way. So much for that idea." (I remember saying this one time just after reading Hans Küng.) But more learning, talking, thinking, reading, and discernment eventually led me to see that I had not understood matters adequately and later, for good reasons, I changed my thinking.

In the years before my wife, Emily, and I became Catholic, I had a list of theological points about Catholicism that I simply could not square with my best understanding of truth. Since I knew that being received into the full communion of the Catholic Church meant affirming that I believed everything that the Church affirmed to be revealed by God as true, these items presented seemingly-insurmountable hurdles. Thankfully, I had many knowledgeable Catholic friends and resources to turn to in order to help sort out the truth about those issues. One by one, as I increasingly learned things I simply had not understood correctly, that list began to shrink. Eventually it disappeared. But earlier, I had no idea that I would be able to reconcile my beliefs with the items on that list with any intellectual integrity.

The moral of the story is this: focus on your discernment of the possibility of becoming Catholic. Be patient. Give yourself time. Try to restrain yourself from making premature, seemingly-self-assuring declarations either for or against Catholicism. And see how it turns out in the end. Eventually, you will be in a position to make definitive statements. But don't rush them in the meantime.

46. Download and read the 1999 "Joint Declaration on the Doctrine of Justification," agreed to by the Vatican and the Lutheran World Federation and affirmed in 2006 by the World Methodist Council. A truly world-historical religious event took place in 1999. Unfortunately, most American Christians apparently failed to notice it. That event was that the Catholic Church, after decades of hard ecumenical conversation with Lutherans, officially and publicly reconciled and ended its core historical disagreements with Lutheranism on the key doctrine of justification. Lutheranism did the same with the Catholic Church. Both Catholicism and Lutheranism lifted their five hundred year-old mutual anathemas against each other and are now working on further strengthening their relations.

The official 1999 "Joint Declaration" document is available on the Vatican website.[1] Download it and read it carefully. You will be amazed.

Do not fail to grasp the massive significance of this event. The Protestant doctrine of justification (through faith by grace alone) was *the* "material principle" of the Reformation. It was one of the two central principles that the Reformers advanced as absolutely necessitating the Reformation, despite the breakup of Christendom it caused. Along with the Reformation's "formal principle" of *sola Scriptura* (which we will examine next), the right doctrine of justification was essentially what the

---

1. Online: http://www.vatican.va/roman_curia/pontifical_councils/chrstuni/documents/rc_pc_chrstuni_doc_31101999_cath-luth-joint-declaration_en.html.

Reformation was about. Differences over the nature of justification were at the heart of the Reformation's struggle and break from Rome. And now those differences have been reconciled.

The Catholic Church has significantly rethought since Luther's day how it expresses[2] its doctrine of justification and salvation. Today Catholicism is, even from a traditional Protestant perspective, orthodox on the matter. The Joint Declaration on the Doctrine of Justification should satisfy the theological scruples of any reasonable Protestant. Catholicism today teaches salvation by grace and Christ alone, not earned by good works. In short, when it comes to the decisive doctrine of justification today, here is the news: *the Reformation is over.*

The Catholic *Catechism*[3] is also quite clear about the source of all justifying and saving merit being grounded in Christ and grace alone. "Our justification," it teaches, "comes from the grace of God. Grace is favor, the free and undeserved help that God gives us to respond to his call to become obedient children of God" (1996). "The first work of the grace of the Holy Spirit is conversion. . . . Moved by grace, man turns toward God and away from sin, thus accepting forgiveness and righteousness from on high." "This vocation to eternal life is supernatural. It depends entirely on God's gratuitous initiative, for he alone can reveal and give himself. It surpasses the power of the human intellect and will" (1998). "The preparation of man for the reception of grace is already a work of grace" (2001). "No one can merit the initial grace of forgiveness and justification" (2010).

> Justification has been merited for us by the Passion of Christ. . . .
> It conforms us to the righteousness of God, who justifies us. It has
> for its goal the glory of God and of Christ, and the gift of eternal
> life. It is the most excellent work of God's mercy (2020).

"The divine initiative in the work of grace precedes, prepares, and elicits the free response of man" (2022). This is not the Catholic Church you were warned against—the one that supposedly believes in salvation by good works. The time has come to update your map of reality.

One can only wonder why so few evangelicals noticed the world-historic fact of the 1999 "Joint Declaration on the Doctrine of Justification."

---

2. See step #58.

3. References to *The Catechism of the Catholic Church* are given parenthetically in the text.

Perhaps they were distracted by preparing for Y2K. Or perhaps the obvious implication of the "Joint Declaration" was simply too hard to face—namely, that, on the point of justification, the Reformation is over, and so, necessarily, the evangelical party is also over.

The truth is: reconciliation has been achieved—time to return home. Time to wake up and smell the coffee, and undo the divisions of the past. Can evangelicals deal with that? I fear that what *should* be met with joy and celebration by evangelicals will instead elicit indifference and nit-picky resistance. Hopefully not.

But this book is not about all evangelicals. It is about you. And if this good news doesn't throw you into an evangelical paradigm crisis—perhaps along with what comes next—I do not know what will or could.

47. Realize that the doctrine of *sola Scriptura* is itself not biblical but, ironically, is received and believed as a sacred (Protestant) church tradition. As an evangelical, you grew up accepting as an obvious, sacred truth the doctrine of *sola Scriptura*—the Bible alone and no other human tradition as authority. This was not a point of orthodoxy that needed active justification and defending. It was simply taken for granted as a self-evident truth that informed all other thinking.

Stop taking *sola Scriptura* for granted. Start asking if it actually makes sense, even when taken on its own terms. If *sola Scriptura* is correct, then, for starters, to be an internally coherent and foundational belief, it needs to be authoritatively established by Scripture and by Scripture alone. But it isn't. As strange as this might sound, the Bible nowhere says that Scripture or the written word of God is the sole and sufficient authority for Christian faith and practice. It just doesn't. You can spend the rest of your life looking for Bible verses that say that and you will never find them. If anything, you will find passages commending both the word of God and the tradition of faith. Then you start wondering how you never noticed that before.

Because this matter is so central to the Protestant-Catholic difference, it is worth some attention to specific relevant texts.

Matthew 15:1–6 and Mark 7:1–9 are two New Testament texts to which advocates of *sola Scriptura*, including some classical Protestant confessions of faith, typically appeal. Here Jesus criticizes a particular religious group of his day, the Pharisees, who he said "nullify the word of God for the sake of [their] traditions" (*paradosis*) and "rules taught by men." Jesus is criticizing the Pharisees for insisting that his disciples engage in a ritual washing of hands before eating meals, a practice originally prescribed for Jewish priests eating consecrated food in the temple, but later required by the Pharisees as ritually binding for all meals.[4] Jesus condemns this, and then extends his attack by criticizing the Pharisees' violating the command to "Honor your father and mother" by allowing children to devote money to God ("corban") instead of supporting their parents.

So . . . how does this passage teach *sola Scriptura*? Well, um, it doesn't. Jesus here criticizes the Pharisees, a particular religious sect of his day[5], for imposing a priestly cultic practice (hand washing) well beyond its intended scope, and for encouraging Jews to use religious rationalizations to break one of the Ten Commandments (by neglecting the material needs of parents). Jesus was *not* making a general point about *sola Scriptura* or the epistemic illegitimacy of tradition per se. That just isn't there. What we can learn from this text is that human traditions should not cause us to break or distort God's laws and so "nullify the word of God." But that is quite a different matter than establishing the epistemic principle of *sola Scriptura*. Only very poor proof-texting could make this passage prove *sola Scriptura*.

If Jesus was indeed opposing the validity of tradition per se, then the New Testament would be violating that teaching when it elsewhere commends Christians to follow apostolic traditions, which it does. In 1 Cor 11:2, for instance, Paul writes, "I praise you for remembering me in everything and for *holding to the traditions*, just as I passed them on to you." The word for "tradition" here is the same Greek word, *paradosis*, used in Jesus' criticism of the Pharisees. (Protestant Bible translations often use the word "teachings" here, instead of "traditions," to avoid the obvious problem that a better translation would raise.)

Also, in 2 Thess 2:15, one of Paul's earliest written letters, he says, "So then, brothers, stand firm and hold to the *traditions* (*paradosis*) we passed on to you, whether by word of mouth or by letter." Note here that apostolic tradition has been conveyed by Paul both in writing and *orally*—and that both forms of tradition are authoritative. Again, in 2 Thess 3:6, Paul refers to the life-guiding authority of tradition: "Now we command you, brethren, in the name of our Lord Jesus Christ, that you

---

4. Setzer, "Tradition of the Elders," 638–39; Baumgarten, "Pharisaic *Paradosis*," 63–77.

5. Of which the apostle Paul had also been a part, per Gal 1:14.

keep away from every brother who leads an unruly life and not according to the *tradition* which you received from us."

Furthermore, Paul writes in 1 Cor 11:23 that the tradition he teaches he originally received from God: "For I received from the Lord what I also passed on (*paralambanō*) to you." In 1 Cor 15:3, Paul repeats himself: "For what I received I passed on (*paralambanō*) to you as of first importance." Elsewhere, Paul distinguishes between "the traditions of men" (problematic) and those "of Christ" (good) (Col 2:8). So, apparently, there are apostolic traditions "of Christ" that Christians should follow.

In fact, Paul's teachings in his letters draw upon numerous established Christian traditions of confession, liturgy, and acclamation (1 Cor 12:3; Phil 2:11; Rom 10:8–9), creedal formulations (1 Cor 15:3–5; Rom 1:3–4, 3:24–26; 2 Tim 2:8; possibly Rom 4:24–25 and 1 Thess 1:9–10), and hymns (Phil 2:6–11; Eph 5:14; possibly Col 1:15–20). Paul's moral teachings, recorded in the Bible, also draw upon some extra-Christian traditions from Cynic and Stoic moralist, Jewish *halakah*, and dominical teachings (that is, related to or coming from Christ), which were also likely reflected in early Christian catechetical materials.[6] In short, Paul himself drew on the authority and teaching value of tradition himself.

Jesus' criticisms of the traditions of the Pharisees, therefore, cannot be understood to support *sola Scriptura*. Nor can the New Testament testimony about tradition (*paradosis*) and the handing on of it (*paralambanō*) be read as evidence validating the doctrine of *sola Scriptura*. If anything, when read for what it actually says, it supports the Catholic idea of an authoritative apostolic tradition—different from merely human traditions and those which nullify God's word—which is passed on to believers both in writing and orally.

A second standard attempt to try to prove the biblical basis of *sola Scriptura* appeals to 2 Thess 2:1–2: "Concerning the coming of our Lord Jesus Christ and our being gathered to him, we ask you, brothers, not to become easily unsettled or alarmed by some prophecy, report or letter supposed to have come from us, saying that the day of the Lord has already come." So, where exactly is the *sola Scriptura* here? Paul is neither saying specifically nor establishing a general principle here that *only* the Bible is an authority for the church (remember, again, most of the New Testament documents did not even exist when Paul wrote these words, nor was any of it to be canonized for three more centuries). All Paul

6. Thompson, "Tradition," 944.

is saying is that he has already taught the Thessalonians about Christ's second coming and so they should not to be troubled by stories that teach something different—even if they come in epistles that have the appearance of being Paul's own. Once again, this has nothing to do with *sola Scriptura*.

A third passage sometimes suggested as supporting *sola Scriptura* is Gal 1:8–9: "But even if we or an angel from heaven should preach a gospel other than the one we preached to you, let him be eternally condemned! As we have already said, so now I say again: If anybody is preaching to you a gospel other than what you accepted, let him be eternally condemned!" Again, this text says nothing about *sola Scriptura*. All it says is that Christians should not accept a version of the gospel that differs from the gospel of grace that Paul originally taught the Galatians, the tradition he handed on to them—and so that they should reject the false teachings of Judaizers among them on circumcision and dietary laws. The Protestant intent to strip the Church of the authority of historical tradition with its teaching of *sola Scriptura* is simply irrelevant to this passage.

Some believers in *sola Scriptura* also point to Rev 22:18–19 as supportive biblical evidence. It says this: "I warn everyone who hears the words of the prophecy of this book: If anyone adds anything to them, God will add to him the plagues described in this book. And if anyone takes words away from this book of prophecy, God will take away from him his share in the tree of life and in the holy city, which are described in this book." But the only way this text could possibly be relevant to *sola Scriptura* is if one presupposed that "this book" referred to here is the Bible, and if church tradition was "adding" to it. But, again, the canonical New Testament did not exist when this passage was written, so that is impossible.

Furthermore, the text itself is plain that it is referring not to the entire word of God written, all scriptures, but to "the prophecy of this book" and "the book of this prophecy." The prohibition here, in short, is against adding to or taking away from the book of Revelation—something which, of course, no Catholic has any interest in doing. Again, the theory of *sola Scriptura* fails to find biblical validation.

The same logical problem applies to Deut 4:2, which some think teaches *sola Scriptura*. It says, "Do not add to what I command you and do not subtract from it, but keep the commands of the Lord your God that I give you." The problem, however, is that, "if we were to apply a parallel [to Rev 22:18–19] interpretation of this verse, then anything in the Bible beyond the decrees of the Old Testament law would be considered non-canonical or not authentic Scripture—including the New Testament . . . . The prohibition . . . against 'adding,' therefore, cannot mean that Christians are forbidden to look to anything outside the Bible for guidance."[7]

Yet another Bible passage to which advocates of *sola Scriptura* point is 2 Tim 3:14–17. What this text actually says when one pays close attention and does not presuppose *sola Scriptura* before even reading it, however, is instructive on the matter of Scripture and tradition. Paul[8], writing to Timothy, has been denouncing "evil men and imposters." He then says to Timothy: "But as for you, continue in what you have learned and have become convinced of, *because you know those from whom you learned it*, and how from infancy you have known the holy Scriptures, which are able to make you wise for salvation through faith in Christ Jesus. All Scripture is God-breathed and is useful for teaching, rebuking, correcting and training in righteousness, so that the man of God may be thoroughly equipped for every good work."

Note, first, that there actually isn't a hint of *sola Scriptura* here. This text tells us that Scripture is divinely inspired and useful for leading to salvation and righteousness. Quite so. But it does not say that Scripture should be the only and sufficient authority for the Christian church. Furthermore, as noted above, the Scripture to which Paul is here referring is the Old Testament Law and Prophets—not the New Testament, which, again, did not exist in canonical form at the time.

Also, notice that in this passage Paul appeals to the quality of the *people*, from whom Timothy learned about Christian faith, as a kind of authority ("because you know those from whom you learned it"). This may include Paul himself. But it also definitely refers to Timothy's mother and grandmother, who earlier in this letter Paul mentions as the source of Timothy's faith: "I have been reminded of your sincere faith, which first lived in your grandmother Lois and your mother Eunice, and, I am persuaded, now lives in you also" (1:5).

---

7. Peters, *Scripture Alone?*

8. Biblical scholars disagree whether Paul himself is the author of the "pastoral epistles" or whether one of Paul's later disciples wrote in Paul's name. The matter is not relevant for present purposes, but, if nothing else than for convenience sake, I will write as if Paul himself was the author.

So, not only does this passage not teach *sola Scriptura*, it actually emphasizes the kind of *social* basis of the inter-generational passing on of the faith tradition as an authority that rightly lends credibility to the faith. That is a lot like what the Catholic Church teaches about the authority of the Christ-authorized apostolic tradition guarded and passed on from generation to generation by the Church's teaching office and pastoral leaders. That too is consistent with another New Testament passage, 1 Tim 3:15, in which Paul, saying nothing about Scripture, actually writes that it is *the church* that is the basis of the truth: "If I am delayed, you will know how people ought to conduct themselves in God's household, which is *the church* of the living God, *the pillar and foundation of the truth.*"

Proponents of the *sola Scriptura* doctrine of the Bible sometimes offer one other approach in its "biblical" defense. That is to point to what the Bible says about "the word of God," which they take to mean the Bible. The idea here is that the Bible says in many places many laudatory things about the word of God. Like the Scriptures examined above, however, this approach also fails to validate *sola Scriptura* as biblical.

One problem here is that the phrase "the word of God" means different things in the Bible, oftentimes not referring to Scripture.[9] In some cases, it means God's direct speaking to humans (e.g., Num 3:16; Josh 19:5). In other cases, particularly in the Psalms, the focus is on the act of God's speaking itself. Sometimes, "word of God" indicates the subject matter which God conveys to people with whom he communicates; other times to the specific words themselves. "The word of the Lord" can also concern God's message to the prophets to be proclaimed to his people ("The word of the Lord came to me . . ."). It also indicates the actual thoughts and will of God, in contrast with his name, person, or presence. In the New Testament, the "word of God" also sometimes refers to the *orally preached gospel message* (e.g., Acts 4:31, 6:7, 13:5,7). In other passages, the "word of God" is clearly Jesus Christ himself (John 1:1-2; Rev 19:13). And in certain New Testament passages, "the word of God" indicates the written Scriptures of the Old Testament (e.g., John 10:35; 2 Pet 1:19).[10]

---

9. The Old Testament uses three different Hebrew words for "word," which are translated into the one English word "word"—'*ēmer*, *ne'um*, and *dābār*.

10. McDonald, , "Word, Word of God, Word of the Lord," 1185–88.

Since the documents which comprise what we call the New Testament were written centuries before they were canonized as Christian Scripture, however, none of the biblical phrases, "the word of God," can be taken to refer to the Bibles that we now carry in our hands—unless we want to indulge in retrospective projections and anachronisms involving many centuries of magnitude. Christians in the sixteenth and twenty-first centuries may call the Bible "the word of God." But that does not mean that our Bibles are actually what texts in the Bible were referring to when they said "the word of God." So whatever good things the Bible may rightly say about "the word of God," at most they may refer to the Old but not the New Testament.

Another difficulty in this defense of *sola Scriptura* is that, even if we mistakenly understood the "word of God" to mean the Bibles in our hands, nowhere do scriptural claims about the "word of God" ever say what the doctrine of *sola Scriptura* claims: that the Bible is and should be the only and sufficient authority guiding the beliefs and practices of God's people, to the exclusion of sacred Church tradition. No passage says that or anything quite like it. Yes, the "word of the Lord" is perfect, living, active, right, true, stands forever, and so on. Of course. But where in that is *sola Scriptura*? It's just not there—not unless one injects a pre-committed belief in *sola Scriptura* into those texts and then does not think too hard about it.

The hard bottom line, in short, is that the Bible itself does not teach *sola Scriptura*. That makes *sola Scriptura* itself an incoherent belief—in that the sole and sufficient source of authority that *sola Scriptura* upholds does not itself uphold *sola Scriptura*. The doctrine of *sola Scriptura* could thus only be correct if an extra-biblical authority made it so—something, at best, like sacred church tradition. But that would make *sola Scriptura* dependent upon the very thing it is designed to deny, namely, the authority of sacred church tradition. Hence, the doctrine is self-defeating. To believe in it necessarily means one in fact (regardless of what one says) believes in the authority of sacred church tradition. There is no way to get around that.

Well, so where did this Protestant doctrine come from, if not the Bible? The answer is that the sixteenth-century Protestant reformer, Martin Luther, was rightly criticizing a number of abuses and corruptions in the Catholic Church of his day, as we saw above, particularly in areas of popular piety and devotion. When Catholic leaders did not respond well, he quickly decided that he needed to challenge not only these abuses but to reject the entire basis and organization of the Church. It was not enough merely to reform Catholicism—a project with which, unfortunately, the Catholic Church of Luther's day was not cooperating. Luther decided that he had to completely reject, renounce, and damn Catholicism in its entirety as a work of the devil. All of the circumstances of the times and of Luther's personality considered, this is somewhat understandable. But it was the wrong move. The Catholic Church needed reforming, not rejecting and demonizing.

In order to justify his radical break from the Catholic Church, Luther needed a clear epistemological rationale—that is, a theory of how Christians know what they know. Without such a compelling and decisive theory to justify his actions, Luther's break from Catholicism would have amounted to little more than a well-intentioned but sinful schism. The theory that Luther advanced to justify his break with Rome was *sola Scriptura*. About that he was adamant. He pounded his fist on the table about it in defiance of the previous 1,500 years of church history on the matter. Besides the fact that Luther was in his personality, by all accounts, impetuous and stubborn—for better or worse—he *had* to be adamant about *sola Scriptura*. For without that key belief, his developing anti-Catholic project was misguided and destructive. With it, however, it could make sense and appear necessary, whatever the consequences.

This is all difficult for evangelicals to recognize and accept, of course. But, when faced honestly, it is simply a fact. *Sola Scriptura* is not itself a biblical teaching, but is received as part of Protestantism's sacred tradition. It was needed to justify Protestantism's separation from Catholicism. And only on that basis is it a sacrosanct Protestant doctrine not to be questioned. But that realization itself calls the doctrine fundamentally into question. Evangelical Protestants cannot have it both ways. Either *sola Scriptura* is true and then we must admit the legitimacy of (Protestant) sacred church tradition—and, if so, then the dismissal of the authority of church tradition *as a category*, including then perhaps Catholic Church tradition, is unwarranted. Or, *sola Scriptura* is not true, and then we have no reason in principle not to admit the authority of Catholic Church tradition. Either way we cannot evade the authority of sacred church tradition. The only question is whether tradition is taken on Catholic or Protestant terms and why.

At this point, some Protestants may admit the necessity of authoritative church tradition in principle, but still reject Catholic sacred tradition. They may do this because, they claim, some Catholic traditions not only go beyond what the Bible explicitly teaches—which they admit in principle to be okay—but actually, they believe, positively violate some clear biblical teachings. In short, sacred tradition that is consistent with the Bible is one thing, but tradition that contradicts the Bible is another.

First we need to go back and take a second look at the alleged lack of biblical support for certain Catholic teachings over which Protestants habitually stumble. We will do that below, where we will see much more biblical support in fact than Protestants usually ever realize. Second, by here admitting in principle the authority of some sacred church tradition that is formally extra-biblical but does not positively contradict the Bible, one has taken an enormous step away from evangelicalism's Bible-only-ism. That opens a huge can of worms that turns out to make a mess of the evangelical paradigm. That will come in due time. Meanwhile, there are other steps to take first.

48. Consider the positive plausibility of an authoritative oral tradition passed on from Christ to the apostles to the Church. The authority of Catholic sacred tradition is grounded in part on a particular belief. That is that Christ taught his apostles by his life, death, and resurrection truths that were not necessarily recorded in the Gospels or other parts of the New Testament—yet which are dominical and apostolic and have been passed down through apostolic succession from bishop to bishop, and thus to all of the Church. Protestants generally do not trust that kind of authority because it resides in an institution and not in written words on a page. But it is worth considering the case for the plausibility of such a belief.

To begin, we should note the obvious: Jesus did not write books or manuscripts. The only record we have of Jesus writing anything was with his finger on the ground (John 8:8). Otherwise, Jesus seemed content to convey all that he had to say orally. Furthermore, nowhere does Scripture say that Jesus instructed his disciples to write down what he taught them or what they had learned during their life with him. Nor did they seem in a rush to do that. The materials that were eventually written into what we have as the four Gospels were passed on by early Christians in an oral tradition for decades before they were committed to writing. If, as Protestants insist, written Scripture is the only and sole Christian authority, then isn't it odd that the apostles did not do a better job of getting the truth of revelation of the Gospels written down sooner?

Furthermore, during the intervening decades, the early church worked only with its oral and liturgical traditions. Yet it was able to organize, function, and grow effectively. Between the years 40–150 CE, according to the best calculations, the Church grew in size from approximately 1,000 believers to 40,500 believers—a multiplication of about forty times in size.[11] That tells us that the Church relying on an authoritative, apostolic oral tradition is not only theoretically possible; it was actual and effective in the life of the Church. Oral tradition was clearly used by God—and, from a Catholic perspective, ordained by God—to help advance the life and work of the Church.

We have already seen that Christian churches of this era usually possessed various hand-copied manuscripts of many (but not all) of the documents that would eventually be included in the New Testament scriptures (as well as other documents considered authoritative but not eventually included). Yet we have also seen that those documents were not collected together and authoritatively defined by the bishops of the Church as Christian scripture until as late as the end of the fourth century. So how did the Church function without the canonized "Bible" that we now hold in our hands? The best estimates show that the Christian Church sustained a growth rate of 40 percent per decade between the years 40–350 CE—which translates into a sustained 3.42 percent annual rate. That rate grew the Church from approximately 1,000 believers in the year 40 CE to 33,882,000 in the year 350 CE. That means that Christian adherence grew in that time period from a mere 0.0017 percent to fully 56.5 percent of the total population of the Greco-Roman world.[12]

In short, the church grew amazingly fast and functioned well for centuries without having in its hands the Bible as we today know it. How? The Church historian, Eusebius of Caesarea, writes at the beginning of the *fourth century* that, "they proclaimed the knowledge of the kingdom of heaven through the whole world, *giving little thought to the business of writing books.*"[13] The early church was spread through oral preaching and instruction.

11. Stark, *Rise of Christianity*, 7.

12. Ibid., 6–7.

13. Eusebius, *History of the Church*, 24.

Back to the apostolic era, the apostles appear mostly to have communicated the gospel and Christian moral teachings orally, by *speaking* with people. The apostle Paul certainly wrote a number of letters to different churches he had helped establish. But for the most part they were occasional and problem-driven. As far as we know, Peter wrote a few letters, John wrote a few, and James is attributed as having written one. But from the pens of the other apostles, we have nothing. Again, putting all that was to be known and said about the Christian faith systematically into writing simply was apparently not a big priority for the apostles.

If anything, actually, the Bible itself suggests that at least some apostles preferred to communicate much of what they had to teach orally rather than in writing. The apostle John, for example, states this explicitly: "I have much to write to you, but I do not want to use paper and ink. Instead, I hope to visit you and talk with you face to face" (2 John 12); and "I have much to write you, but I do not want to do so with pen and ink. I hope to see you soon, and we will talk face to face" (3 John 13–14). Funny how easy it is for evangelicals to read over such verses and miss their larger implications.

It is also clear that Jesus taught and did much more with his disciples than is recorded in the four Gospels. The Gospel of John, for example, provides a highly detailed account of Jesus' life and teachings. But, having provided that extended written testimony, John notes this in his last verse: "Jesus did many other things as well. *If every one of them were written down, I suppose that even the whole world would not have room for the books that would be written*" (John 21:25). John also notes that, "Jesus did many other miraculous signs in the presence of his disciples, which are not recorded in this book" (20:30). So, the apostles actually had voluminous knowledge of Jesus' incarnation, life, teachings, crucifixion, and resurrection, only a fraction of which ended up written in the Gospels. Of course that knowledge would have informed their teachings in and to churches between Christ's ascension and their deaths.

Not only that, but Jesus himself promised that he would send his Spirit to teach them all things and remind them "of everything I *said* to you" (John 14:26). Again, the emphasis here is on oral tradition. Jesus never commanded his disciples to write down what he said and did. He promised the Holy Spirit to help teach and remember what Jesus himself had said with his mouth.

Even after Jesus' resurrection, he spent 40 days with his apostles, continuing to teach them about the kingdom of God (Acts 1:3: "After his suffering, he showed himself to these men and gave many convincing proofs that he was alive. *He appeared to them over a period of forty days and* spoke *about the kingdom of God*.") Of all that Jesus taught the apostles during those forty days, the Bible provides only five verses' worth of instructions (Acts 1:4–8)—that concerned staying in Jerusalem until being baptized by the Holy Spirit and then being sent out as witnesses to the world. Everything that Jesus taught the apostles orally for forty days about the kingdom of God surely involved more than those simple instructions. And surely the apostles remembered it and passed it on (*paralambanō*) in the coming years.

It helps in all of this to remember that accurate and extensive written records are an opportunity and concern of particularly *modern* people.[14] Even primitive printing presses were not invented until the fifteenth century. For most people in most of human history, authoritative written documents were quite limited in their use and circulation. Many people were simply illiterate. So it was very natural for oral traditions to be considered trustworthy and authoritative and to be relied upon to pass on important beliefs, practices, and truths. That the Christian Church also did this for centuries is not at all odd. By contrast, the modern, Protestant insistence on the written word in the Bible as the only and sufficient Christian authority for faith and practice relies on an impossible anachronism that artificially projects a modern standard of authority and means of knowledge conveyance retrospectively back into a pre-modern reality that operated by different but reliable and legitimate standards.

Back to the scriptural witness: Jesus clearly *entrusted his apostles* to carry out the work of the church as the most visible embodiment of the kingdom of God after his ascension and the coming of the Holy Spirit at Pentecost. For instance, he explicitly empowered the disciples and the Church with the authority to judge truth and forgive sins: "I tell you the truth, whatever you bind on earth will be bound in heaven, and whatever you loose on earth will be loosed in heaven" (Matt 18:18; also see Matt 16:19). Jesus promised that disciples who have faith in him "will

14. More specifically, reliance on accurate and extensive written records is a particular concern of modern *Western* people, who rely heavily on attorneys using contract law to govern economics and social relations broadly—unlike even modern business and economic relations practiced in many non-Western parts of the world.

do even greater things than [perform miracles like Jesus did], because I am going to the Father" (John 14:12). Jesus commanded Peter, the obvious leader of the apostles, to "feed my lambs, tend my flock, feed my sheep" (John 21:15–17). And he gave Peter, and, perhaps, by extension, the other apostles and the Church more broadly, the keys of the kingdom of heaven (Matt 16:18–19).

In the Council of Jerusalem (Acts 15), the apostles certainly seemed to feel authorized to make authoritative pronouncements without citing Scripture ("It seemed good to the Holy Spirit *and to us* . . ." [28]). This seems consistent with Jesus' promise that, "when he, the Spirit of truth, comes, he will guide you into all truth" (John 16:13). And what the members of that Council decided then became authoritative for all of the churches, as Acts 16:4 says: "As they traveled from town to town, they delivered the decisions reached by the apostles and elders in Jerusalem for the people to obey."

We also just noted in step #47 above that the New Testament itself contains explicit references to an authoritative apostolic tradition that was passed on orally, at least in part (e.g., 1 Cor 11:2, 15:3; 2 Thess 2:15, 3:6; Col 2:8). We also saw that Paul's own writings drawing upon established early church traditions (e.g., Rom 1:3–4, 3:24–26, 10:8–9; 1 Cor 12:3, 15:3–5; Eph 5:14; Phil 2:6–11; 2 Tim 2:8). So, the authors of the New Testament themselves are not only familiar with but using an authoritative oral tradition. This is precisely the kind of deposit of faith which church leaders understood themselves to be responsible to protect and pass on to future generations.

To follow up on these matters, I strongly suggest that you read Yves Congar's *The Meaning of Tradition* (San Francisco: Ignatius, 2004 [1964]), Mark Shea's *By What Authority?: An Evangelical Discovers Catholic Tradition* (Our Sunday Visitor, 1996), and perhaps George Tavard's *Holy Writ or Holy Church: The Crisis of the Protestant Reformation* (London: Burns & Oates, 1959). Pray and ask God to show you the truth concerning these issues.

49. Read John Cardinal Henry Newman's *The Development of Christian Doctrine*. Newman, a superb writer, makes in this book the definitive case for the reality and necessity of development in Christian doctrine. This book will disabuse you of the myth that everything important that the church needs to and does know is found directly in the Bible. It is a landmark work well worth reading.

50. Start reading the documents of the Second Vatican Council, the *Catechism of the Catholic Church*, and Catholic Social Doctrine. The time has come to start digging into real Catholic doctrines and teachings. There are various ways to do this. But the best way is to read the most important documents. Buy and read the *Catechism of the Catholic Church*, *Vatican Council II: Constitutions, Decrees, Declarations*, and *Catholic Social Thought: The Documentary Heritage* or the *Compendium of the Social Doctrine of the Church*. Take note of teachings you already believe, teachings that may make you uncomfortable, and teachings with which you think you have real problems. You will have to sort through these issues as things progress.

Start to absorb the ways that Catholic teachings *express* themselves differently from evangelical styles, even when the content is quite similar to evangelical beliefs. You are getting into a somewhat different culture with some characteristically different terms and expressions (more on this below). Start familiarizing yourself with them. But mostly start to drink in the coherence, historicity, and depth of the Catholic faith in the form of its central teachings.

51. Find some knowledgeable, committed Catholic friends who can help answer your questions. The time has also come—if you have not done this already, which would have been good to do—to start expressing any concerns you have and getting reliable answers to your questions. Books are only going to take you so far. You need some ongoing relationships with different kinds of Catholics with whom you can work through your confusions, concerns, doubts, and questions. This may include clergy, religious (nuns, sisters, brothers, etc.), or laity. Some you will find some more helpful than others. Keep searching and asking. Keep your antennae up for new people you might meet who can help you out. Ask around. You will find that the right kind of people for this job will be more than happy to help you. Make sure to find and make use of them. Ask them to pray for you and your process of discernment. Do not try to do all of this in your head by yourself.

52. Embrace the social and communal nature of salvation and church. Until now, as an American evangelical you have believed that Jesus saves individuals; and that Christian churches consist of saved individuals voluntarily banded together in like-minded, local groups for worship, teaching and fellowship.

Time for a new vision. God has saved a *people*, not atomized in-dividuals. Redemption is cosmic and a mystery, not private, voluntary, and transparent. The Church is irreducibly a sacred, organic *community* of God's people, formed sacramentally into the mystery of the Body of Christ. The Church is not made by volitional human decisions. It is Christ's existing Body on earth into which the baptized are born to new life. Both Christian salvation and church are communal, social, visible, embodied, and materially constituted by and in the Holy Spirit through the sacraments.

The Church is not something you choose. It is something for which you are chosen. Church is not a matter of so many consumer prefer-ences to meet one's needs. (Did you know, incidentally, that the English word "heresy" comes from the Greek word *hairetikos*, meaning "able to choose"?) There is one church and it has a very particular place in it for you. So expunge the individualistic outlook and volitional agency you have inherited mostly from modern liberal individualism and its assumptions about autonomous human agency, not from scripture or the Christian tradition. The Catholic Church badly needs the best of what evangelicals have to bring it. But it does not need the standard evangelical mentality of individualism and autonomous choice-making. Leave that part behind.

53. Change your idea of what "catholic" means. It is time to drop the Protestant notion that "catholic" simply means the abstract universal idea of all true believers everywhere at all times. That is a start, perhaps, but seriously incomplete. Catholic Christianity entails a lot more than that. It means living in full relational communion with all other catholic believers in heaven and on earth. It means sharing the same faith once delivered to the Church (Jude 3) which is commonly affirmed and taught by Church teachers. It means being tied to your parish, to priests, and to a bishop who are all themselves tied by historic succession and confirmation to the real, global body of all other Catholics. It means be-longing to the oldest, the largest, and the most continuously stable social and spiritual institution on earth.

Being Catholic for you now no longer means being part of a cat-egory. It means real relationships, real belonging, real community, real accountability, real commonality, real human ties that span the globe, pull together all of redemption history, and reach into every nation on earth. That is how you need to start understanding what it means to be catholic. It means, in short, to be Catholic.

54. Let liturgy sink in and transform your approach to worship. A big part of your move to Catholicism will involve understanding and embracing liturgy as a very different way of worshipping God, praying, and celebrating the Eucharist. The chances of your ever becoming Catholic are slim if you do not learn to "get" liturgy—or, rather, allow liturgy to *get you*. And it might take some time and effort.

We are not talking here about an alternative style that one may or may not prefer. Liturgy involves a rather more profoundly different, basic approach to history, prayer, the communion of saints, the act of worship, human subjectivity, Christian formation, sense of the movement of time, and more. "Getting" liturgical worship is not something that can be readily explained in words or put into a formula. It has to happen through lived experience, through a personal and communal process of doing, learning, and growing in understanding. It is something one is formed into. Whether step-by-slow-step or all in one fell swoop, you will eventually come to see the awesome difference that liturgy makes in worship and spiritual formation.

The format and content of Catholic worship services today go back to and are based upon the very earliest records and practices of the Christian church. Catholics today say the words, pray the prayers, and perform the liturgical acts that Christians have spoken and performed for almost 2,000 years. By contrast, most evangelical formats and styles of worship are based, at best, on principles invented in the seventeenth century (e.g., the so-called "regulative principle"). At worst, they are made up situationally, on the spot, according to things like local pastors' opinions, what seems "relevant" or appealing to people at a point in time, or what "praise band" talent a church happens to enjoy.

As a result, increasingly, many evangelical worship services, cut off as they often are from historical tradition, emphasize cognitive teaching, individual subjectivity, aesthetic enjoyment, and worshippers feeling "blessed," "spoken to," or having had "meaningful" experiences. Again, that is so modern. In fact, Christian worship has little to do with individual subjective experience—what one "gets out of it" is nearly irrelevant. Christian worship is a collective *act* offered, with all of the saints, present, past, and future, to God; as well as a collective, objective receiving of Christ's body and blood in the Eucharist. That is the liturgy.

You may be the sort of evangelical who has the advantage of a jump start on liturgy by virtue of having spent time in an Anglican or Episcopalian church. If so, that will be a big help in your becoming Catholic. Whatever else are the many problems besetting modern Anglicanism and the American Episcopal church, and there are many, they at least still do possess the *Book of Common Prayer* which structures and guides Anglican worship. Anglican liturgy is beautiful, life-forming, and perhaps more accessible to ordinary evangelical sensibilities than the Catholic Mass.

(At the same time, if you have been or currently are in the Anglican church, you also know or are in the process of realizing that the Anglican communion is coming apart at the seams, its "instruments of communion" have become dysfunctional, the American Episcopal church has been moving decisively away from historic theological orthodoxy for a long time, and there appears very little hope of a truly catholic Anglicanism in the United States (the AMIA and "Network" churches notwithstanding). So, Anglicanism is a very useful and helpful "train stop" on the way to Catholicism, but, when it comes to being truly catholic, it simply no longer appears to be a viable final destination—even *if* the Anglican account of its catholicity made sense, which in the end it does not.)

But most readers of this book have not been formed by the Anglican liturgical tradition. Some evangelical churches today do try to insert bits and pieces of historical liturgy into their otherwise typically evangelical Protestant services. That is a step in the right direction that reflects a good intuition. But in order to really work, liturgy needs to hang together as a whole, not be pulled apart and experimented with in pieces. It is not enough simply to test the temperature of the water with one's toes, so to speak. One needs to dive into liturgy and enjoy (or not) the swim, however cold or warm the water feels at any given time.

One of the excellent things about liturgical worship is how active and participatory it is. Many evangelicals wrongly assume that liturgical worship is stale, rote, and passive. Like anything, it can of course become that. But, in its essence, liturgy is anything but stale, rote, or passive. In liturgy, the congregation actively participates with full body and voice in many ways, from start to end, with the clergy, musicians, cantors, readers, and servers, with water, oil, ashes, bread, and wine. Liturgical worship is in fact one of the most active, participatory styles of church worship possible. "Liturgy" thus itself actually means "the work of the people," which is exactly what it is.

The main difference from other more "active" styles of worship—such as "holy-roller" Pentecostal or "open floor" Quaker services—is that liturgy does not require the people in worship to spontaneously make up their own prayers, congregational responses, songs, readings, sermon topics, and so on. All of that done today in liturgy follows the way Christians have been doing it for nearly two millennia. What is done in liturgical worship, therefore, participates in the best of all that has been learned and done in Church history, rather than what was thought up or felt the previous week or even on the spot.

If anything, it is actually the typical Protestant worship service that lacks much activity and participation. Many of them consist of congregants sitting in pews for an hour or more listening to one or two people up front do most of the talking. The assumption seems to be that church is about didactic learning—bookended with some singing at the start and end. The "Congregational Prayer" of many Protestant churches often consists of pastors praying at the pulpit for an extended list of items for a very long time. Congregational confessions of sin are usually done entirely quietly, inside the minds of each person. The congregation is sometimes told to stand and sing, or perhaps to recite the Apostles' Creed and the Lord's Prayer. Otherwise, their active involvement in the service is in fact rather limited. The contrast between this and real liturgical worship is quite stark.

Many evangelicals have of course recognized this problematic fact of relatively extensive congregational non-participation in their churches. The charismatic movement was in a sense one response to it. But that only goes so far. The relative informality of many evangelical "seeker-friendly" churches is another response. But that too usually makes changes only at the margins of the standard format. Today's "emerging church" movement is also in part, I think, another attempt to address this routine congregational passivity in worship. But in the end, I suggest, it is not enough to simply adjust the standard evangelical service format. What evangelicals really need is the formative power, beauty, and active involvement of all believers that comes in traditional liturgical worship.

If you think you'll have a hard time with liturgy, perhaps begin by reading a liturgy-friendly book by a good evangelical, like Mark Galli's *Beyond Smells and Bells: The Wonder and Power of Christian Liturgy* or Thomas Howard's *Evangelical is Not Enough: Worship of God in Liturgy and Sacrament.*[15] Ask some people who know liturgy to take you to Mass with them and to help explain what is going on. Eventually, you will have to learn what liturgy is about by simply doing it. Be prepared for that learning to take a year or two. Go into it by temporarily suspending your familiar notions about worship and lowering your expectations concerning how liturgy will or will not make you feel. At first you will most likely feel lost and confused. Be patient. It takes time, but it eventually makes some sense.

The day will come, believe me, when you will simply not be capable of worshipping well in the old free-form, "spontaneous"-prayer, wonder-bread-cubes-and-tiny-grape-juice-cups, one-guy-up-front-talking-the-whole-time way. You'll know then that you have nearly crossed the continental divide and will be looking down on a whole new promised land of Christian life and worship. That will be a major, major step toward the destination.

55. Reorganize your basic sense of time by the Christian calendar year. A larger part of becoming a liturgically-formed Christian involves learning a transformed sense of time. Most of the marks and flows of time in your life till now have been determined by the institutions and imperatives of the secular world—school schedules, workdays and weekends, punch-in time clocks, vacation weeks, plane and train schedules, spring and summer breaks, and so on. Guess what? The Catholic Church has an ancient, highly-developed system of marking and living time that is shaped by an historically Christian sense of reality.

I am talking here of course about the liturgical calendar, the Christian year—Advent, The Twelve Days of Christmas, Epiphany, the Feast of the Presentation of Our Lord, Ash Wednesday, Lent, Easter, Ascension, Pentecost, Trinity Sunday, Corpus Christi, Ordinary Time, All Saint's Day. We are talking about Holy Week and the Easter Triduum—Palm Sunday, Tenebrae, Holy Thursday, Good Friday, the Easter Vigil, Easter Sunday. We are talking about Morning Prayer, Evening Prayer, daily lectionary (scripture) readings, and Night Prayer to end the day. We are talking about days strewn throughout the year designated by the Church to remember and honor the lives of the many saints. It all hangs together and moves in a grand cycle by which you can live your life.

---

15. Beyond that, perhaps try reading von Hildebrand's *Liturgy and Personality*, which is dated but still contains some of the ideas I am suggesting here.

The Christian liturgical calendar involves a lot to take in, to get up to speed on. But the marking and flow of time is a fundamental force shaping our human lives. And lives formed by a Christian approach to time tend over time to become more Christian. The significance and power of the cosmic story of redemption becomes more real, more embodied, more formative as it is dramatized across the year and within each day. The flow of the seasons, our waking and sleeping, become connected to Christian meanings and teachings. Christian discipleship is thus pressed home by means of a dimension of creation and life—time—that is both deeply natural and human.

So, for example, the awareness of our mortality, which is crucial for a Christian life, is put into searing focus on Ash Wednesday, as the priest bodily crosses our foreheads with the ashes of the previous year's burnt palm branches and tells us one-by-one, eye-to-eye, "From dust you have come and unto dust you shall return." It is powerful.

Here again we return to the basic question of Catholic Christianity's use of the mundane and material to learn and to live the faith. Protestants, again, strip down nearly all of this. Catholicism, by contrast, is eager to know and live the faith with and through bread, wine, water, oil, palm branches, ashes, incense, banners, bells, chimes, crucifixes, tapestries, statues, icons, vestments, processions, chapels, cathedrals, standing, kneeling, prostrating, and much, much more. And one of the main organizing frameworks in which much of that happens is the Christian liturgical calendar, which imbues time, memory, and movement with Christian significance. Time to learn and live it.

56. Read stories of evangelicals who have already become Catholic. Many evangelicals have already converted to Catholicism. Reading their stories helps you to realize that you are hardly alone. Many others have already shared the same feelings and concerns you have and have lived to tell of them. A bit of searching will turn up a number of relevant books. Some of the following will be worth your time: *Journeys Home* (Marcus Grodi), *By What Authority?: An Evangelical Discovers Catholic Tradition* (Mark Shea), *Born Fundamentalist, Born-Again Catholic* (David Currie), *Chosen: How Christ Sent Twenty-Three Surprised Converts to Replant His Vineyard* (Donna Steichen), *Surprised by Truth: Converts Give the Biblical and Historical Reasons for Becoming Catholic* (Patrick Madrid), *Crossing the Tiber: Evangelical Protestants Discover the Historical Church* (Stephen Ray), *Home at Last: Eleven Who Found* *their Way to the Catholic Church* (Rosalind Moss and Michael Sheehan), *Rome Sweet Home: Our Journey to Catholicism* (Scott and Kimberly Hahn), *Return to Rome: Confessions of an Evangelical Catholic* (Francis Beckwith), *Lead, Kindly Light: My Journey to Rome* (Thomas Howard), *Classic Catholic Converts* (Charles Connor), and *The Catholic Church and Conversion* (G. K. Chesterton). Knowing that you share the journey with many others and hearing their stories will prove helpful.

57. Start shifting from a literal, linear order of thought to an analogical and symbolic imagination. Your paradigm revolution will have to involve a change in the way you think and imagine. Protestantism forms a mindset that tends strongly to be linear, literal, either/or, univocal, didactic, and rationalist. Catholicism thinks quite differently. Catholic thought is more analogical, both/and, metaphorical, curvilinear, symbolic, and multi-directional. It's a difference you need to recognize and shift with.

In Catholicism, for instance, time is not always a linear movement literally forward. Divine reality in Catholicism is bigger than time, it transcends time in a way that makes time relative and different parts of time interconnected. Thus, the celebration of the Mass as "sacrifice" is not for Catholics a literal re-sacrificing of Christ's body. That is how it seems to the Protestant mind, because Protestants view time as linear, literal, and unidirectional. Hence, they believe that the Mass violates Heb 9:25–28. But that imposes a Protestant mindset on a Catholic practice and culture. The sacrifice of the Mass for Catholics means that in that place and time the people of God actually participate in the one and only sacrifice of Christ on the cross that happened once for all but is eternally given. The sacrifice of the Eucharist transcends and relativizes time, it connects different points of time, and so through the sacrament we today are put in immediate touch with the real sacrifice of Christ on Golgotha. How's that to blow your mind?

The University of Chicago theologian, David Tracy, provides a language for this Protestant-Catholic difference in thought and imagination in his book, *The Analogical Imagination*. We might think of the general Protestant mentality as mapping onto what he calls a "dialectical" mentality, versus the more Catholic "analogical" tendency which he contrasts.[16]

16. In Tracy's thinking, the two do not align with these traditions strictly, as some Protestants (e.g., Schleiermacher) tend toward an analogical imagination, whereas some Catholics (e.g., some liberation theologians) can be dialectical in their method. Still, the comparison maps well enough to make the point.

The Catholic priest and sociologist Andrew Greeley writes similarly about "the Catholic Imagination" in his 2001 book by the same title, in which he emphasizes the Catholic instinct for seeing the mysterious in the plain, the sacred in the material, the holy lurking just below the surface of the ordinary. In the kind of analogical imagination toward which you need to now shift, everything is not simply what it is, only and literally that, and nothing else. Rather, our understanding comes from seeing how some things are *like* other things, how certain symbols *point to* other realities, how differences and similarities can work *together* to create coherent, harmonized understandings of reality.

Catholics, therefore, are much friendlier to what (for Protestants) seem like contradictions, to both/and understandings, metaphorical images, symbolic representations, and non-literal readings and interpretations. In some sense, Catholicism is more confident than Protestantism in its understanding of its apprehension, definition, security, and coherence of Christian truth—it has, after all, been working with the same basic approach for two millennia, and it enjoys the Church Magisterium to guard the deposit of faith.[17] So Catholicism tends to feel more relaxed and at ease with differences, tensions, metaphors, and ambiguities in its thought and imagination. This is, again, a very different way of thinking, which takes a paradigm shift to acquire. So keep working on and praying about that.

58. Distinguish between formulations of truth and the truths that the formulations express. This step follows from the previous one. For evangelicals, things say what they mean and mean what they say. Lines are drawn, people get clear on where they stand, and clarity and consistency throughout is paramount. That is its literal, either/or, univocal approach at work again. That view also reflects Protestantism's central emphasis on *the word*. As Protestant pulpits replaced Catholic altars, as printed Bibles displaced icons and devotional practices, Protestantism made *words*—discrete written and spoken units of language—*the* medium for grasping and conveying Christian truth. Correct words, for Protestants—particularly for evangelical rationalists—are therefore nearly themselves sacred, because Christian truth itself is represented directly in the right words.[18]

17. For an excellent explanation of the Magisterium, see Dulles, *Magisterium*.

18. One important exception to this in Protestantism is Karl Barth. See Torrance, "Karl Barth and the Latin Heresy," 465–72.

Catholics also care very much about right words. But their approach to words is a bit different in a way that turns out to make a big difference. Catholicism, in short, recognizes *a gap between words and what the words express* or represent. For Protestants, *the words are the truth.* That is why one must get them exactly right. For Catholics, by contrast, words *formulate expressions* of truth. There is not in Catholicism a literal, exact, univocal correspondence or identity between words and truth. Much of truth, especially truth that directly concerns God, is in Catholicism a mystery. Ultimately the truth *is* God. And God is not words.[19]

So we use words to understand and express those mysteries to the very best of our ability. That is what humans—even those in possession of divine revelation—do. But the words themselves can never fully capture or embody the truth. The words point us to the truth. They are good witnesses to or mediums for expressing truth. But the truth itself does not consist of the assemblages of words.

This results, in part, from what the Church recognizes as the challenges to human understanding of the hidden mysteries of God. These, Vatican I declared, "by their nature so far transcend the human intellect that even if they are revealed to us and accepted by faith, they remain concealed by the veil of faith itself and are, as it were, wrapped in darkness."[20] The Church thus recognizes that "even though the truths which the Church intends to teach through her dogmatic formulas are distinct from the changeable conceptions of a given epoch and can be expressed without them, nevertheless it can sometimes happen that these truths may be enunciated by the Sacred Magisterium in terms that bear traces of such conceptions."[21] Thus, the Vatican's Sacred Congregation of the Doctrine of the Faith has stated:

> It has sometimes happened that . . . certain of these formulas gave way to new expressions which . . . presented more clearly or more completely the same meaning. As for the meaning of dogmatic formulations, this remains true and constant in the Church, even when it is expressed with greater clarity and [is] more developed.[22]

19. I am obviously here distinguishing between human words and Christ as *the* Word (John 1:1).

20. Vatican Council I, *De Filius*, chapter 4, page 808.

21. Congregation for the Doctrine of the Faith, *Mysterium Ecclesiae*, 5.

22. Ibid.

The same document also quotes Vatican II in saying that over time, "there is a growth in the understanding of the realities and words which have been handed down."[23]

As a result of this approach, Pope John XXIII was able to open the Second Vatican Council with these words concerning Christian doctrine: "This certain and unchangeable doctrine, to which faithful obedience is due, has to be explored and presented in a way that is demanded by our times. One thing is the deposit of faith, which consists of the truths contained in sacred doctrine; another thing is the manner of presentation, always however with the same meaning and signification."[24]

Commenting on this in 1973, the Vatican noted that, "What is new and what he [Pope John XXIII] recommends in view of the needs of the times pertains . . . to modes of study, expounding, and presenting that doctrine, while keeping its permanent meaning."[25] In 1971, Pope Paul VI had already reinforced that point, saying, "Nowadays, a serious effort is required of us to ensure that the teaching of the faith should keep the fullness of its meaning and force, while expressing itself in a form which allows it to reach the spirit and heart of the people to whom it is addressed."[26]

Why does this difference matter? For starters, it provides for what we might call a "confident humility" about doctrinal formulations. On the one hand, Catholics confidently believe that they understand and declare what is true. On the other hand and simultaneously, Catholics remain aware that their verbal formulations of those truths are not themselves *the* truth per se, but expressions *of* the truth. That means that the Church can rightly claim that what it declares in words is really the truth, but also remain open to the fact that it may need to adjust its verbal formulations of the truth as its understanding deepens in new times.

The implications are huge. Catholicism can thus at once claim infallibility for some of its teachings and at the same time *revise* the verbal expression of those teachings. Even the doctrine of papal infallibility does not claim that the verbal formulations per se that are promulgated by popes are infallible. Rather, it is the real *truths* which their verbal

23. Ibid.

24. John XXIII, "Alloc. in Concilii Vaticani inauguratione," AAS 84, page 792, quoted in *Mysterium Ecclesiae*, section 5.

25. *Mysterium Ecclesiae*, section 5.

26. Paul VI, Exhortation *Quinque iam anni*, 100.

formulations express that are infallible.[27] In short, we haven't gotten at all wrong what we say is true, even though the way we say the truth might not be quite right or adequate.

What that means is that Catholicism has a built-in self-understanding and mechanism for *reforming* itself. Irony of ironies! Protestants lambast Catholicism for being (allegedly) irreformable. In fact, however, Catholicism has reformed, does reform, and in the future will reform itself, in significant ways. It does so, not through shifty and dishonest means, but rather in ways that make total sense, given its own understanding of the relationship between words and truth.

Study historical change in the Catholic Church. You will see that the Church recurrently talks about "deepening its understanding" and "rereading its doctrines and teachings" in light of "new circumstances" and "current challenges" that require "updating," "better expressions of insight," and "more illuminating formulations" of the truth. This outlook is precisely what moved the historic changes promulgated by the Second Vatican Council—which confessed that the Church is "always in need of being purified."[28]

This does not, however, mean that the Church is forever changing its mind, jumping around, or entertaining radical revisions to its doctrines. Far from it. It *does* mean that the Catholic Church is open in a self-consistent way to learning new, better, and more accurately expressive ways to formulate the unchanging truths of its authoritative verbal statements. In this way, liberal Protestantism's boundless spirit of radical revisionism is avoided. But so is confessional and conservative Protestantism's tendency toward the ossification of verbal confessions, catechisms, and positions in particular formulations of words that must be defended at all costs till the end of time.

59. Decide once and for all that there is something fundamentally and deeply wrong with denominationalism. As an evangelical, the American denominational religious system is second nature to you. Differences of denominations seem to have always existed and likely always will exist. How else could anyone accommodate the vast differences between distinct types of Protestants? In fact, if you are the kind of person who likes free markets, you might positively *like* America's

27. See Heft, "Humble Infallibility."
28. *Lumen Gentium*, 8.

denominational system. Different kinds of believers with different preferences and needs can find in this system at least one kind of church that will suit them well. And since more people's religious needs are met by a greater variety of types of churches, then more Americans will be more religious in the aggregate, since they will not be pushed out of the religious market by a lack of attractive faith-based "products." Isn't that what makes America great?

It is time to expunge that kind of thinking from your mind for good. All it does is turn Christianity into a consumer commodity and abet the disunity and divisions that, according to John 17, undermine the credibility of the gospel. Furthermore, what makes America or American religion great is by no means what makes the Christian church faithful. The Christian church is not like ice cream, coming in 69 flavors for individuals to pick and choose according to their personal tastes. The Church is one, holy, catholic, and apostolic. It preaches one Lord, one faith, one baptism. It is called by Christ, prayed for by Christ, to *be one* as Jesus and the Father are one (John 17:20–24).

Denominationalism makes a visible and material mockery of all of that. Denominationalism is the institutional validation and embodiment of Christian division and disunity. It violates what the Bible plainly teaches about Christians agreeing, loving, being reconciled, and living in unity. Denominationalism is from a Christian perspective—whatever else is good or not good for America—simply sinful, unacceptable, and intolerable. It is time now for you to accept that and work out the consequences.

60. Understand Catholicism's internal unity in diversity. Protestants and evangelicals tend to grumble about Catholicism's alleged "uniformity." In fact, they have it completely backward. Contrary to Protestant and evangelical assumptions about "Roman" uniformity, Catholicism's "universality" necessarily makes room for and actually comprises a huge amount of internal diversity of various sorts.[29]

Catholicism is not a church of uniformity except on central matters. In Catholicism, there are clear boundaries on the outside—its authorized teachings. And there is a clear center on the inside—Christ and the Eucharist. But between them, there is a lot of room for healthy (and sometimes unhealthy) differences, arguments, and cultural expressions.

29. See, in particular, *Gaudium et Spes*, 92.

Here we go back to getting the right idea of what a *tradition* is. Evangelicals tend to think of church traditions as rigid and erroneous weights of the dead past that obstruct the vibrant and relevant possibilities of the present. But that outlook is seriously flawed. Much better and more realistic it is to think about tradition roughly the way Alasdair MacIntyre defines it in his book, *After Virtue*. That is something like "an historically extended, socially-embodied argument" that argues in part about "the goods that constitute the tradition."[30] That understanding of tradition makes sense dynamically of both the shared commitments and various differences existing within any living tradition. And that is something like what Catholicism is.

With its true source of unity actually secure (unlike in evangelicalism), Catholicism can afford to allow a variety of good forms of diversity to flourish within. Thus, in many ways, Catholicism entails much greater unity-in-diversity than do many Protestant denominations, which tend toward tight internal homogeneity and big between-group differences.

61. Realize that "authoritative" does not equal "authoritarian." Americans are a people who arguably suffer (and, in other ways, benefit) from an instinctive suspicion of any institutional authority. Evangelicals are Christians who are naturally apprehensive about most forms of organized church authority. American evangelicals therefore tend to be allergic to anything that sounds, smells, or feels like human authority at work. Authority is often confused by American evangelicals with authori*tarianism*. That is unfortunate, if understandable. It also is at least somewhat unbiblical.

It is pretty hard to get around the idea that authority matters in Christian reality. We Americans may not like it, but authority is real, and right authority is legitimate. Jesus said that all authority has been given to him (Matt 28:18). According to the Gospels, Jesus authorized the apostles and the Church to use the keys of the kingdom, to retain and forgive sins, to discern truth from heresy, to exercise discipline (Matt 16:19, 18:15–18). Lone Ranger Christianity is a problem. Everyone-decides-for-themselves Christianity is a joke. Reality in a Christian mode—which, Christians believe, is the only reality that exists—simply cannot dispense with authority. Christianity is not a faith for ecclesial libertarians or anarchists. The only question is who or what in the Christian world has legitimate authority and how it is rightly exercised.

30. MacIntyre, *After Virtue*, 222.

Become Catholic. Resist authoritarianism. But also learn to appreciate and—yes—at times to submit to legitimate authority in the church. That very idea, just the word "submit" itself, causes many of us to grind our teeth in rebellion. But that is not necessarily because we are good Christians. It is often because we are liberal, individualistic children of the American Revolution, mass-consumerism, and heirs of the Baby Boomers' cultural revolution of the 1960s and 70s. For some it may also be because they had restrictive or even abusive parents. But if we actually took the Bible seriously, we would not have a problem with proper authority well exercised in the Church. We would be grateful for it. We *need* an authori*tative* Church, though clearly not an authoritarian one.

Heaven help us. These are difficult and complicated matters. And the Catholic Church does not always properly carry out what it rightly safeguards. All the more reason it needs you. But, stepping back to view the larger concern here, however you and I end up sorting through them, if you want to become Catholic, it is important to remember that an authoritative Church is very, very different from an authoritarian Church. Resist the latter. But look for, love, appreciate, and follow the former.[31]

62. Come to realize that Catholicism itself suffers from being deprived of its "separated brethren," by having evangelicals and other Protestants estranged from it, living in impaired communion, and thus dividing the Body of Christ. It is very easy to show the weaknesses, problems, and failings of the Catholic Church. They are evident and sometimes pathetic and angering. But why is that? Well, people in the Church on earth will of course always be beset by sin—that we know. But a full answer requires a more penetrating analysis than this.

Suppose I took your body and cut it down the middle into two parts, and then cut one of the parts into little bits. How healthy would you be? Would you have problems? Would you be weak? Would you fail to flourish and live up to your full potential? Rhetorical questions, these. In fact you would be dead.

That is what the Protestant Reformation (which would be more accurately described as the "Great Western Schism") did to the Church Catholic of the West—it split the Body of Christ into parts and shredded

---

31. At the same time, as I say below in step #80 below, do not think that the Catholic Church, which does speak with proper authority, provides absolute *certainty*. It does not and cannot. Certainty—in the sense of absolutely indubitable, positive knowledge—is simply not given by God to any humans. Faith, belief, trust, and confidence are rather the calling and way of Christians.

one of the parts into pieces. The Catholic Church owns its share of the blame for that schism. But that does not change the fact that the schism was sparked by Martin Luther, that Protestants left Catholicism, and that the Church has ever since been a divided body. That is all water under the bridge. But the organizational consequences still affect the church today.

Of course, Church division in (small "o") orthodox Christianity was begun in 1054, after many centuries of tensions, with the breaking apart of the Latin West and Rome from Constantinople and what became Eastern Orthodoxy.[32] Thankfully, that division of Christendom is now in the active process of being healed. Rome and many Eastern Churches are being reconciled as you read this. Full reconciliation is possible within our lifetime—a hope toward which we must live, as I note below.

Meanwhile, Catholicism and Protestantism remain divided. The Body of Christ in the West continues after five hundred years to be split in two, torn apart by the Reformation's rupture and Protestantism's subsequent fracturing. Is it any wonder that the Catholic Church is weak, has problems, fails to be and do what it could and should? The Body is cut apart. What else should we expect? The Reformation thus does not call for celebration. It calls for sorrow, repentance, and reconciliation.

Imagine, for a moment of utopian dreaming, the Christian Church of the West (Roman Catholicism and the various branches of Protestantism) being reunited. Imagine a big Christian family reunion at which all of the estranged children of former siblings and cousins in faith, who long ago left the family mansion in angry rebellion to build their own huts on the fringes of the great family estate, came together to be reconciled, to forgive, and to share again in family communion and fellowship. What a party that would be!

Meanwhile, should we be surprised to find that the old, grand, historic family mansion had fallen into disrepair after half of the family abandoned it to live on the fringes of the family estate—and at least some of those who remained have been influenced by the mansion-despising attitudes of those who left? Think what might result from real Christian unity, if God were to make that possible? How much stronger and healthier might the Body of Christ be if it was not torn into pieces? How powerful and vibrant could the Church become if in unity all of today's separated evangelicals and other Protestants brought together in it all

32. None of this even addresses the implications of the Oriental Orthodox Churches, about which see Jenkins, *Lost History of Christianity*.

of their gifts, talents, energies, and devotion? We are so used to division that that is almost unimaginable. But that itself is a sign of our pathetic condition. You now need to imagine it.

It is a cruel and ignorant joke to tear the Body of Christ into pieces and then to turn around and criticize it for being weak and unhealthy. The correct explanation of Protestantism's sickness and evangelicalism's woes is to understand them as the natural consequence of being amputated parts of a dismembered Body. The Catholic Church's weaknesses and problems are also partly caused by the divisions that continue to tear Western Christendom into pieces. When we get the right perspective and image, we begin to see the causes of the ailments. The only option, then, having seen them, is to put yourself in the service of reconciliation and unity of the Church visible.

five

More Revolutionary Science

We are part way there. Your paradigm crisis is underway. Let's keep learning about the revolutionary science of the Catholic paradigm, focusing in what follows more clearly on Catholic theological beliefs.

63. Learn the distinction between the seven sacraments and the many sacramentals. Evangelicals often freak out about all of the devotional practices and doo-dads with which they see Catholics messing. A big part of their problem in this, however, is their not understanding the fundamental difference Catholicism makes between the sacraments and sacramentals. The names sound similar. But they indicate different things.

In Catholicism, sacraments are "outward signs of inward grace." There are seven sacraments, according to Catholic teaching: baptism, confirmation, holy Eucharist, penance, anointing of the sick, matrimony, and holy orders. Those are all serious, central, and believed to be instituted by Jesus Christ. The sacraments also always themselves give grace, objectively, as long as believers do not willfully place spiritual obstacles in the way.

Sacramentals, however, are not sacraments. They are different. Sacramentals are material objects or actions set apart as blessed by the Church to evoke respect for what is sacred, provoke good thoughts, increase devotion, and turn believers away from sin. Examples of Catholic sacramentals, as objects and actions, include making the sign of the cross, folding hands, genuflecting, holy water, crucifixes, medals, rosary beads, scapulars, prostration, statues, icons, candles, nativity scenes, incense, vestments, religious habits, palm branches, ashes, Advent wreaths, bells, blessed fire, the washing of feet, and so on. Many of these are explicitly known as not instituted by Christ but rather by the Church's tradition and discipline. Furthermore, sacramentals are not taught to give grace themselves, but only evoke pious (in the good sense of the word) dispositions, devotion and love for God, and remorse for sin.[1]

Note, as an aside, that evangelicals of course have their own "sacramentals"—things like WWJD bracelets, fish signs, steeple bells or chimes, regular "quiet times" and devotions, folding hands and closing eyes during prayer, crosses (empty, instead of crucifixes), all of the plaques, figurines, needlepoint, and other display items and collectables noted in chapter 1 above, sometimes crosses worn on chains, sometimes the "Christian flag," sometimes candles, sometimes stained glass, and so on. These are not called "sacramentals" by evangelicals, are not often explicitly theologically justified, and are not officially blessed by evangelical churches. Otherwise, sociologically, at least, they function similarly to Catholic sacramentals.[2]

Sacramentals are important in Catholicism. But they are not central, nor claimed to be divinely instituted. They are simply a variety of particular means learned by Christians through history that help lead believers toward truth and right living. They are good "ways to trip over God," as a Catholic Director of Christian Formation I know likes to say. As helps and not obligations, sacramentals are not mandatory for faithful Catholic living, the way that sacraments are. When you become a Catholic, therefore, you will not be required to pray the rosary or put a statue of Mary in your yard. The sacramentals are more like blessed resources to help you on your Christian way, to the extent that they do in fact help you. Learning this distinction between sacraments and sacramentals should help orient you to Catholic ways of life, clarify what in Catholic practices are more and less central, and perhaps relieve you from the mistaken idea that to be Catholic you must engage in every one of these devotional actions and objects.

1. *The Catechism of the Catholic Church* has enlightening teachings on sacramentals; another potentially helpful resource is Hahn, *Signs of Life*.

2. Theologically, however, the efficacy of Catholic sacramentals is defined in not merely psychological, sociological, or symbolic terms, but in relation to the liturgy of the Eucharist.

64. Recognize the distinction between "revealed truth" and "church disciplines." A next step parallel to the last is to learn the difference between what Catholicism teaches as revealed and what it teaches as church disciplines. Again, they are not the same. Revealed truths are dogmatic. They consist of the "deposit of faith" concerning the entire revelation of Jesus Christ about Christian doctrine and morals. Dogmas are recognized and affirmed by the teaching Magisterium of the Church and in their truth cannot change. The intentional denial of revealed truth is what defines heresy. That God is Trinity and that the Son is both fully God and fully human are, for example, revealed truths. If you want to be Catholic, you must believe the Church's teachings on revealed truths.

Ecclesiastical disciplines are something else. Disciplines are rules, regulations, laws, and directions set down by the Church to guide the faithful toward the perfection of the Gospel. Disciplines are taught by the Church but not claimed to be revealed by God. Nor are they claimed to be infallible. Abstaining from eating meat on certain days of the year is one example of a Church discipline. Monastic vows to obedience and poverty are also disciplines. These can change and have been different in the past.

Yet another matter of Church discipline, and not divine revelation, is the required celibacy of Catholic priests. This is a big issue for Protestants, as well as some Catholics, so it is worth understanding that the Catholic Church does not claim that priestly celibacy is a matter of divine revelation. Nor is it held as an infallible teaching. It is rather something that the Church itself, over the centuries, has decided to set down as a practice to follow for what it believed at that time (and still) to be in the service of the good of God's people and the Church.

It is important to realize in all of this, however, that Church disciplines may and do change over time. Circumstances and eras, viewed by the discerning judgment of the Church, can and do change disciplines. At one time, for example, it was not a Church discipline to abstain from eating meat on Fridays. Then it became a taught discipline. And now that is no longer a discipline, outside of Lent. These changes are not inconsistencies in Church practice or flip-flops in its teaching. They are well-considered changes that are consistent with the very notion of a discipline itself as defined by the Church.

Some implications follow. The day may come, for example, when the Catholic Church changes its teaching about the ecclesiastical discipline of a celibate, diocesan priesthood.[3] The Church already now allows married priests under some circumstances. When times and circumstances change, the Church could very well decide more widely to allow married diocesan priests. Those changes do not appear to be on the immediate horizon and may never happen.[4] On the other hand, few Catholics in 1958 had any idea that the major changes brought by Vatican II were only a few years away.

Furthermore, you should know that, while you must believe revealed truths if you want to be Catholic, you do not need to believe in and endorse Church disciplines. You only need to be willing to accept and cooperate with or practice them as they are relevant to you and as asked at a given point in time by the Church. So, you may not only choose not to take vows of poverty, celibacy, and obedience. You can also be a good Catholic and, for example, personally not support diocesan priestly celibacy. You can take a break from giving something up for Lent one year if you must. Because these are Catholic disciplines, not revealed truths, all of that is possible.

At the same time, such openness to potential transformation in Church disciplines does not mean that Catholicism puts everything on the table for negotiation and change. All that is taught to be revealed truth, what is dogmatically defined, is in fact not up for discussion, is not open for revision. If you cannot affirm your belief in that, then you shouldn't and can't become Catholic. The only aspect of revealed truth that could possibly change, as we just noted, are some of the verbal formulations that express it, not the truth itself. Furthermore, at any given point in time, the Church may declare that some disciplines (the current position of Rome on priestly celibacy, for example) are not going to change in the near future—though, again, in due time those disciplines could change.

3. Celibacy would likely be treated differently when it comes to priests in religious orders (such as Franciscans and Dominicans) versus those who serve dioceses directly under bishops. Celibacy, along with poverty and obedience, are often constitutive rules defining the very existence of religious orders. Celibacy could more easily be removed for diocesan priests, by comparison.

4. The matter of possible female priests is particularly complicated and debated today, with some, though not all, arguing that this could never change. Both the previous and the current popes strongly opposed women's ordination to the priesthood, declaring the matter definitively settled. While that claim is stronger than saying it is a mere discipline, it still stops short of defining male priesthood as "revealed" in the strong sense. The debate remains in play. More time will be needed to settle the question.

Here again, Catholicism balances openness to change in different circumstances on some matters with a resolute steadfastness in proclaiming the teachings of revealed truths, the deposit of faith once delivered to the saints, whatever the circumstances. In your movement toward Catholicism, it is important that you understand these important distinctions.

65. Correct your understanding of the sacrifice of the Mass.
Time to get more theological. You may have been taught as an evangelical that the Catholic Mass tries to sacrifice Christ's body over and over again, a repetition that is clearly invalidated by Hebrews 9 and 10. But that is simply factually wrong.

The Catholic Church actually teaches that the sacrifice of the Eucharist in the Mass "makes present and real" and "re-presents the sacrifice of" the cross (*Catechism* 1362, 1363, 1366). But the sacrifice is not repeated, it does not "crucify Christ again and again," as some critics of Catholicism wrongly insist. What happened once and for all on the cross is simply brought to the present, memorialized, made real, and applied in its fruits. "The sacrifice Christ offered once for all on the cross," teaches the *Catechism*, "remains ever present" in the Eucharist (1364). The Mass does not re-create Christ's body and blood, but rather connects cognitively and ontologically back to his original body and blood shed for us—an event that, though taking place in space and time, is not bound by space and time. "In the Eucharist, Christ gives us the very body which he gave up for us on the cross, the very blood which he 'poured out for many for the forgiveness of sins'" (1365). The key point is thus made perfectly clear in the *Catechism*: "The sacrifice of Christ and the sacrifice of the Eucharist are *one single sacrifice*" (1367, italics in original).

Here again, as explained above, Protestants need to get out of their limited, linear, and irreversibly sequential view of time and how it works, and instead try to understand Catholicism from within a Catholic view of time, which is quite different. For Catholics, by the power of the Holy Spirit, a Eucharist celebrated in the twenty-first century transcends the normal boundaries and flows of created time and mysteriously re-presents and makes real in a bloodless way the actual, original, and final bloody sacrifice of Christ on the cross (*Catechism* 1367). Pretty wild.

So you don't need to fret about the idea that Catholics re-crucify Christ in the celebration of the Eucharist at Mass. The next time an evangelical tries to tell you that's what Catholics believe, you can advise them to actually read the *Catechism of the Catholic Church* on the point and to stop spreading myths. And when you eventually become Catholic yourself, you will personally participate in the mystery of the cross in the bread and the wine made present to share with you and incorporate you into his Body. Meanwhile, as you are working on learning about these issues, again, pray and ask God to guide you into the truth.

66. Correct your understanding of the Real Presence of Christ in the Eucharist (which the doctrine of "transubstantiation" has been an important attempt to specify theologically). I don't know about you, but I was told growing up that, according to Catholics, going down their throats as they ingest the consecrated bread and wine are actually the real, literal, fleshy and bloody flesh and blood of Jesus Christ—or so they think. A magical form of cannibalism, it was intimated to be, brought about in Catholic minds by the hocus pocus[5] of priests. Creepy.

Wrong again. The Catholic Church does teach without apology the *Real Presence* of Christ in the Eucharist, such that in the latter "the whole Christ is truly, really, and substantially contained" and that this "is a substantial presence by which Christ, God and man, makes himself wholly and entirely present" (*Catechism* 1374). The Church also teaches that Real Presence involves "the conversion of the bread and wine into Christ's body and blood," and that "there takes place a change of the whole substance of the bread into the substance of the body of Christ our Lord and of the whole substance of the wine into the substance of his blood" (*Catechism* 1375–76).

But here is precisely one of those points where you have got to stop thinking with your standard Protestant, literal, either/or imagination, and starting thinking instead with a Catholic, both/and, analogical imagination. Stop trying to impose a Newtonian mechanical mindset on what is really an Einsteinian quantum theory, so to speak. The Catholic Church, quoting Thomas Aquinas, also teaches—without contradiction, when properly understood—that "the true Body of Christ and his true Blood is something that 'can*not* be apprehended by the senses . . . but *only by faith*, which relies on divine authority"(*Catechism* 1381).

Now, if what I was taught as a child that Catholics believe was true, then the body and the blood would be perfectly able to be apprehended

---

5. Many believe, incidentally, that this phrase has its origin in the corruption or parody of the Catholic liturgy of the Eucharist, the Latin version of which contains the phrase, "*Hoc est enim corpus meum*."

by the senses—quite repulsively so. That the Catholic Church clearly says that they cannot shows that the Protestant understanding is off. If the Protestant understanding of Real Presence and transubstantiation was correct, then the Catholic *Catechism* could also not (which it does) approvingly quote these verses by Thomas Aquinas on the matter (1381):

> Godhead here in hiding, whom I do adore
> Masked by these bare shadows, shape and nothing more,
> See, Lord, at thy service low lies here a heart
> Lost, all lost in wonder at the God thou art.
>
> Seeing, touching, tasting are in thee deceived;
> How says trusty hearing? That shall be believed;
> What God's Son has told me, take for truth I do;
> Truth himself speaks truly or there's nothing true.

The *Catechism*'s (1381) added approval of St. Cyril's writing the following reflects the same outlook: "Do not doubt whether this [Real Presence] is true, but rather receive the words of the Savior in faith, for since he is true, he cannot lie."

Ask yourself: if the vulgar Protestant account of transubstantiation was correct, how could Christ be "in hiding" and "masked by these bare shadows" in the bread and wine? Why and how would our human senses be "deceived" by the sacramental elements? Why would Catholics swallowing actual flesh and blood be tempted to "doubt whether this is true?" It makes no sense.

Next question: does this real-presence doctrine, this transubstantiation view, have any *biblical* basis? Let's see. Well, how's this?

> I tell you the truth, *unless you eat the flesh of the Son of Man and drink his blood, you have no life in you. Whoever eats my flesh and drinks my blood has eternal life*, and I will raise him up at the last day. For *my flesh is real food and my blood is real drink. Whoever eats my flesh and drinks my blood* remains in me, and I in him. Just as the living Father sent me and I live because of the Father, so *the one who feeds on me will live* because of me. (John 6:53–57)

And this?

> I am the bread of life. . . . Here is the bread that comes down from heaven, which a man may eat and not die. I am the living bread

that came down from heaven. *If anyone eats of this bread, he will live forever. This bread is my flesh*, which I will give for the life of the world. (John 6:48–51)

Or this? "Take and eat, this is my body. . . . Drink from it, all of you, this is my blood" (Matt 26:26–28). I'm not sure how the Bible could be more clear. So, why do Protestants want to be people who react by saying, "How can this man give us his flesh to eat? This is a hard teaching. Who can accept it?" (John 6:52, 60).

Once again, a key distinction is important to grasp here. "Substance" concerns what something *is in itself*, what we might call its "essence," not what it looks, feels, and tastes like. The technical theological term for the latter is "accidents." The bread and wine themselves do become in *"underlying reality"* the body and blood of Christ—even if they appear to be bread and wine, as, at an accidents level, they are. But that does not mean you are literally eating skin and muscle and drinking intervascular fluid at the level of accidents—as if Christ's body was merely human and not resurrected. That interpretation is only the stuff of anti-Catholic horror stories told to little children to scare them well away from priests and Rome.

At the same time, lest we take Real Presence too lightly, ask yourself this: if Jesus was really only talking *figuratively* about eating his body and drinking his blood, as only a "sign" to help his disciples remember him, then why did so many disciples abandon him after he said it?: "On hearing this, many of his disciples said, 'This is a hard teaching. Who can accept it?' Aware that his disciples were grumbling about this, Jesus said to them, 'Does this offend you?' . . . From this time many of his disciples turned back and no longer followed him." If Jesus has only exaggerated about eating and drinking his body and blood, then why did he not call these disciples back and explain to them the easier teaching that he *really* meant? And, for that matter, why were early Christians accused by those who persecuted them of cannibalism?[6] Apparently the offending teaching in fact was not easier, and the accusation wasn't terribly far off, even if it was not entirely accurate.

Do not be creeped out by the Real Presence, even transubstantiation, in the Eucharist. Rather, receive with gratitude that "sacred banquet of communion" (*Catechism* 1382) that Christ offers you and which unites

6. McGowan, "Eating People," 431–42. Pagans too had difficulty with the Catholic imagination.

you with him in it. It's a fantastic mystery, a free means of grace. Through it, be, with Aquinas, "lost in wonder at the God" who is in it for you.

67. Consider the possibility of purgatory. Evangelicals, in fact nearly all Protestants, choke on the Catholic belief in purgatory. You need not. The common Protestant idea of purgatory is a "place" between heaven and hell where Christians who were not good enough during their lives "go" to be subject to suffering before they are let into heaven— just to make sure they have paid enough for their sins before they are rewarded with eternal life. Protestants protest against that purgatory because it is part of the alleged Catholic belief in salvation by good works and the insufficiency of the grace of Christ. Plus, Protestants say, the idea of purgatory has no biblical basis.

The last point first. It is actually not accurate to say that the Bible does not refer to something like purgatory, rightly understood. 1 Cor 3:11–15 teaches this:

> No one can lay any foundation other than the one already laid, which is Jesus Christ. If any man builds on this foundation using gold, silver, costly stones, wood, hay or straw, his work will be shown for what it is, because the Day will bring it to light. It will be revealed with fire, and the fire will test the quality of each man's work. If what he has built survives, he will receive his reward. If it is burned up, he will suffer loss; he himself will be saved, but only as one escaping through the flames.

As I note elsewhere in this chapter, we are dealing with mysteries here about which we ought not to claim that we know too much. But this passage certainly suggests that, before taking one's final place in heaven, believers pass through some kind of fiery purification process which burns away the elements of lives that are weak and impure. The passage clearly is not talking about hell and damnation, as it concerns those who have built on the foundation of Jesus Christ and who in the end are "saved." Yet these Christians are only saved after the quality of the lives they have built is "shown for what it is" as "revealed through fire" and "as one escaping through the flames."

Understanding such a Bible passage to be indicating some kind of final purging of sin from our lives (and not simply its guilt) in the movement toward heaven is hardly far-fetched. In fact, numerous Church Fathers—including Ambrose, Jerome, Augustine, Gregory, and Origen— interpreted this Scripture passage as evidence for the existence of an intermediate state in which the dross of lighter sins are burned away and the purified soul thus saved.

Church Fathers and respected theologians across church history have also believed that Matt 12:32 ("anyone who speaks against the Holy Spirit will not be forgiven, either in this age *or in the age to come*") implies the existence of such an intermediate state in which sins may be finally purged and forgiven. Augustine of Hippo, for example, writes in *City of God* that the fact "that some sinners are not forgiven either in this world or in the next would not be truly said unless there were other [sinners] who, though not forgiven in this world, are forgiven in the world to come."[7] Gregory the Great, the Venerable Bede, St. Bernard, and others shared that same view.

Such a belief in purgatory many Church Fathers also understood as supported by the passage in 2 Macc 12:43–46, which is part of the Scriptures nearly all Christians used from at least the third century until the fifteenth century. That passage (which we will examine more closely below) describes the Jewish practice of offering sacrifices for the sins of the dead, in anticipation of the resurrection. Psalm 66:10, many believe, also alludes to purgatory: "For you, O God, tested us; you refined us like silver" (also see Isa 48:10; Dan 11:34–35; 1 Pet 1:7). Many theologians have also connected prayers and good works offered on behalf of those in purgatory as not unlike the sacrifices that Job customarily offered on behalf of his children, in case they had sinned during their feasts (Job 1:4–5). Job, apparently, did not do wrong in offering sacrifices to God for the purpose of purifying not his own sins but the sins of his children.

If any of this makes sense, then what is purgatory? Well, as the name suggests, it is a process of purging of sin, of the burning away of remaining impurities in the lives of Christians. The *Catechism* (1030–1031) discusses purgatory as follows: "All who die in God's grace and friendship, but still imperfectly purified, are indeed assured of their eternal salvation; but after death they undergo purification, so as to achieve the holiness necessary to enter the joy of heaven. The Church gives the name Purgatory to this final purification of the elect, which is entirely different from the punishment of the damned." Purgatory is *not* punitive (which is something many medieval believers did not fully understand). It is refining. That is almost the full extent of it. And remember, too, that the

7. Augustine, *City of God*, XXI, 24.

timing of all of this could well "occur" outside of created time in ways we can not imagine. That too has important implications.

A key underlying difference between Catholicism and Protestantism that helps to generate their differences over purgatory is this: Catholics hold a substantive notion of sin's presence and operation in life, and believe that sin itself needs to be ontologically transformed in the lives of people so they can live in God's presence eternally. Justification and sanctification are intrinsically connected here. Protestants, by contrast, focus primarily on the declared, legal, "forensic" status of individuals' guilt for sin. What matters more than what crimes one has actually committed is how clean one's official criminal *record* looks to God, the legal verdict that is declared for the criminal. Therefore, when it comes to salvation, Protestantism is less concerned with the actual reality of sin in people's lives than with the legal status of the sinner before God. What matters is justification, conceived of as a forensic declaration of innocence; sanctification as the actual reduction of actual sin in people's lives is subsequent and secondary.

For Protestants, therefore, purgatory makes no sense. It is unnecessary. Christ offers believers an "as if" status of innocence before God the Father and so clears the way to heaven immediately—despite the fact that most of us die with lives still tainted by sin. Catholics, however, believe that the forgiveness of Christ is wrapped up with the actual, substantive, ontological negation of the power of sin in our lives. Not only are we declared "as if" innocent in God's judgment ("God sees Christ instead of you"), Christ's atonement actually works to make us innocent in ontological fact. This is both achieved once-and-for-all on the cross and at Easter for every one of God's children, but is also a real process worked out in our lives in history. (Note the both/and nature of this understanding yet again.) Since most of us die with sin still more or less present in our lives, purgatory is a final means by which God provides for that sin to be burned from our lives, so that we can enter God's presence not merely "as if" innocent, but actually and in fact innocent. Even so, that work of purging from sin is always from start to finish the result of God's love and grace in Jesus Christ.

If you become Catholic, you'll have to reckon with purgatory as a belief. (And, if Catholicism is right, whether or not you become Catholic you will have to reckon with purgatory as an experienced reality.) What that means is something like you believing that, since the sins that remain in our lives when we die cannot survive with us in God's presence in heaven, our remaining sins will need to be purged from our lives, as if by fire, in something like an intermediate state on the way to heaven. You have been taught not to believe that. But if you shift your thinking on purgatory, you will have some scriptural warrant for believing it and will be in the good company of many Church Fathers and theologians—including St. Augustine, one Church Father whose teachings the Protestant Reformers saw themselves as following and upholding.

At the same time, one should not make too much of purgatory, one way or the other—as Protestants have often done by blowing it hugely out of proportion. The Catholic Church does not. The doctrine of purgatory is the focus of only two of the 2,865 paragraphs that constitute the *Catechism of the Catholic Church* (and then is merely mentioned in only one other paragraph). That gives purgatory 0.000698 of all of the content of Catholic teachings as represented in the *Catechism*. So, please keep purgatory in that kind of perspective.

68. Correct your understanding of Mary's Immaculate Conception. Not many evangelicals—or Catholics, for that matter—understand the Catholic doctrine of the Immaculate Conception. But not many evangelicals like it either. This is not the place for a full theological exposition of the matter. But it is worth here simply correcting one often-misguided notion.

Many evangelicals, to the extent that they even think about it, suspect that the Immaculate Conception means that Mary somehow did not need to be saved from her sins, because she was perfect. Many also often suppose that Mary's perfection results from her own merit or goodness. Such a suspicion fits the view that Catholics worship Mary, somehow considering her to be quasi-divine, not human. But none of that is correct.

The doctrine of the Immaculate Conception teaches that Mary, "full of grace" (Luke 1:28), was from conception "preserved immune from the stain of original sin" (491). But it was *God alone* who was the agent of this preservation—in order for her to be able to bear the baby Jesus free from sin—and *based completely on the "retroactively-applied" saving merits achieved by Jesus Christ.*[8]

The underlying idea is that if Mary was a sinner, then Jesus would have inherited the sin of his human parent. The Incarnation therefore

---

8. For an award-winning examination of the biblical basis of the notion of merit itself, see Anderson, *Sin*.

needed a mother preserved from the stain of original sin to bear the Son sinless.[9] God achieved that by applying back to Mary the saving merits of her Son, Jesus, which were won later in history for the salvation of the world in his temptations, on the cross, and through his resurrection more than three decades after he was born. (Notice here again that a Catholic view of time in God's redemptive hands—as not necessarily linear, sequential, and irreversibly completed—is essential for grasping the logic and importance of this doctrine.)

Here then is what the *Catechism* teaches on the matter. "To become the mother of the Savior, Mary was *enriched by God* with gifts appropriate for such a role. . . . In order for Mary to be able to give free assent to her faith to the announcement of her vocation, it was necessary that she be *wholly borne by God's grace*" (490). God, in effect, did it all with and for Mary. Mary's Immaculate Conception was thus the key aspect of *her* redemption from sin, different in mode perhaps from the way you and I are redeemed, but still fully the kind of salvation from sin by God just as you and I also need. "Through the centuries the Church has become ever more aware that Mary, 'full of grace' through God, was *redeemed* from the moment of her conception" (491). In Mary's case, you might say, salvation was "preemptive," while in ours it is "subsequent"—though in all cases, of course, it transpires through the eternal foreknowledge and will of God in the person and work of Jesus Christ.

The *Catechism* thus teaches that Mary's Immaculate Conception happened "from the first moment of her conception, by a *singular grace and privilege of almighty God* and by *virtue of the merits of Jesus Christ, Savior of the human race*" (491). Again, Mary's preservation from original sin "*comes wholly from Christ*: she is *redeemed*, in a more excellent fashion, *by reason of the merits of her Son*" (492). Mary, therefore, is every bit the subject of *God's* salvation, blessing, and blamelessness in Christ as is every other Christian (492). The Immaculate Conception is thus only

---

9. Many Protestant Reformers who denied the Immaculate Conception got around this by advocating the theory that the stain of inherited, original sin is passed down to children only through fathers, not mothers, so that Mary did not need to be sinless to bear a sinless Son. This view was supported in their minds by Rom 5:12, which says that sin entered the world through a man, and 1 Cor 11:3, which says that the "head" of every woman is a man. Women, therefore, do not pass down the stain of sin through generations, fathers do; and since the Holy Spirit is perfect, so was the incarnate Son. I do not advise you to find this explanation compelling.

and entirely achieved "by the grace of God" (493) and not any of Mary's own merit or goodness. Misunderstanding corrected.

Finally, you might, as an aside, be interested to know that Martin Luther defended his belief in Mary's Immaculate Conception to his death. "It is piously and suitably believed," he wrote, that the infusion of Mary's soul upon her conception "was without any sin, so that while the soul was being infused, she would at the same time be cleansed from original sin and adorned with the gifts of God to receive the holy soul thus infused. And thus, in the very moment in which she began to live, she was without all sin."[10]

69. Correct your understanding of the veneration of Mary and the saints. Evangelicals commonly believe that Catholics worship Mary and the saints, including statues of them, which are idols. If this were true, then you should not become Catholic. As it turns out, however, that is not true. It is yet another Protestant misunderstanding and distortion.

The problem here is that Protestants fail to grasp some subtle but crucial distinctions in Catholicism between "adoration" and "veneration." For most Protestants, these are merely different labels for "worship," which belongs to God alone. But in Catholicism, veneration and adoration are two very distinct things—and that difference matters a lot. Adoration belongs only to God, not to any created being, including Mary. But, by contrast, it is right and good to regard Mary and the saints with veneration.[11]

These distinctions are easily lost in the English language, which tends to collapse all such nuances into the simple idea of "worship"—of which, again, God is the only legitimate object. But Greek makes the distinctions clearer. *Latria* (adoration) is the worship and homage that is rightly given only to God. *Dulia* (veneration, devotion), by contrast, is the recognition and honor rightly evoked by excellence observed in created persons. The highest form of *dulia*, reserved only for Mary, the Mother of God, Catholics call *hyperdulia*, since she as the Mother of God stands out as first and most shining among all the saints. Such differences are alien to evangelicals. But they were understood in the early

10. Luther, *Works*, IV:694.

11. To better grasp a Catholic theological understanding of Mary, read Rahner's *Our Lady and the Church* and Newman's *Mary*.

days of the Church and officially recognized by the Seventh Ecumenical Council, the Second Council of Nicaea, in 787 CE.

Protestants may object that humans should never venerate any humans, no matter how saintly they were or are. But that is naïve, even hypocritical. Evangelicals themselves in fact venerate all sorts of their own "saints," as I point out below, including C. S. Lewis, Billy Graham, Martin Luther (ironically), and so on. That is not only natural, it is entirely legitimate, when deserved. Nothing in scripture or doctrine denies the validity of recognizing, honoring, and praising that which is excellent and inspiring among humans, especially among Christian role models. Furthermore, the situation here is not zero-sum: offering *dulia* to human saints needs not detract *latria* from God. In fact, it can increase it, as we will see below.

We can even observe various forms of *dulia* in the Bible. Paul commands believers in Philippi to *honor* Epaphroditus because of the heroic works he had done in service to Paul (Phil 2:25–30). Paul himself *praised* the Corinthian believers for remembering him and holding to the traditions which he passed on to them (1 Cor 11:2). Paul urged the Corinthians to *imitate* his worthy example (1 Cor 4:16). The author of the book of Hebrews similarly urges readers to observe the lives of their leaders and to *imitate* their faith (Heb 13:7). The same author also holds a litany of people of God—Abel, Enoch, Noah, Abraham, Isaac, Jacob, Joseph, Moses, the people of Israel, Rahab, Gideon, Barak, Samson, Jephthah, David, Samuel, and prophets and martyrs—as *models* of faith to *inspire* Christians to throw off sin and live with perseverance (Hebrews 11 and 12). It is commendable, Paul writes, for Christians to seek their own *honor* in doing good; God will indeed reward that with honor (Rom 2:7,10; also see 1 Pet 1:7). God himself crowns humanity with *honor* (Ps 8:5; see Ps 71:21). God bestowed *honor* upon Solomon (1 Kngs 3:13). And God the Father *honors* believers who serve Jesus (John 12:26; also see Ps 84:11). So for Protestants to suggest that no human, however excellent in good things, deserves any recognition, honor, praise, or admiration is silly.

Even Martin Luther, despite criticizing the Catholic doctrines of Mary's intercession and mediation, insisted on venerating Mary: "The veneration of Mary is inscribed in the very depths of the human heart," Luther taught.[12] In his last sermon at Wittenberg, in January 1546, Luther

---

12. Luther, *Works*, X:313.

preached: "Is Christ only to be adored? Or is the holy Mother of God rather not to be honored? This is the woman who crushed the Serpent's head. Hear us[, Mary]. For your Son denies you nothing."[13] John Calvin, too, no fan of Catholic Mariology, nevertheless conceded that, "It cannot even be denied that God, in choosing and destining Mary to be the Mother of his Son, granted her the highest honor."[14]

Okay, then. Catholicism says that many Christian believers from and since the apostolic era have lived excellent lives worthy of *dulia* by the Church on earth; that it builds the faith of living Christians to honor them; and that it honors God himself, the author of salvation, when his people venerate Mary and the saints. I do not have space here to develop a full-blown explanation of Catholic doctrines of Mary or the saints. You'll have to read about that elsewhere. Meanwhile, some teachings of the Catholic *Catechism* and Vatican II are helpful for setting those teachings in a larger context.

First, the Catholic Church is perfectly clear that worship and adoration (*latria*) belong to God alone: "Adoration is the first act of the virtue of religion. To adore God is to acknowledge him as God, as the Creator and Savior, the Lord and Master of everything that exists, as infinite and merciful Love. 'You shall worship the Lord your God, and him only shall you serve,' says Jesus, citing Deuteronomy" (*Catechism* 2096, also see 2628).

Second, therefore, Catholic teaching is explicit about the difference between venerating Mary and adoring God, noted above. For instance, the Catechism says that, "The Church rightly honors the Blessed Virgin with special devotion [*dulia*]. From the most ancient times, the Blessed Virgin has been honored with the title 'Mother of God'. . . . [Yet] this very special devotion differs essentially from the adoration [*latria*] which is given to the incarnate Word and equally to the Father and the Holy Spirit, and greatly fosters this adoration" (971).

Third, Catholics venerate Mary and the saints not as quasi-polytheists but in order to grow closer to God and to recognize the unity of the Church:

> It is not only by reason of their example that we cherish the memory of those in heaven; we seek, rather, that by the practical

13. Luther, *Works*, LI:128–29.
14. Calvin, Commentary on Luke 11:27, in *Calvini Opera*, 348, 350.

fraternal and sororal charity the union of the whole church in the Spirit may be strengthened (see Eph 4:1–6). Exactly as Christian communion among pilgrims brings us closer to Christ, so our communion with the saints joins us to Christ, from whom as from its fountain and head flow all grace and life of the people of God itself. It is most fitting, therefore, that we love those friends and co-heirs of Jesus Christ who are also our sisters and brothers and outstanding benefactors [i.e., saints in heaven], and that we give due thanks to God for them. (*Lumen Gentium* 76)

Fourth, offering *dulia* to the saints in heaven is itself a form of *latria* for God. "Every authentic witness of love . . . offered by us to those who are in heaven tends toward and terminates in Christ, the crown of all the saints, and through him in God who is wonderful in his saints and is glorified in them" (*Lumen Gentium* 76–77). Again, the flow of every kind of Christian honor, veneration, and praise for human saints continues to its final destination in God alone.

Fifth, for this reason, veneration for Mary, who is not divine, is regularly connected to a higher worship of her divine Son, Jesus. Regard for Mary, in other words, is recurrently paired with adoration of Jesus, in a way that consistently emphasizes the superiority of Christ. "What the Catholic faith believes about Mary," the *Catechism* teaches, "is based on what it believes about Christ" (487). The Churches, it also says, have always "developed their prayer to the holy Mother of God, centering it on the person of Christ" (2675). "Jesus, our *only mediator*, is the way of our prayer," it repeats again. "Mary, his mother and ours, is wholly transparent to him: she 'shows the way'" (2674).

Sixth, Catholicism offers a reflective, historically-rooted doctrine about the place of material and pictorial images in the veneration of saints and Mary. Central to that reflection is the recognition of the implications of the history-changing centrality of *the incarnation* of God the Son in the person of Jesus Christ. The incarnation links the material world to the heavenly realms in a way previously unknown in God's economy of salvation. Heaven and earth, divinity and humanity are brought together in Christ. The material and sensory are put to the service of the triune God in a way not entirely known in the old covenant. Thus, "by becoming incarnate, the Son of God introduced *a new 'economy' of images*" (*Catechism* 2131). Because of this historic change, the Church teaches this about images of Mary and saints:

> The Christian veneration of images is not contrary to the first
> commandment which proscribes idols. Indeed, "the honor ren-
> dered to an image passes to its prototype," and "whoever vener-
> ates an image venerates the person portrayed in it" [St. Basil]. The
> honor paid to sacred images is a "respectful veneration" [*dulia*],
> not the adoration [*latria*] due God alone. (*Catechism* 2132)

Consequently, it is important to understand that, when it comes to
images of God, such as paintings of Jesus or crucifixes, "religious worship is not directed to images themselves, considered as mere things, but
under their distinctive aspect as images leading us on to God incarnate.
The movement toward the image does not terminate in it as image, but
tends toward that whose image it is."[15] It is simply false, therefore, to
say, as more than a few evangelicals do, that Catholics worship icons or
images. Correction: they *use* icons and images to aid their worship of the
true God.

Finally, the Church since Vatican II has been extremely careful to
curb misunderstandings and abuses of the veneration of Mary and the
saints in practices of popular piety. Vatican II, for instance, teaches that,
"The various forms of piety toward the Mother of God" must be pursued
"within the limits of sound and orthodox doctrine" in order to "ensure
that while the mother is honored, the Son . . . is rightly known, loved,
and glorified and his commandments are observed" (*Lumen Gentium*,
VIII, 4, 66). The *Catechism* likewise teaches that, "Pastoral discernment
is needed to sustain and support popular piety and, if necessary, to purify
and correct the religious sense which underlies these devotions so that
the faithful may advance in knowledge of the mystery of Christ" (1676).
Vatican II therefore offers this pointed, balanced advice for practical
implications:

> [The Church] strongly urges theologians and preachers of the
> word of God to be careful to refrain as much from all false
> exaggeration as from too summary an attitude in considering
> the special dignity of the Mother of God. Following the study
> of sacred scripture, the Fathers, the doctors and liturgy of the
> church, and under the guidance of the church's magisterium, let
> them rightly illustrate the offices and privileges of the Blessed
> Virgin, which always refer to Christ, the source of all truth,
> sanctity, and devotion. Let them carefully refrain from whatever

15. Aquinas, *Summa Theologia*, II-II, 81, 3 *ad* 3.

might by word or deed lead the separated sisters and brothers [i.e., Protestants] or any others whatsoever into error about the true doctrine of the church. Let the faithful remember moreover that true devotion consists neither in sterile or transitory feeling, nor in an empty credulity, but proceeds from true faith. (*Lumen Gentium*, VIII, 4, 67)

In short, many standard evangelical understandings of Catholics paying regard to Mary and the saints are off beam. They need to be corrected. Meanwhile, you must learn the distinction between *latria* and *dulia*, so that you can worship God alone and properly venerate those who have run the race before us in a manner worthy of honor, praise, and imitation.[16]

70. Clarify your understanding of the Assumption of Mary. Evangelicals—again, if and when they ever think about it—tend to picture the Assumption of Mary as some kind of magical ascension into the blue—as if, at some point in her life, Mary's body simply began floating up into the sky until it "reached heaven." Not quite. This doctrine simply says that Mary, "when the course of her earthly life was finished, was taken up body and soul into heavenly glory" (*Catechism* 966).

Whether Mary first died and then was assumed into heaven or whether her assumption took place at the end of her still-alive life, the Catholic Church does not declare. Sometimes the Church speaks of the Assumption as or coming after her "dormition." Different views on this are accepted. Furthermore, the Catholic Church distinguishes between Christ's *ascension*, which took place by his own power, and Mary's *assumption*, which was not brought about by her own capacity but by the power of God.

Of course the Bible never says that "Mary, the mother of Jesus, was assumed body and soul into heaven." This doctrine is viewed by the Church, rather, as a theological implication of the Immaculate Conception, Christ's resurrection, Mary's identification with the Ark of the Covenant, and Mary's role as symbol of the church and pledge of the resurrection on the last day. In order to understand that, you'll have to do more reading elsewhere. Meanwhile, you can be assured that this is not simply a doctrine pulled out of the air by a power-hungry pope looking for some way to make up an unbiblical "human tradition."

16. For a thoughtful discussion about this and related matters, see relevant chapters in Duffy, *Faith of Our Fathers*.

In fact, throughout Church history, various fathers, theologians, and doctors have understood a variety of scripture passages (e.g., Rev 12:1–2; Ps 8:6; Luke 1:28 overcoming the curses of Gen 3:16; Song 8:5; 1 Cor 15:21–26; Isa 30:16; Ps 45:9–17) as foreshadowing the Assumption of Mary, which the Church only in time came to understand and express theologically in fuller depth. Such Bible verses of course make no sense when read within the Protestant paradigm. But that again only shows the data-signifying and thought-shaping power of paradigms. If you care about this enough to read in greater depth, you will find that Catholic thought on the matter actually makes some sense, granted a few Catholic presuppositions and tendencies.

And if you remain skeptical, you can at least rest in the knowledge that the Bible teaches that both Enoch (Gen 5:22–24) and Elijah (2 Kngs 2:11), and arguably Moses (putting together Deut 34:6; Jude 9; and Matt 17:3), were assumed into heaven[17] and that the Bible does not say that Mary was not assumed into heaven. You might also keep in mind that Martin Luther himself endorsed this doctrine four centuries before it was authoritatively defined, writing that, "There can be no doubt that the Virgin Mary is in heaven. How it happened we do not know."[18] Here too, however, it is worth keeping this doctrine in perspective—in all 2,865 paragraphs comprising the Catholic *Catechism*, the Assumption appears in a total of *one* (966).

71. Improve your understanding of papal infallibility. I am not sure what you picked up along the way. But from my earlier decades spent in the evangelical world, the idea I got about the Catholic doctrine of papal infallibility was something like this: The pope thinks he's perfect. The pope has grabbed all power to himself so that he can promulgate all kinds of strange ideas. The Catholic Church operates arbitrarily and without any accountability. The pope has turned himself into a god. The Church can never change its mind or reform itself. Etcetera.

Those kinds of ideas turn out to be rather hysterical in their inaccuracy, when one learns the truth about papal infallibility. I do not suggest, once the facts of the matter are properly understood, that all

17. According to Jewish Midrash, eight people have gone alive to heaven: Elijah the Prophet; Serach, the daugher of Asher, son of Jacob; Eliezer, servant of Abraham; Jaabez, son of Rabbi Yehudah ha-Nagid; Bithian, daugher of Pharaoh; Ebed Melech, the Ethiopian; Enoch; and Hiram, king of Tyre.

18. Luther, *Works*, X:268.

evangelicals are going to convert and start coming to Mass on Sundays. But at least then the real differences can be addressed, instead of fictions that do nothing but divide Christians for no reason. In any case, before you become Catholic you should understand the facts.

First, papal infallibility does not mean that everything a pope says is perfect. Only a limited set of papal pronouncements made under very specific conditions are held to be infallible. One is that the pronounce-ment be proclaimed "by a definitive act of doctrine pertaining to faith or morals" (*Catechism* 891). Most of what popes say are not a "definitive act of doctrine," so is not held to be infallible.

Further, infallibly held beliefs may only be those which are pro-mulgated as "being divinely revealed" and therefore "must be adhered to with the obedience of faith" (*Catechism* 891). Finally, infallibly held beliefs may "not . . . admit any new public revelation as pertaining to the divine deposit of faith" (*Lumen Gentium* 36). So there is no room here for introducing as-if divinely revealed doctrines, definitions and beliefs which do not already belong to revelation itself as the Church under-stands it. Much of what that Catholic Church teaches, including matters of Church disciplines and government, is not considered infallible.

Second, papal infallibility is not grounded upon the *person* who oc-cupies the seat of the bishop of Rome. The person generates no authority. It is rather the *office* of the bishop of Rome—as "head of the college of bishops . . . in virtue of his office"—that is to be understood as giving rise to infallibility. And the ultimate source of the authority of that office is believed to be none other than Jesus Christ. Furthermore, infallibility is not the result of divine "inspiration," but of the "assistance" of the Holy Spirit, which is an altogether different matter. The pope is not inspired in what he declares.[19]

Third, invocations of papal infallibility are rare. Only two instances are quite clear in the entire history of the Church. One is Pope Pius IX's definition of the dogma of the Immaculate Conception of Mary in 1854. The other is Pope Pius XII's 1950 definition of the dogma of the

---

19. Catholics have a certain amount of reserve for speaking about the Bible, which is taken to be normative and infallible. Papal and Vatican statements are not "inspired," in this sense. The pope, the magisterium, and the Church as a whole is only "assisted" by the Holy Spirit in coming to clearer understandings of normative teachings of the Bible and tradition.

Assumption of Mary. Beyond that, there is no clear consensus on what other pronouncements might claim the status of infallible.[20]

Fourth, the Church has declared that infallible papal definitions are *not* "absolute." This fact was established by leaders of the First Vatican Council in 1870—particularly by Vincent Gasser, the Council's head of its theological commission. Gasser made clear in a four-hour presentation with questions and answers, explaining what the dogma did and did not affirm, that papal infallibility was "in no way (*nullo modo*) . . . absolute, for such infallibility belongs to God alone. Every other form of 'infallibility,'" Gasser continued, has its limits and conditions.[21]

Fifth, papal decrees promulgated as infallible never come from unilateral statements of popes—even though in theory they could in the rarest of circumstances. Instead, they are heavily informed through both consultations with many other, if not all, Catholic bishops and with the "sense of the faithful" (*sensus fidelium*—which is something like the Church's people's supernaturally-formed consensus about matters of faith and morals) (*Catechism* 91–93). One should also distinguish between infallible papal pronouncements and teachings of Church Councils (e.g., Real Presence, the relationship between faith and reason, the Nicene Creed, etc.) which the pope concurred as being infallible—even as our understanding and appreciation for them can and do develop over time.

20. According to Francis Sullivan in *Creative Fidelity*, additional documents promulgated *ex cathedra* include "Tome to Flavian," Pope Leo I, 449 CE, on the two natures in Christ, received by the Council of Chalcedon; Letter of Pope Agatho, 680 CE, on the two wills of Christ, received by the Third Council of Constantinople; *Benedictus Deus*, Pope Benedict XII, 1336 CE, on the beatific vision of the just prior to final judgment; *Cum occasione*, Pope Innocent X, 1653 CE, condemning five propositions of Cornelius Otto Jansen; and *Auctorem fidei*, Pope Pius VI, 1794 CE, condemning seven Jansenist propositions.

21. See Heft, "Humble Infallibility"; Heft, *John XXII*, 207ff. Some readers, particularly perhaps those who tend to think in binary terms, may wonder what "non-absolute infallibility" could look like. A non-absolute teaching, even an infallible one, is acknowledged to be humanly conditioned and potentially able to be improved upon or developed. If infallible statements were "absolute," they could never be improved or "developed" (to use a key concept with which Cardinal Newman blessed us). Thinking of "absolute" in the theological sense, meaning "perfect," we say that only God is absolute truth. That is what Gasser was saying. Every human effort to articulate God's absolutely true revelation is conditioned by our limited capacity to capture God's truth in human words. But that does not mean that an infallible statement can be falsified. It is true and never to be reversed or rescinded—otherwise, what is the point of claiming that the Church can under certain strict conditions make binding (true) statements on "faith and morals" that communicate God's truth? Thanks to Jim Heft for helpful ideas here.

So, arbitrary, unilateral pronouncements by popes at this level just do not happen. The pope simply could not exercise this gift of infallible definition if he were separated from the rest of the Church.

Sixth, one must recall the distinction explained above between the truth a theological formulation expresses and the formulation itself. They are not the same. As Thomas Aquinas wrote, "The act of the believer does not reach its end in the proposition, but in the revealed reality itself."[22] Thus, even when the Church propounds a doctrine to be "irreformable," because declared infallible, it also recognizes that there are still a number of conditions that make Church pronouncements historically conditioned and therefore in need of possible development over time. Those factors of historical conditioning include:

> (1) the limited state of human knowledge at the time of the original definition; (2) the changeable conceptions and thought patterns that belong to a certain period of time; (3) the specific concerns that motivated the definition; and (4) the limited expressive power of the language used at the time of the definition. In light of these limitations, what become "irreformable" are not the words or definitions, which are open to improvement, but their meaning.[23]

Thus, again, the Vatican's Sacred Congregation of the Doctrine of the Faith has declared, "it sometimes happens that some dogmatic truth is first expressed incompletely (but not falsely), and at a later date, when considered in its broadest context of faith or human knowledge, it receives a fuller and more perfect expression."[24]

Finally, I suggest that you read J. M. R. Tillard's *The Bishop of Rome* (London: SPCK, 1983), which will provide a better perspective on the nature of the papacy more generally.

72. Clarify the theological idea of Merit. The word "merit" as a theological concept sends shivers down the spines of most evangelicals. Merit has to do with being good and earning something. And that has to do with works-righteousness and salvation by good deeds. And that has to do with Catholicism and heresy and a rejection of the Bible.

Again, not really. The Catholic Church does on occasion use the terminology of merit—perhaps unfortunately, given its troubled history

22. *Summa Theologiae*, II-II, Q. 2, Art. 2.

23. Heft, "Humble Infallibility."

24. Congregation for the Doctrine of the Faith *Mysterium Ecclesiae*, section 5.

with its "separated brothers and sisters." But in *every* use of the term, all human merit comes from God as a gift of free grace. Never does any person earn their own merit or meritoriously deserve anything good from God as a result of their own doing apart from what God provides them as a gift. Listen to what the *Catechism* (2006–11) teaches: "With regard to God, there is no strict right to any merit on the part of man. Between God and us there is an immeasurable inequality, for we have received everything from him, our Creator." And this:

> The merit of man before God in the Christian life arises from the fact that *God has freely chosen to associate man with the work of his grace.* The fatherly action of God is first on his own initiative, and then follows man's free acting through his collaboration, so that the merit of good works is to be attributed in the first place to the grace of God, then to the faithful. Man's merit, moreover, itself is due to God.

In short, God provides all the merit in question, then humans follow God's lead and run with it. Yet all the merit that humans may "have" completely comes from God alone.

Continuing: "Filial adoption, in making us partakers by grace in the divine nature, can bestow *true merit* on us as a result of God's gratuitous justice. . . . The merits of our good works are gifts of the divine goodness" (2009). Then the *Catechism* quotes Augustine of Hippo: "Grace has gone before us; now we are given what is due. . . . Our merits are God's gifts" (2009). The same theme continues: "Since the initiative belongs to God in the order of grace, *no one can merit the initial grace* of forgiveness and justification, at the beginning of conversion. . . . *The charity of Christ is the source in us of all our merits before God*" (2010–11).

In brief, Catholicism does talk about merit in discussions about grace and salvation. But what the Church says about merit bears no resemblance to evangelicalism's mistaken caricature of it. Yes, you possess merit before God. But, even though it is true merit, and even though somehow in this mystery you really participate in that, this merit that you possess is not your own making or earning. It is all grace and completely from and about Jesus Christ.

73. Get over indulgences. They do not matter much in theory, and do not matter at all in any reality that will affect you. Johann Tetzel is not knocking at your door. They won't affect your life as a Catholic in the slightest. Focus on more important issues instead. Maybe someday you will figure indulgences out.[25] But you do not need to focus on that now.

74. Think harder about praying for the dead. If you have experience in the Anglican church, this will not be an issue for you. If you do not, this may be a strange part of Catholicism that could take some getting used to. Catholics (and Anglicans and the Eastern Orthodox) pray for the dead. What about that?

Okay, why should we not pray for the souls of the dead? We care about them, sometimes dearly love them. As we bury them or later remember them in our minds and hearts, what exactly is wrong with asking God for "the repose of their souls" or to receive them into his eternal kingdom? It seems odd that we should suddenly stop caring about the deceased, or that we must after the point of their death say nothing at all anymore to God about them. C. S. Lewis put the matter this way:

> Of course I pray for the dead. The action is so spontaneous, so all but inevitable, that only the most compulsive theological case against it would deter me. . . . At our age the majority of those we love best are dead. What sort of intercourse with God could I have if what I love best were unmentionable to him?[26]

Protestants often quote that "man is destined to die once, and after that to face judgment" (Heb 9:27), arguing that once someone is dead, their fate is sealed, so there is no use praying for them.[27] The context of that verse, however, places it in a complex argument about the finality of Christ's death, not a discussion having to do with when and what exactly happens to humans after they die and whether prayers for them are valid. Catholics too believe that judgment comes after death. But that fact does not say how "soon" after death judgment comes, nor does it prove that one cannot or should not pray for their souls. That is just not there.

Many evangelicals also argue that prayers for the dead are useless, since the opportunity the dead had to choose Christ (while living) is now gone. They had their chance when they were alive, but now that they're dead, the window of grace for salvation has closed for good. But this

25. If so, the place to start will be: United States Conference of Catholic Bishops, *Manual of Indulgences*.

26. Lewis, *Letters to Malcolm*, 107.

27. For a highly readable and informative survey of the history of Protestant/Catholic differences on the matter of the dead, see Eire, "Eternity Reformed," chapter 4 in Eire, *Very Brief History of Eternity*, 100–156.

logic comes more from the rhetoric of an evangelistic revival meeting ("If you were to die tonight . . .") than from clear scriptural teaching.

In fact, the Bible is quite murky about what exactly faces the dead upon their death and before the final judgment at the end of time. Not all Christian theologies have asserted that the window of salvation closes immediately upon bodily death in this world. C. S. Lewis, for instance, an evangelical saint, certainly didn't think all eternal fates were sealed the very second that people's hearts stopped beating—just read *The Last Battle* and *The Great Divorce* to see that. Perhaps a bit more humility about what we "know" about post-mortem human fates and an openness to praying for the dead, as the Church has done for nearly its entire history, are in order.

But, many evangelicals say, the Bible never teaches us to pray for the dead, so doing that goes beyond biblical teachings. Well, that may depend in part on what you mean by "the Bible." A passage in the Catholic scriptural canon—what some call the "Deuterocanonical" books, scriptural texts received from the Septuagint, which is the Koine Greek translation of the Hebrew Bible completed in the second century BCE—namely, 2 Maccabees (12:42–45), clearly commends praying for the dead. It says this:

> The noble Judas [Maccabeus] exhorted the people to keep them-selves free from sin, for they had seen with their own eyes what had happened because of the sin of those who had fallen. He also took up a collection, man by man . . . and sent it to Jerusalem to provide for a sin offering. In doing this he acted very well and honorably, taking account of the resurrection. For if he was not expecting that those who had fallen would rise again, *it would have been superfluous and foolish to pray for the dead*. But if he was looking to the splendid reward that is laid up for those who fall asleep in godliness, *it was a holy and pious thought*. Therefore he made atonement for the dead, that they might be delivered from their sin.[28]

Protestants reject 2 Maccabees and other books as not canonical scrip-ture, disparaging them as "The Apocrypha." What that means, however, is that the *Protestant* Bible does not obviously teach prayers for the dead, at least at first glance.

28. Prayers for the dead are offered in Judaism in Jewish services, which include this prayer: "Have mercy upon him; pardon all his transgressions . . . Shelter his soul in the shadow of Thy wings. Make known to him the path of life."

But why, you might ask, do Protestants reject the Deuterocanonical books of Scripture? A big reason, it turns out, is because one of them, 2 Macabees, commends prayers for the dead, as we just saw, and Protestants could not accept that—having already rejected the practice as too Catholic.[29] In short, Protestants were by definition anti-Catholic; one Catholic teaching to which they objected came from a certain set of scriptural texts; so therefore those books, Protestants decided, *must not* be scriptural. Martin Luther argued something very similar for the same reason, by the way, about the Book of James, Hebrews, Jude, and Revelation—though that is a different story. But this is a case of the tail wagging the dog. Nobody should decide what is Scripture based on whether they do or don't like what it says—that simply takes authority away from scripture and places it in preconceived theological beliefs.

In any event, to come back to the point, it is simply false, granted a Catholic view of Scripture, at least, to say that God's people offering prayers for the dead is "unscriptural." To settle the issue, then, the argument must move to a different level about the canonical status of the Deuterocanonical texts.

(I cannot go into a debate about that here. But I will offer two points about which evangelicals are often unaware. First, the Deuterocanonical books Baruch, Tobit, Maccabees, Judith, Sirach, Wisdom and parts of Daniel and Esther were all included in the Septuagint that Jesus and the apostles read as Scripture. Second, the New Testament itself in at least some and possibly many places references Deuterocanonical books. Heb 11:35b, for example, references 2 Macabees 7:1–19. First Peter 1:6–7 references Wisdom 3:5–6 and Sirach 2:5. First Peter 1:17 references Sirach 16:12. Numerous other similar instances can be found. One [Protestant] scholar finds that the New Testament references or alludes to the Deuterocanonical books at least a hundred and fifty times [though Protestants predictably dispute these claims].[30] That itself does not *prove* that the Deuterocanonical texts should be considered scriptural, since the New Testament also quotes some clearly non-scriptural sources [such as the Cretan philosopher Epimenides in Titus 1:12; also see 1 Cor

29. And not found in the Masoretic Hebrew text, which they preferred.

30. McDonald, *Formation of the Christian Biblical Canon*. On a parallel note, Jude 14–15 and 2 Pet 2:4–5 also quote the Book of Enoch, which is included in the biblical canon of the Christian Oriental Orthodox churches of Ethiopia and Eritrea (although Enoch is not part of the Deuterocanonical books recognized as Scripture by Catholicism).

15:33 and Acts 17:28]. Still, the Deuterocanonical books belong to the [Alexandrian] Jewish, not a pagan, tradition. And the New Testament references them not as general cultural heritage but as if they held some status of authority in the faith. And that gives us reason to question the simple Protestant dismissal of the Deuterocanonical texts as obviously unscriptural.)

Beyond that, however, it *may in fact be* that even the *Protestant* New Testament contains a case of an apostolic prayer for the dead. In 2 Tim 1:16–18, Paul writes: "May the Lord show mercy to the household of Onesiphorus, because he often refreshed me and was not ashamed of my chains. On the contrary, when he was in Rome, he searched hard for me until he found me. *May the Lord grant that he will find mercy from the Lord on that day.*"

Some biblical scholars believe for three good reasons that Onesiphorus was dead when Paul wrote this, and so Paul was asking the Lord in a prayer to show Onesiphorus mercy. First, Paul speaks of Onesiphorus here in the past tense, as if he is no longer around in the church community that was his own. Second, Paul references Judgment Day with the phrase, "on that day" in which mercy is needed—suggesting a parallel to 2 Maccabees in praying for mercy in anticipation of the resurrection and judgment of the dead. Third, later in the very same epistle (4:19), Paul conveys his request to "Greet Priscilla and Aquila and the household of Onesiphorus." Paul is seemingly distinguishing in that one phrase the living from the dead—for if Onesiphorus was still living, why would Paul not send him greetings directly? Why instead did he greet other individuals (Priscilla and Aquila) and then only members of Onesiphorus' household, but not Onesiphorus himself?

But if Onesiphorus was dead, then Paul was in fact here in Protestant Scripture petitioning the Lord for his soul—in brief, Paul was praying for the dead. Thus, an evangelical case of an "argument from silence" in scripture about prayers for the dead—aside from suffering the weaknesses of all arguments from silence—may not be quite as airtight as evangelicals often presume.

Still, as an evangelical, you very likely assume that once a person dies, they are gone, kaput, cut off from those of us still living. They may be "in heaven" praising God. Or they may be decomposed, awaiting the final Resurrection Day. But either way, they certainly are not connected or accessible to you or me. There exists, in Carlos Eire's words, a "spiritual apartheid" that completely separates the living and dead.[31]

Now, question that assumption. Why should that be the case? Catholicism offers a different view of the matter. The Church toward which you are moving understands itself as comprised in part, in large part, in fact, of dead believers. The Church, here and now, entails and involves all believers, past (dead), present (living), and future (as yet unborn). As the *Catechism* (954–55) says:

> Some of [the Lord's] disciples are pilgrims on earth. Others have died and are being purified, while still others are in glory, contemplating in full light God himself triune and one, exactly as he is. . . . So it is that the union of the wayfarers with the brethren who sleep in the peace of Christ is in no way interrupted, but on the contrary . . . this union is reinforced by an exchange of spiritual goods.

When we pray, we pray with the whole Church. And that means that we pray alongside of the faithful dead. Get used to it.

Here again the different Catholic view of time and eternity, which Protestants often have difficulty grasping, comes into play. Eternity is not an infinite length of our created time. That is linear, literal thinking—and quite unbiblical. Eternity, biblically speaking, is *outside* of time, defined by the being of God who is the author and judge of time. What happens after death, therefore, when deceased persons may exit time, is a mystery that we cannot make rational sense of in terms of our temporally-bound experience. It is also a mystery the details about which God has seen fit to tell us very little in the Bible.

One might reasonably conclude that we should approach this subject with humility and not presume to know everything about prayers for the dead being supposedly useless. In that case, we might look to the long practice of the Christian Church offering prayers for the dead. Consider, for instance, that the surviving late-second century Christian tomb of Abercius of Heiropolis bears this inscription: "Let every friend who observes this pray for me."[32] The Roman catacombs where dead Christians were laid also have inscriptions, like "Peace be with them," "May God refresh the soul of Marcus," and "May you live among the

31. Eire, *Very Brief History of Eternity*, 123.

32. In his entire inscription, of which this is only one part, Abercius speaks "from the dead" in the first person.

saints." The Church Father Tertullian wrote around the turn of the third century that, "The widow who does not pray for her dead husband has as good as divorced him." We know that St. Perpetua in the year 202 CE prayed for her late brother. In the third century, in his list of rules, Cyprian presupposed that the Church prayed for the dead. And in the ninth book of his *Confessions*, Augustine of Hippo prays for his deceased mother, Monica. Christian prayers for the dead thus have a much longer historical lineage than the Protestant prohibitions of them. That matters. Once again, as you sort through these issues, pray and ask God to guide you to understand the truth.

75. Think hard about prayers not only for but also with and to the dead. Next step: Catholics not only pray for the dead. They also pray to and *with* the dead. If you want to become Catholic, you're going to have to get a grip on what that's about. Let us build upon what we have just learned about prayers for the dead and approach the matter from a few other angles.

The first and simplest thing to consider is this. Asking other believers to pray with and for us is actually not strange. Evangelicals do it all the time. "Could you pray for me? I'm really struggling with this problem" or "Please pray for my cousin's son, who was in a bike accident." That is what Catholics also do—only, in addition to asking living believers, they also ask those in heaven to pray with and for them as well. So, if anything is at issue, it is not asking others for prayer, but simply the earthly deadness of some of those asked.

Next, you need to attend to a particular but very important point about the preposition "to" here, over which Protestants have needlessly stumbled for five hundred years. Catholics talk about prayers *to* Mary and the saints. That may be infelicitous wording in English, because it is easy, though wrong, to assume based on it that this means that Mary and the saints are the "final destinations" or "ultimate targets" of those prayers. They are not. Christians pray to Mary and the saints not so their prayers can stop with them. They do so in order that Mary and the saints may also pray alongside of Christians in bringing their prayers to God, the final destination of *all* prayers. So, whenever you hear the phrase "pray to" anyone in heaven other than God, you can rightly translate that in your head into "pray along with the help and additional prayers of support of" those others. That is the intended meaning.[33]

33. Of course some Catholics have historically and may currently misunderstand

About that the Catholic Church is clear. "The Church," the *Catechism* for example says, "loves to pray in communion with the Virgin Mary, to magnify with her the great things the Lord has done for her, and to entrust supplications and praises [for God] to her" (2682). The same is true of all of the saints: "Being more closely united to Christ, those who dwell in heaven fix the whole Church more firmly in holiness. . . . They do not cease to intercede with the Father for us. . . . So by their fraternal concern is our weakness greatly helped" (956). And about the great "cloud of witnesses," the *Catechism* says this:

> The witnesses who have preceded us into the kingdom . . . share in the living tradition of prayer by . . . their prayers today. They contemplate God, praise him, and constantly care for those whom they have left on earth. When they entered into the joy of their Master, they "were put in charge of many things." Their intercession is their most exalted service to God's plan. We can and should ask them to intercede for us and for the whole world. (2683)

Of course, one may object to anyone in heaven other than Christ interceding to God for us (per 1 Tim 2:5). But that is a separate matter which I address below. My more limited point here is simply that prayers "to" Mary and the saints, as Catholics express it, are really prayers *to God*. They are prayers offered up to God with the help of additional prayers of support from Mary and the saints—just like you might ask a friend or family member to pray for and with you.

Hence, the Protestant criticism that Catholics "pray to Mary and saints" is linguistically not incorrect but is substantively misinformed. Really, Catholics pray *to God* with perhaps the requested aid and added prayers of Mary and the saints. That makes a huge difference, which might make a big difference in your readiness to become Catholic.

Okay, consider next the question of whether prayers to and with the dead are biblical. In fact, whether or not you've ever noticed it or connected it to this issue, the Bible actually portrays heaven as a place where angels and elders in glory, who encircle the Lamb on the throne, carry bowls of incense full of "the prayers of the saints" to offer to God.

---

and abuse this doctrine in their popular devotional piety—just like some evangelicals misunderstand and abuse certain evangelical teachings, such as "putting out a fleece" or "finding 'God's will'"—turning Mary and the saints into divine objects of prayerful worship. But that itself does not make the doctrine wrong, but only something good being misunderstood, abused, and in need of correction.

Revelation 5:8–9 says: "The twenty-four elders fell down before the Lamb. Each one had a harp and they were holding golden bowls full of incense, *which are the prayers of the saints*. And they sang a new song." Three chapters later, Revelation 8:3–4 depicts this scene: "Another angel, who had a golden censer, came and stood at the altar. He was given much incense to offer, *with the prayers of all the saints*, on the golden altar before the throne. The smoke of the incense, *together with the prayers of the saints*, went up before God from the angel's hand."

Good heavens! So angels and elders in heaven are offering up to God the prayers of Christian believers in bowls of smoking incense? It appears so. These passages seem to allude to other scriptural images which connect the prayers of God's people on earth and incense rising to heaven, including Ps 141:3 ("May my prayer be set before you like incense; may the lifting up of my hands be like the evening sacrifice") and the many offerings and prayers ritually made in the Old Testament tabernacle and temple. Oh, and in Acts 9:40, the apostle Peter prays for a dead woman.

What does this mean? None of it, admittedly, is a clear, straightforward, didactic teaching that believers on earth should pray with and to the dead. But it does give a picture consistent with the possibility. At the very least, even based only on these passages, we can observe that it is erroneous to say that the idea of (living) believers praying with and to the dead in heaven is absolutely "unbiblical." In fact, Martin Luther himself taught that "angels in heaven pray for us (as Christ himself also does) . . . [just as] saints on earth . . . do likewise."[34]

Next, think about this: your evangelical background has probably taught you to think of prayer primarily as worship and intercession. "Prayer" to you likely means offering praise or thanks and asking for things. "Dear God, thank you so much for your love. Please give me the wisdom to know how to deal with my difficult situation." Or, if you are less spiritually mature: "Please give me this job I really want." If that is what prayer is, then praying for, to, and with dead Christians might seem odd. Why praise them when only God deserves all praise? Why ask dead people for stuff when God is the one who gives it?

Aside from understanding the difference between *latria* and *dulia* noted above, it is helpful to realize that Catholics actually think about

34. Smalcald Articles of 1537, Part II, Article II, quoted in Tappert, *Book of Concord*, 297.

prayer a little differently than evangelicals. Prayer is not simply praise and intercession. Prayer is, first of all, "the raising of one's mind and heart to God" (*Catechism* 2559). Prayer can also involve "the requesting of good things from God." But more fundamentally, "prayer is the living relationship of the children of God with their Father who is good beyond measure, with his Son Jesus Christ, and with the Holy Spirit. . . . Thus, the life of prayer is the habit of being in the presence of the thrice-holy God and in communion with him" (*Catechism* 2559, 2565).

Prayer in Catholicism has to do with more than a discrete communication, like a telephone conversation. Prayer is more broadly about focusing attention on, living in relation to, and being in the presence of and in communion with God. That broadens out what is going on in Christian prayer in a way that is relevant to the present question. Specifically, it provides a model in which it makes more sense to pray with even the dead, the saints in heaven.

Consider the following somewhat curious, though not irrelevant, point as well. The Bible contains diverse passages suggesting that something about the cross of Christ has in some way broken down the barrier between the living and the dead—between those who may still hear the gospel message and those heading toward the final judgment. Matt 27:51–53, for instance, tells us this about what happened when Christ died on the cross:

> The curtain of the temple was torn in two from top to bottom. The earth shook and the rocks split. The tombs broke open and the bodies of many holy people who had died were raised to life. They came out of the tombs, and after Jesus' resurrection they went into the holy city and appeared to many people.

Okay, that is wild. What is up with *that*? And how could that even have happened, if (allegedly, per Heb 9:27) death immediately sends all people to their final judgment and fate? Not only that, both Peter and Paul raised people from the dead (Acts 9:40, 20:9–12). And the apostle Paul writes of people being "baptized for the dead" (1 Cor 15:29–30). Hmm.

Then 1 Pet 3:19 tells us that when Christ died he "preached to the spirits in prison who disobeyed long ago." Many call it "the harrowing of hell." Strange stuff—this going back and forth of Christ between the living on earth, the "spirits in prison," and then back to the living again, before ascending to heaven. Perhaps these were the fallen angels referred to in 2 Pet 2:4–9 and Jude 6–7. Perhaps they were more than that. Again, much is mysterious here. But maybe there actually is something about the cross and the kingdom of God that starts to break down the immediate and final divorce of the living and the dead which many Protestants seem so intent on maintaining. And perhaps that adds a bit more weight to the idea that believers on earth are not wrong to pray to God with and through the saints in heaven.

That would certainly make sense in light of Hebrews 11 and 12, which recount the many people of God in history who lived by faith and then died, concluding the point by observing that living believers "are surrounded by such a great cloud of witnesses" (12:1). Note that the readers of Hebrews are not here told simply to look back into history and recall the lives of the dead, in order to learn some lesson for today. No, the former people of great faith, long since dead, actually currently *surround* Christian believers like a "cloud," and that fact should affect how they live their Christian lives. If the Protestant view of the dead was accurate, how could that be and why should it matter? The Catholic view, however, again, is that this "great cloud of witnesses" is in fact very real and present, is indeed a help in our lives now, and rightly affects our awareness, including our prayerful thoughts with them to God.

It is for these reasons that the Catholic Church teaches that, "It is not merely by the title of example that we cherish the memory of those in heaven; we seek, rather, that by this devotion to the exercise of fraternal charity the union of the whole Church in the Spirit may be strengthened. Exactly as our Christian communion among our fellow pilgrims brings us closer to Christ, so our communion with the saints joins us to Christ, from whom as from its fountain and head issues all grace, and the life of the People of God itself" (957).

In this, the Church appeals to the teaching and testimony of many Church Fathers, including the early martyr Polycarp (70–155 CE), who wrote: "We worship Christ as God's Son; we love the martyrs as the Lord's disciples and imitators, and rightly so because of their matchless devotion towards their king and master. May we also be their companions and fellow disciples" (*Catechism* 957). Companions and fellow disciples the martyrs could not be to Polycarp or you or me, if upon the moment of their deaths they were whisked off to judgment and then heaven, totally sealed off from living believers. Only inside the *heads* of living believers could the dead ever be what Polycarp describes. But, then again,

Protestantism is primarily a religion of the head, as we've already noted. Yet that does not make its view of prayers with the dead correct.

76. Don't get freaked out by certain bits of Catholic terminology. If you have not picked this up by now, be aware that Catholic lingo involves certain terms that will likely freak you out. But you don't need to be freaked out. You need to learn what the terms mean and maybe identify other terms you can rightly translate them into, if that helps you. I'll mention only a few here.

Probably my favorite of these freak-out words is "cult." When evangelicals hear "cult," they immediately think Jim Jones, David Koresh, drinking Kool Aid, burning compounds, and so on. But the specific use of "cult" in Catholicism, which is actually pretty rare, comes from the Latin word *cultus*. It is a technical term for devotions or venerations which are usually not part of the official public liturgy. Sometimes it conveys the broader meaning of practices associated with worship, such as in the Catechism's discussion of the "disparity of cult" that pertains when married spouses come from two different religions. In almost all cases, in Catholicism, when you hear or read the word "cult," therefore, you can translate it in your mind into "practice of devotion or (if God is the object) worship."

Another of these words is "Extreme Unction." That sounds pretty extreme and maybe painful. In fact it only means "final anointing," in the sense of "anointing the sick with oil," particularly as a part of last rites when there is an immediate danger of death. So, when you hear "extreme unction," think "anointing the very sick" (per Jas 5:13–15).

Yet another Catholic term that may ring strangely in your ear is "charism." This is not the word charismatic, as in the movement, with its end accidentally cut off. "Charisms," rather, are "graces of the Holy Spirit which directly or indirectly benefit the Church, ordered as they are to her building up, to the good of men, and to the needs of the world" (*Catechism* 799). When you hear the word "charism," just think "spiritual gifts" or "ministries given by God to be used for the good of others."

Okay, so I've got you rolling on this. Now if you want you can figure out "Triduum," "concupiscence," "venial sins," "beatific vision," "catechumenate," and so on. The point here is not to write a glossary of all Catholic terms.[35] The point is to inform you in advance that you will in your journey to Catholicism surely come across technical terms over which you

---

35. *The Catechism of the Catholic Church* has a good one.

could, but need not, stumble. What you need to do is to ask or read about them and learn the reasonable concepts to which they actually refer.

77. Start questioning the human control impulse of artificial birth control. The Catholic Church is, of course, from most evangelical perspectives, crazy for resisting the convenience and control offered by The Pill, diaphragms, condoms, intrauterine devices, and other technologies of birth control. What a pre-modern, regressive, fertility-obsessed institution the Catholic Church is! Abortion is in most cases wrong. But birth control and sterilization, you have been raised to believe, are just fine—good gifts from God for couples who want to put off having children till later and limit the total number of children they eventually bear. Evangelicals should have no problem with birth control, you think.

Okay, so, what follows is a very difficult idea for evangelicals to grasp. But give it a try. Here it is: question whether there just *might* perhaps be something not quite right about the human "control" embedded in the heart of birth control.

It might help for starters to learn what most evangelicals do not know, that artificial contraception was condemned by every major branch of Christianity, including Protestantism, until well into the twentieth century. It was not until 1930 that Protestants began changing their minds on the matter. In that year, the Anglican church first accepted birth control as legitimate in Christian ethics. Over the subsequent thirty years, Protestant denominations then increasingly accepted the acceptability of birth control. Ever since, contraceptives have become a non-issue in Protestant, including evangelical, ethics. In short, in only a handful of decades, Protestantism completely reversed its view on the Christian morality of artificial contraception. That itself of course proves little. But it may give one pause to consider the longstanding, historical Christian opposition to birth control and the recentness and rapidity of the dropping of that opposition.

Consider too that the widespread diffusion of technological means of controlling fertility in the latter half of the twentieth century was an essential factor in disassociating in our culture sexual activity from procreation and parenting—with consequences of promiscuity and more that normally alarm most evangelicals. For nearly all of human history, those two were closely linked, for obvious biological reason. Modern contraceptives pulled them apart. Sex became something separate from pregnancy. Increasingly it became a matter of personal self-expression, an obvious step in romantic love, even a recreational activity.

That helped produce the sexual revolution of the 1960s and 70s—for better and/or worse. (And then it did not take long for evangelical sex manuals to hit the market, explaining how conservative Christians too were *Intended for Pleasure* in *The Act of Marriage* and so should learn how to *Turn Up the Heat* and *Fire Up Your Sex Life with the Song of Solomon* in *A Celebration of Sex* toward *Enjoying God's Gift of Sexual Intimacy*. Good stuff. Wouldn't want to be irrelevant to the culture—not to mention left out of the fun.)

You do not need to figure out or decide anything now about birth control. All you need to do is to crack open the door to this question: is all of the technologically-driven human-control imperative involved in birth control really an unambiguous good?

78. Notice who takes the most resolute and unapologetic stand to defend life, marriage, and family. Do you think it matters that Christians actively defend the right to life from natural beginning to end? Do you believe that marriage and family are not simply human social constructions that might be re-defined at will, but rather created institutions of God for the flourishing of humanity? Then take stock of who actually lays it on the line for these commitments. Who offers the deepest, most robust, and theologically-grounded justification for these positions? It is the Catholic Church. No evangelical, much less generally Protestant, denomination or group is as clear, consistent, and forceful in defending life, marriage, and family as the Catholic Church. Happily, however, the Church manages this strong position without—as so many evangelical leaders in recent decades have—being sucked into a consistently conservative or right-wing agenda on all issues. Catholic Social Teachings are simply too strong to allow the Church to be blown about so easily.

79. Face the Future: Protestant and evangelical anti-Catholicism feeds primarily off of the past, focusing especially on the "Dark Ages" and the sixteenth and nineteenth centuries. But it is not the ninth or sixteenth or nineteenth century anymore.

Christians today and into the future *do* need to "live in the past" when it comes to learning from Christian historical tradition. We do need "the living faith of the dead." But we cannot afford to live in the past in ways that merely sustain ancient, needless conflicts and divisions. The larger challenges facing Christians today are immense and growing. It is time to stop nurturing dated animosities from centuries ago and instead to focus on the challenge of being the Church and living faithfully in the present and into the future.

Okay, so now you are beginning to grasp the "revolutionary science" of the Catholic paradigm. For you to become Catholic, you need to see that the Catholic paradigm makes better sense of reality than the Protestant paradigm. Catholicism not only presents an alternative view that explains a lot on its own terms. It also explains the many anomalies in the evangelical paradigm noted above which evangelicalism cannot explain—while raising far fewer of its own new problems as anomalies for its own paradigm. In other words, to shift the image, the Catholic story tells its own narrative, but *also* tells the evangelical story within its own story, in a way that makes better sense of the problems in evangelicalism's story than the evangelical story can make sense of itself.

As a reminder, the point of religious transformation, of which you are on the cusp, does not in the end involve lining up one argument against another. It rather requires a paradigm shift—a fundamental reorientation to the basic approach to and understanding of being a Christian. You cannot argue yourself into Catholicism, in the end. But you can see the many anomalies that simply do not fit the evangelical paradigm. And you can, in an "ah-ha!" vision of insight, come to realize that the Catholic paradigm simply works better—all things considered—than the evangelical paradigm. At which point, your paradigm shift is underway.

If so, then you are getting close to having no good reason not to become Catholic, not to set into motion some final steps toward making that happen. Having completed the seventy-nine steps elaborated above, one simply cannot remain in the same place and retain one's intellectual integrity and spiritual honesty. Becoming Catholic may not be easy for you in practical terms. But, again, who ever said that faithful Christianity would be easy?

Keep praying about all of this. And let's keep moving forward.

six

Shifting and Solidifying Careers

If you are still with me at this point, having completed the first seventy-nine difficult steps, I assume that you are serious about the possibility of becoming Catholic. Good. This chapter focuses on steps you need to take next to move from your current position to actually becoming Catholic for real. You have already done most of the hard work and are now looking down the home stretch. There is not a lot of track left now between you and your reception into the full communion of the Catholic Church. If that is where you think you want to go, then proceed with the following.

80. Do not become Catholic because you think it will give you certainty. Some evangelicals find Catholicism attractive because they think it offers them certainty about Christian beliefs. Previously, they thought an inerrant Bible alone provided certainty. Then they began to see the real problems with that approach, some of which we have noted above. What then to do? Looking to Rome, some decide that the Catholic Church Magisterium provides the epistemic certitude that conservative Protestantism taught them to desire. Catholicism appeals to such people in these cases because it seems to provide that absolute certainty.[1]

Don't do that. Don't think that way. Establishing certainty is a distinctively *modern secular* project, not a Christian one. It was Descartes, empiricism, scientism, and the logical positivists who taught us to

---

1. See McKnight, "From Wheaton to Rome," 451–72.

151

prioritize and search after an indubitable and universal foundation of certainty in human knowledge (which only fairly recently we have realized actually does not exist). Christ, by contrast, calls us to drop what we want and expect, to believe, and to learn the truth from and follow him.

So, do not become Catholic in order to replace a misguided theory about the Bible with a misguided expectation about the Church Magisterium. The main attraction of both of those, of course, is to make people feel more secure about what they think they know. But managing feelings of (in)security is not what Christian faith is about. So don't replace an old foundationalist Protestantism with a new (falsely) foundationalist Catholicism.[2]

The Catholic Church provides Christian believers today very many good things. One of them is a highly coherent account of Christian faith and life, rooted both in scripture and historical tradition, which makes well-warranted claims about the truth of things and calls for lives lived in the light of that truth. Having studied the matter and for good reasons believed its teachings, you can believe with great confidence that what the Church teaches as true really is true.

But confident belief and certain knowledge are not the same things. The Catholic Church does not offer certainty in human knowledge in the way that some ex-evangelicals seem to want to have it. So forget about that. Learn, have faith, seek understanding, and be prepared to give an account. Be forgiven and forgive. Be formed by the sacraments and practices of the Church, particularly the Eucharist, and learn Christian love for God and your neighbor. That's it.

81. Tell your Catholic friends, contacts, or a local priest that you are considering becoming Catholic and continue conversations with them about why, what that means, and what is involved. Again, this is very much a social process and you need to work out all of these steps with Catholic contacts, friends, a priest, and acquaintances who can help you. Don't do this on your own.[3] Seek out faithful Catholics

2. There are obviously a number of complex philosophical issues at play here. For a deeper examination of some of them, see Smith, *Moral, Believing Animals*, ch. 3; Smith, *What is a Person?*

3. If you literally cannot find Catholic friends or contacts locally, go to a local parish and talk to people. And try contacting a national organization designed to help people become Catholic, such as the Coming Home Network (http://www.chnetwork.org/), the Paulist National Catholic Evangelization Association (http://www.pncea.org/), or, for those raised Catholic, Catholics Come Home (http://www.catholicscomehome.org/).

who know what they are talking about, who are serious about their own faith, and are invested in helping you.

Ask your questions. Express any doubts you might have. Raise any issues that are bothering you. Seek clarification on areas of confusion. Get the best handle you can on what you might be getting yourself into. Ask for prayer. And enjoy the relationships and conversations along the way.

82. Identify any of your remaining reservations about or disagreements with Catholicism and talk with others who can help you with them. Perhaps you have a list of things about which you have reservations or possible disagreements with Catholicism. Perhaps not. Make sure you have sorted through your issues. Do not go into the Church with unaddressed and unresolved reservations or disagreements. Face whatever issues you may have, put them on the table, and work them out. Reading can help. The right conversations can help. Pray to God to give you an open but discerning mind as you sort out your issues. One way or another, work on them.

83. Visit your local Catholic parish for Mass and pay close attention to your instinctive reactions. It makes sense at this point to, if you have not already, attend your local Catholic parish and maybe some others and see what you think. Remember, you are no longer church shopping. You are learning about the Church that would be yours if you become Catholic. Ideally you already know some people who attend there. Spend enough time to get a feel for the place. Introduce yourself to the priest and others on staff. Read their materials. Become familiar.

While you're there, it is possible that you will have some residual if not strong Puritan impulses well up within you. Pay attention to them. Some Catholic parishes are wonderful. Others are frankly just bad, at least in some ways. Your Puritan instincts will show themselves the more the parish you visit is closer to bad. By "Puritan" I mean accepting only the pure. Puritanism is making sure that everything is correct and ideally getting better, and that all of the people involved in any church are serious, worthy, and creditable. The Puritan impulse is to quickly criticize when particular things (e.g., sermons, teachings, music, aesthetics, the singing) are not up to par, and to feel some sense of superiority when other people seem lax or uncommitted. The Puritan way is to demand that things be purified as a condition of staying, or else leaving and doing things more purely elsewhere.

Of course it is good to want to do things better, to improve and strengthen the Church. But as a general mode of instinctive operation, Puritanism verges on the sins of presumptuousness, arrogance, and self-righteousness. Work on containing any of your overly-critical and separatist Puritan instincts.

A related word of advice: keep pathetic American Catholics in perspective. There are many out there—untaught, uncommitted, culturally accommodated. But the sociological fact is this: there are also very many pathetic, untaught, uncommitted, and culturally accommodated American evangelicals and confessional Protestants out there too. Pathetic Catholics per se do not invalidate Catholicism any more than bad marriages invalidate marriage. Pathetic Catholics need to be taught, challenged, and nurtured—like struggling Christians of every church in every era. If Catholicism is the authentic Christian church, as I am suggesting here, then that is all the more reason for committed believers to get into it and, with humility, work to strengthen it, as possible (as well as to learn and grow themselves).

In my experience, one of the very nice things about Catholic Churches is how diverse, ordinary, and natural they are and feel. So many evangelical churches, by contrast, seem to me to be very earnest in *trying so hard* to be and do something or other—to be sincere or happy or vibrant or dynamic or appealing or whatever. By contrast, in my experience, most Catholic parishes are simply unperturbed in doing the regular business of being Church. They've been doing it for 2,000 years and will keep doing it till Christ returns.

Another difference I have noticed is that most Catholic Masses that I have attended are populated with the hoi polloi of the world, the great unwashed, ordinary folk who forgot to brush their hair and don't sing all that well. All in all that is a good thing, I think. One way that Catholics talk about their Church is, "Here comes everybody." Jesus loves everybody. To the extent that we in our hearts do not want to be just part of "everybody," that we want somehow to be better, cleaner, smarter, and righter, then learning to sit with the hoi polloi is good for us.

Start getting comfortable being with that. They're God's people. To be Catholic is to be universal, and that means being adequately inclusive and so living with a great deal of diversity in unity.

84. Stop expecting church to be your one-stop center of personal and community life. Evangelicals are not always aware of it, but many expect their churches to be the center not only of their spiritual but also their social lives. They not only want worship and teaching in church. They also want nursery, VBS, Sunday school, reading groups, support groups, play groups, small groups, discipleship groups, Bible studies, food pantries, Christian libraries, middle-school youth group, high-school youth group, retreats, ski trips, men's breakfasts, choir, missions prayer teams, short-term mission trips, church softball teams, marriage counseling, pastoral counseling, stewardship committees, community outreach committees, diaconal ministries, and on and on. Usually that stuff is taken for granted in evangelicalism.

But when you start to contemplate church as a place primarily to worship, celebrate Eucharist, baptize, and send members "forth into the world to love and serve the Lord," you start to realize how central social life is in evangelical churches.

The epitome of this taken-for-granted evangelical subcultural centering of social life in church may be the quest for intimate community that drives so many evangelical small groups. I remember once not long ago hearing an evangelical pray to God to give their church "intimacy." There was once a time in my life—in what feels like a former life—when I would have understood that prayer petition. But by the time I heard that prayer for "intimacy," I realized there was something fundamentally misguided about it. Christ does not command us to achieve intimacy. Strongly desiring relational intimacy is mostly the result of our late modern alienation and social isolation, not a priority of Christian discipleship. Yet much of what drives the life of many evangelical churches is the quest to build intimate, supportive communities of like-minded people.

I am not suggesting that Catholic parishes are devoid of community or that Catholics lack or do not care about relational intimacy with others—far from it, in many cases. But the typical feel and value of Catholic Churches is nonetheless simply not the same as most evangelical churches. Few Catholics today expect their parishes to serve as one-stop centers of their fulfilled personal and social lives. Christian life is lived out in family and in the world. Important relationships can come in all sorts. What Catholic Mass is primarily about instead is Eucharist, liturgy, and baptism. More broadly, Church is about a shared identity in Christ, sacramental life, and formation in right Christian living. That does not require that everyone know each other well, much less experience "intimacy" together. It does require that people participate in the liturgy, worship God, celebrate the sacraments, and do good in Christ's name.

(To nuance this picture, however, once you become Catholic, you might consider joining a Catholic lay movement. Catholicism does not have parachurch ministries the way American evangelicalism has. But it does have hundreds of vibrant lay movements which you might consider joining. The Vatican provides an authorized list of these lay movements on its website.[4] These lay movements tend to specialize in different charisms, which they believe they have received from God. It may be that you belong in one of them.)

At some point, it may hit you—probably immediately, if you have little ones—that the Catholic Church you are visiting does not have a nursery service for toddlers. Some do. Many don't (though some have "crying rooms" for babies). The frequent lack of nurseries in Catholic Churches in part reflects a different view of church services. For Catholics, church is not primarily a time of cognitive education, which requires age-appropriate segmentation and curricula, but centrally of worship and celebration of the Eucharist. Catholic liturgy is also something that one learns by being a part of and participating in. And there is no better time to start that, Catholics suppose, than as a child. Even toddlers and children, the idea is, can and do learn prayer, song, procession, offering, scripture, response, and so on by being part of the body as it worships and celebrates. Why stash little ones away in a nursery downstairs with volunteers, who are hard to recruit and who themselves then miss the service, when they can actually be part of God's people in worship? This can make it hard sometimes when children are acting up. But it keeps families together. And even the youngest soon learn that being part of church is a normal part of life in which they can and should participate as they are able. But it's different than the typical evangelical experience and may take some getting used to.

Making the transition successfully from an evangelical to a Catholic culture may require you adjusting your expectations about what Church is, does, and offers in a way that expects less of some things and more of others. You will learn that through experience. Going into the Church, it can be helpful simply to be aware of these differences.

4. Online: http://www.va/roman_curia/pontifical_councils/laity/documents/rc_pc_laity_doc_20051114_associazioni_en.html#PREFACE.

85. Consider the possibility that you have mostly already become Catholic. I do not mean by this that you have been living a double life and your other self has already joined the Church. I mean that, having gotten to this point in the process, it may be that you have already mostly become Catholic *substantively*, at least in your beliefs and proclivities. It could well be that, in your convictions about Christian authority and ecclesiology, in your basic assumptions, outlook, and dispositions, you have already become Catholic. If so, then you probably cannot go back. All that's left is to make official in name, public status, relationship to the Church, and rightly partaking in the Eucharist and the communion of saints what is already mostly real.

This realization struck me some months before my wife and I joined the Catholic Church. At some point, it dawned upon me and I said to my wife, "The fact is, we already *are* Catholic. We have already become Catholic in reality. All that is left to do at this point is own up to that and make it official." I knew then, before I became formally Catholic, that my other options had, in fact, already fallen by the wayside. It was Catholicism or nothing.

If something like this is true for you, then you will know it when you find yourself realizing that you cannot go back to an evangelical approach to the matters of Bible-only-ism and the nature of church. You might, for instance, be trying to talk yourself through the legitimacy of an evangelical position on some matter—testing in your mind whether you could still really remain evangelical—and find yourself saying, "But that way of justifying the matter does not make any sense. What about church history and tradition and teaching authority?" Or you might be struggling to justify evangelical practices of church and hear yourself thinking, "But that simply cannot work, it is an untenable position. I just no longer believe that."

If so, then the matter is largely settled. You might as well admit that you have already crossed the continental divide and are heading down the far slope to another shore of faith. You have already mostly *de facto* become Catholic. What you need to do now is to work out the implications of that fact for your public identity, personal relationships, and official status vis-à-vis the Church. What you need in this case is full communion with your bishop, with the Bishop of Rome, and with all other Catholics around the world. As the Brits say, "There's nothing else for it."

86. Get clear on the official Catholic view of Protestants. A related fact to keep in mind in all of this is the correct Catholic understanding of the status of Protestantism vis-à-vis the Catholic Church. I mentioned this in the Introduction above. Because the matter is so important, it is worth quoting the actual Catholic teachings at length here. Read carefully the following paragraphs of the Catholic *Catechism*, which quote liberally from the Second Vatican Council's "Decree on Ecumenism," *Unitatis Redintegratio* (italics added for emphasis):

> 817: In this one and only Church of God from its very beginnings there arose certain rifts, which the Apostle strongly censures as damnable. But in subsequent centuries much more serious dissensions appeared and large communities became separated from full communion with the Catholic Church - for which, often enough, *men of both sides were to blame.* The ruptures that wound the unity of Christ's Body—here we must distinguish heresy, apostasy, and schism - do not occur without human sin: "Where there are sins, there are also divisions, schisms, heresies, and disputes. Where there is virtue, however, there also are harmony and unity, from which arise the one heart and one soul of all believers" [Origen].

> 818: However, *one cannot charge with the sin of the separation those who at present are born into these communities* [that resulted from such separation] and in them are brought up in the faith of Christ, and *the Catholic Church accepts them with respect and affection as brothers.* . . . *All who have been justified by faith in Baptism are incorporated into Christ; they therefore have a right to be called Christians,* and with good reason are *accepted as brothers in the Lord by the children of the Catholic Church.*

> 819: Furthermore, *many elements of sanctification and of truth are found outside the visible confines of the Catholic Church*: the written Word of God; the life of grace; faith, hope, and charity, with the other interior gifts of the Holy Spirit, as well as visible elements. *Christ's Spirit uses these Churches and ecclesial communities as means of salvation,* whose power derives from the fullness of grace and truth that Christ has entrusted to the Catholic Church. All these blessings come from Christ and lead to him, and are in themselves calls to Catholic unity.

> 838: The Church knows that *she is joined in many ways to the baptized who are honored by the name of Christian, but do not profess the Catholic faith in its entirety* or have not preserved unity

or communion under the successor of Peter. Those who believe in Christ and have been properly baptized are *put in a certain, although imperfect, communion with the Catholic Church.*

Furthermore, the Vatican II document, *Unitatis Redintegratio*, itself teaches that "*Catholics must gladly acknowledge and esteem the truly Christian endowments* from our common heritage which are to be found among our separated brethren. It is *right and salutary to recognize the riches of Christ and virtuous works in the lives of others* who are bearing witness to Christ, sometimes even to the shedding of their blood. For God is always wonderful in His works and worthy of all praise" (4).

In short, by becoming Catholic, you are not implicitly declaring that the evangelicals you "leave behind" are inferior, guilty, worthless Christians—or anything like that. It does not mean you are breaking ties of Christian identification with them. It does not mean you are suggesting that their churches and ministries are of little worth. No. The Catholic Church extends generous and affirming arms to those "separated sisters and brothers" who are children of the Reformation. There remain strong ties of Christian truth between them and a recognition of the truth and value in much of what they do. Making that clear may help in negotiating the meaning of your Catholicism for these relationships.

87. Consider how becoming Catholic will affect your relationships with family and friends. Your becoming Catholic is likely to affect your important relationships. No doubt you have already been thinking and praying about that. In fact, that may be one of the biggest factors with which you are wrestling in considering becoming Catholic: how will it affect my friendships and family relationships? That is very important. But it cannot in most cases be ultimately determinative. I will spare you the relevant Bible verses about seeking first the kingdom, the pearl of great price, "hating" one's father and mother compared to love for Jesus, etc. You know the story.

Two things to keep in mind, however. First, if you have family and friends who will be unhappy with your becoming Catholic, be prepared in advance to distinguish their intellectual from their emotional responses. Sometimes people who oppose Catholicism do so for theological or other reasoned positions they hold. Often, however, as I noted above, people react against Catholicism for visceral emotional reasons. Both are legitimate and deserve engaging—but for what they actually are and not something else. It is what it is. What can be confusing, however, is when the emotions get cloaked in intellectual argumentation, which some people seem to think is more respectable. Sometimes people may pretend to you and perhaps to themselves that they have intellectual, theological, historical, and moral problems with Catholicism, when in fact most of their issues are actually personal, autobiographical, and emotional.

Conversations in those kinds of situations usually don't get very far. That is because you are answering alleged intellectual objections with reasoned arguments, when in fact the person's real issues are deeply emotional. What you need to do then is to recognize that the issues in question are actually affective, not intellectual, and deal with the emotions on that level. One clue that that is happening is when others pose intellectual arguments that actually make no sense or are factually mistaken, and refuse no matter what you tell them to learn anything different or better. Emotions are powerful. They can control the mind. So the trick in such cases is getting these friends and family members to set aside their intellectual arguments and own up to their visceral feelings.

Sometimes people who are against you becoming Catholic are simply worried that they are going to lose you as a friend or son or daughter. That is understandable and you can reassure them that this need not happen. Maybe they just don't like the idea of you introducing a(nother?) point of difference in your relationship in the area of faith. Do not underestimate how profoundly *relational*, not theological, these kinds of issues are. Again, all of that is reasonable and needs to be sorted out. But, in most cases, emotional and even intellectual objections from family and friends ought not to drive your ultimate decision—with the exception of spouses, addressed below. There are larger issues at stake here. Honor your relationships as best as you can. But in the end, with the one exception of marriage relationships being more complicated, you must do what you believe to be right.

88. If you are married and your spouse is not interested in Catholicism, proceed with care. Different people's spouses and marriage relationships are different, obviously, so there is no one-size-fits-all way to proceed here. You have to negotiate your own situation on this matter. Your spouse may be perfectly fine with you becoming Catholic and he or she remaining evangelical or something else. That is not ideal, but it is workable in some cases. Or your spouse may not like you becoming Catholic, but may be willing to have you do it anyway, even if he or she is not interested in Catholicism. That may, in some cases, be the best way to proceed. Then again, your spouse may outright oppose you becoming Catholic and ask, plead, or demand that you not do so. Those are more difficult cases. Go talk to a priest or wise pastoral associate at the Catholic parish with which you have become associated.

As a matter of principle, it is not right to damage your marriage for the sake of becoming Catholic. Holy matrimony itself is one of the Catholic Church's seven sacraments. So it would be perverse if your becoming Catholic injured your marriage. It may be that your desire to join the Catholic Church becomes an occasion for you to exercise greater love, patience, and humility toward your spouse, which honors God and is good for your marriage. You may simply need to face the fact that your marital situation means that you becoming Catholic is going to be a longer, more complicated process than it would have been if you were not married.

It may also be that the process of you and your spouse working through the issue of Catholicism together does good things for your relationship and provides the chance to grow and deepen your love for each other. Furthermore, it might be that your spouse actually has some legitimate concerns about your becoming Catholic, issues that you in fact need to hear and take seriously. God may be using him or her to slow you down, to get you to more carefully work through some consequential matters before you do become Catholic. Remember, the long run is more important than the short run. Being a faithful and loving husband or wife over time is more important than immediately "getting your way" in becoming Catholic.

Keep in mind, too, that for many people the idea of their marriage partner going off to join some other religious tradition can feel very threatening. That is especially true when this involves evangelicals becoming Catholic. Catholicism can seem confusing, alien, and outright wrong for evangelicals who have not personally gone through the process of accumulating anomalies and experienced the paradigm shift described above. Try to remember how Catholicism felt to you when you were at the start or even in the middle of your change process. Offer your spouse plenty of time, space, and reassurance that, whatever happens about Catholicism, all will be well with your relationship and life together. And give your hesitant or resistant spouse at least the same amount of time that you yourself took to work it all out in order to sort out what your becoming Catholic might mean.

Your desire to become Catholic may raise issues for your spouse that are fundamentally about your marriage relationship, not about theology. He or she may worry that, by wanting to become Catholic, you are somehow pulling away. Your spouse may fear that you will make separate Catholic friends that will create an independent life for you which he or she does not share. Your wanting to become Catholic may feel to your spouse like he or she is being sidelined or left behind in your life. Your spouse may worry that this is only the first step in who-knows-what other changes are going to happen in your life that might threaten your marriage. And the more enthusiastic or insistent you are about Catholicism with your spouse, the more you may be intensifying such concerns on their part. Such fears and anxieties are not crazy. Address them.

In all of this, again, make sure to address emotional and relational issues as the kind of issues that they actually are, and not as theological or intellectual issues that are not really in play. Make sure that you can honestly affirm that you have no interest in your becoming Catholic creating distance or unnecessary problems in your marriage. Do all you can to affirm your love for and complete commitment to your spouse. Communicate the clear position that you are not going to do anything unilaterally or arbitrarily about the matter.

Include your spouse in your ongoing discernment as much as you can. Ask them to engage the same questions and issues that have led you to the point that you have now reached on this matter. Be ready to "hold up" on your own process of change in order to be able to better include your spouse in it, to work through the issues together, and perhaps to become Catholic as a couple, not separately. Pray for your spouse. Overall, proceed in a way that will strengthen unity, love, and commitment in your marriage, rather than letting Catholicism become a point of anxiety and conflict.

Do not underestimate your spouse's capacity to change on this matter. Once you attend properly to the emotional and relational matters at issue, and so create a safe context for you together to address your faith concerns in solidarity, rather that at odds, your spouse may very well come along in the process. If you can clear away any unnecessary emotional or relational stumbling blocks that may be getting in the way, you might find yourself able to sort out *together* the issues concerning evangelicalism and Catholicism on which you have been working in your own mind and spirit. Much better for you to take the time to do this together, than to impatiently press to quickly become Catholic on your own and simply let your spouse fend for himself or herself.

If, however, after all of that, your spouse proves to be intransigent on this issue, you will have to figure out where to go from there. No simple formula can tell you what to do. Talk to your Catholic friends. Talk to your spouse's friends. Talk to a priest. Pray for wisdom. Trust God. Do not become resentful.

89. If you are a Protestant minister, don't despair. You may or may not be able to continue being a full-time minister in the Catholic Church. If you are unmarried, you might become a priest or something else. Even if you are married, the Catholic Church accepts as priests some who are married who come into it from other Christian traditions, primarily Anglicanism. Look into that.

In addition, there are many other ways to practice Christian ministry in the Church besides being a priest. Dioceses have various kinds of ministry staff. Parishes have Christian educators. Catholic colleges have chaplains and professors. Catholic lay ministries often have paid leaders and pastors. The Catholic Church is bigger and more complex than you may realize. Do not begin by presuming that there is no place in it for you, for your calling or your gifts. If God wishes to move you into the Church, surely there is.

90. Look with hope for Rome and the East to reestablish full communion within your lifetime. Roman Catholicism and Eastern Orthodoxy, as I noted above, are actively moving toward mutual reconciliation, toward overcoming of the Great East-West Schism of 1054 and thus creating a genuinely global catholic communion.

This may not have been a high priority issue of yours till now. But get it on your radar screen. The unity of the visible Church is immensely important, a matter of basic Christian faithfulness. You happen to live in a time when a nearly-millennium old division between the West and the East may be healed. That would be a truly world-historic event. Pray for it. Understand the full catholicity of your own faith, if you become Catholic, to, in some important way, depend upon it.

91. Read Pope John Paul II's "Theology of the Body" and related works. Catholicism is (in?)famous for its adamant "no sex before marriage" message (picture a frowning nun with ruler in hand slapping kids who get out of line) and the "Catholic guilt" that anything violating that message generates. In fact, however, in recent years the Catholic

Church has articulated a very theologically sophisticated Christian treatment of the spiritual meaning of human bodies, chastity, marriage, and sex.

That takes the form of Pope John Paul II's written works on the "theology of the body." I know of nothing like it in the evangelical publishing world. For unmarried believers who are struggling with issues around sex, and for married couples who are trying to sort out the many issues related to their intimate life—in fact for any Christian at all—the "theology of the body" is a crucial teaching.

I cannot take the time to elaborate the content of this body of work. Here I can simply say that an important step toward your becoming Catholic is to read this stuff. These works provide a rich, sacramentally-grounded rationale for Christian sexual ethics and a compelling explanation for Catholic teachings about the body, chastity, marriage, fidelity, self-giving, openness to bearing children, and more.

I suggest that you read *Theology of the Body in Simple Language* (John Paul II, Sam Torode, editor, 2009). If you want more, read the longer work, *Man and Women He Created Them: A Theology of the Body* (John Paul II, Michael Waldstein, translator, 2006). Pray for understanding and insight as you read. If you can manage the radically counter-cultural Christian message you will find there, you just may never think about these things and live your life the same again.

92. Sort out the meaning of the priest abuse scandals. In recent years it has come to light that some Catholic priests in the United States, Ireland, Germany, and elsewhere had, over a period of decades, been abusing children who were entrusted to their pastoral care. Worse, it has also come to light that some bishops knew that such abuses had happened and failed to take what we now realize would have been the proper steps to immediately remove those priests from the contexts where they could do harm. Some of the priests were given doses of sex therapy and then reassigned to other parishes. These abuses resulted in incalculable pain and destruction in the lives of the abused youth, their families, and communities, which cannot now be undone. Revelations of these abuses and of very poor diocesan decision-making—some would say local cover-ups—concerning them have caused major scandals for the Church, and rightly so. So what ought you to make of this?

The first and most obvious thing to say is that some responsible leaders of the Church operating in different places have sinned badly.

They have acted cowardly, selfishly, and destructively. They have violated all that the Church teaches and stands for. There is no excuse for any of it and no way of undoing in proximate terms the evil that was committed.

Part of the problem involved, it must also be said, reflected not merely the normal human desire to hide wrongdoing. Part of it also involved stupid and imprudent attempts in certain times and places to protect the reputation of the Church, as the Church, in ways that failed to proceed with integrity. What happened also broke the dictates and instructions of Canon Law, to boot. The Church has always condemned such scandalous failures into sin in the strongest of terms. Now it must "own" the rightful condemnation of its own behaviors and actions.

If you did not already realize this, then realize it now: the people—including the leaders—of the Church which you are considering joining are far from perfect. Some are desperately sinful, in different ways, just like much of the rest of humanity, just like you and I may be. To be sure, redemption and sanctification has indeed worked its way deeply into the lives of many Catholics. Many Catholic clergy and laity live impressively holy lives. But for others, real, destructive sins retain a powerful hold. That will never change in any church in history. Still, the Church can and must do better at addressing such evils in its midst.

What needs to continue to happen now in the Catholic Church is repentance, sorrow, confession, reparations, making of amends with victims as best as possible, and learning from the scandals in ways to prevent such evils from happening again.[5] As I write this, the current Pope Benedict XVI has been personally meeting with, listening and apologizing to, and praying with some of the victims of the priest abuses. We can hope that such personal meetings by the pope will continue.

Normally, I consider it best not to identify specific things one thinks that God is doing in history and, if at all, only with the utmost caution. But it is not unthinkable that God is in fact using this priest-abuse evil—for which certain leaders in the Church, and not God, are entirely responsible—to humble and purify the Catholic Church. This is hardly the first time that the Church has needed a very hard humbling, purging of sin, and internal reform.[6] In this case, unlike some times in the past, the force of that demanded repentance cannot be evaded. That is no

5. Worth reading is Cafardi, "Fraternal Correction," 9–11.

6. For some historical context on these matters, see Duffy, "Scandal in the Church," in Duffy, *Faith of Our Fathers*, 149–57.

doubt a good thing, even if that good be outweighed by the suffering and destruction caused in the lives of the young victims. All wish the evil had never happened. But it has. Without discounting the destruction it has caused, one might still look for a redemptive aspect of the entire wreck.

Even so, all of these harsh facts being admitted, it is worth bearing a few other ideas in mind in making sense of the larger matter. Part of the bad decision-making by bishops not to remove abusive priests came from their recurrent belief that enrolling those priests in therapy programs would help to cure their sickness. Decades ago, when most of the abuses happened, such a belief was more plausible. We have since come to learn that this is a naïve expectation. Short-term therapy programs do not reform child abusers. That was a wrong trust in therapy on the part of those bishops, perhaps made easier to rationalize by their desires to avoid the disruptions that removing abusive priests would have caused. But, however reckless and ignorant such beliefs were, at least that is a tad better than their simply knowing about the abuses and doing nothing at all.

Furthermore, while avoiding minimizing the sins in any way or coming off as defensive, it is well worth acknowledging the facts here within their larger context. The actual number of pedophilia cases involved is quite small. The number of abusive Catholic priests and irresponsible bishops is also not large, compared to the total number of priests and bishops in the Church. The vast majority of Catholic bishops and dioceses have had not problems with priest abuse at all. All available evidence tells us that the incidence of sexual abuse of minors by priests is not greater than, and probably is actually far less than, the incidence of sexual abuse of minors by adult leaders in other mixed-age settings, such as public schools, sports teams, and the like.[7] There is no credible evidence causally linking the sexual abuse of minors to celibacy. The Catholic Church has been under particularly intense attack by overtly anti-Catholic attorneys and the *New York Times*, who have also shown no interest in taking on equivalently evil cases of abuse in public schools or elsewhere. One crusading attorney, Jeffrey Anderson, for example, a former-Catholic-turned-atheist who has filed thousands of lawsuits in

7. Some years ago, one of my very own sociology graduate students committed suicide by hanging himself, in order, I learned from his mother afterward, to put an end to his suffering that resulted from being sexually molested by his Boy Scout leader when he was a youth; that molesting man had never been brought to justice and was free and continuing to live his normal life, my deceased student's mother reported.

alleged priest abuse cases, had already by 2002 won more than $60 million in settlements from Catholic dioceses, personally earning up to 40 percent of that money in attorney's fees.[8] Finally, nearly all of the cases of priest abuse happened decades ago, when the training of priests around these issues was nowhere near as good as it is today. None of this of course justifies or excuses any of the priest abuse. But a balanced reading of the debacle requires knowledge of information that will not be highlighted in the *New York Times*.

Stepping back from the whole disaster, for purposes of this book, here is the truth of the matter: if you are looking for a church that does not have big problems, then stop looking. There isn't one. If you do find a church that has no problems, please don't join it. You'll only spoil it with the problems that *you* bring.[9] In any case, whether or not a church has problems should not even be your primary criterion in "choosing" a church. If it is, then you are still stuck in a naïve Puritan Protestantism. What matters in the end, rather, is which church is the right and true church—whatever problems beleaguer it—and what you can do to help it become more faithful.

93. Begin RCIA. No, *RCIA* does not stand for Roman Central Intelligence Agency. It stands for the Rite of Christian Initiation of Adults.[10] This is the rite, or process, by which adults are prepared to be received into the full communion of the Catholic Church. If you want to become Catholic, in most circumstances you need to participate in the formation that the *RCIA* outlines. It may take about a year to complete— a pretty serious and impressive demand—or less, depending on pastoral and spiritual needs. The Church wants to make sure those it receives are well prepared. That is the good news. The potentially bad news is that the implementation of the *RCIA* in some parishes can be quite poor. The quality of preparation varies, frankly. Do your best to find solid, worthwhile, edifying formation in which to participate. Ask around. Get yourself into one that will inform and strengthen you, not frustrate you. Again, as you are guided through the *RCIA*, pray and ask God to lead you into the fullness of truth.

8. Gilgoff, "One Lawyer Behind Many Allegations"; Davey, "Frenzied Pace for Lawyers"; Condon, "Jeff Anderson."

9. Thanks to Jim Heft for this line.

10. See Catholic Church, *Rite of Christian Initiation of Adults*.

94. Start discerning what of your evangelical background you should discard and what you should keep and bring into the Catholic Church. The Catholic Church badly needs evangelicals to return to it, and so bring their commitments, knowledge, gifts, and other contributions to its aid. At the same time, the Catholic Church does not need you to bring with you *all* of your unreconstructed American evangelical subcultural tendencies, sensibilities, and habits. Some are worth replacing with better, Catholic versions.

Stated differently, Catholicism is, on the one hand, incomplete without the particular strengths that you can bring to the Church. On the other hand, American evangelicals need to be changed in the process of becoming Catholic in ways that leave behind aspects of evangelicalism that are simply not worth holding onto. You need to figure out how to understand those differences in your own life and how to work them out in your particular case.

In discerning this balance, these differences, what comes along and what is abandoned, there are no easy formulas or rules. Much of it must be figured out as part of the larger process, along the way. Part of it depends simply on who you are and what you bring. In any case, most important for you to realize, as your final step, is that some of your characteristically evangelical ways need to go. If they didn't go, then becoming Catholic would not signify much. And by letting them go, you'll be the better for it.

Becoming Catholic of course means much more than a change of labels. It means, as this book has stressed, a veritable paradigm revolution, which should change more than a little about your assumptions, thinking, instincts, beliefs, and practices as a Christian. You need, as you proceed, to be ready to change in some significant ways.

At the same time, again, the Catholic Church also needs you to help *her* become strengthened and change in certain ways for the better (though not, of course, acting out of the Puritan sensibilities described above). And that means you should not simply be conformed to some standard Catholic mold—not that such a mold exists. So, even as you sort out ways that becoming Catholic should rightly change you, you should also be attending to the strengths of your background that you can bring along and contribute to the strengthening of the Church.

The specific possibilities are too myriad to name. But you should have a clear enough sense of your own gifts, abilities, insights, convictions, and commitments—all drawn from the best of evangelical well-springs—to be able to identify the positive contributions you can make to the Catholic Church by entering into full communion with her. You should also pray about this and draw upon your family's and friends' knowledge of you to sort it all out. Bring these to your larger discernment process and remain humble and open-minded about the possibilities.

95. Be careful about becoming a stereotypically "More-Catholic-than-Thou" Catholic convert. Converts to any faith tradition are frequently more committed and zealous than those raised in it, who often more easily take their own traditions for granted. This also often holds true for those who become Catholic as adults. That is good and fine. No need to apologize. Again, the Church greatly needs you, with all of your convictions and commitments and gifts, for its renewal and strengthening.

There is a danger, however, which you should consciously avoid, of becoming the stereotypical convert who treats those raised in the Catholic Church with a "more-Catholic-than-thou" nouveau-Catholic attitude. The evident self-satisfaction, condescension, and criticism in that kind of attitude accomplishes nothing positive and can do real damage. Pray to avoid it.

Do not be afraid to take stands, to generate some tensions, in the right situations and for the right reasons. That may be unavoidable and valuable. But also remain self-aware enough to prevent yourself from slipping into any hint of putting yourself on a "neo-Puritan" Catholic pedestal. That will be better for your soul, and, practically, you'll also accomplish a lot more good in the long run.

Okay, that's it. There are no more steps. Those are all that I have to help guide you toward becoming Catholic. If that and a lot of prayer doesn't do it, I don't know what will.

When you have completed *RCIA*, you can be received into the full communion of the Catholic Church. That will be a wonderful day.

Conclusion

Much of what I have written above has focused at a very personal, practical level. I will also end this conclusion at the personal level. But first I wish to set that focus into global, world-historical perspective. Here goes.

Whether or not most people realize it, the fact is that *we live in a time of dramatic, world-historic change in Christianity*. Movements and trends that have consistently shaped history for centuries are now in our lifetime altering course, even being reversed.

Western Catholicism and Eastern Orthodoxy are moving toward the restoration of full communion after nearly a millennium of separation and mutual distrust. The global Anglican Communion, which expanded from England after the sixteenth century, is now breaking apart and throwing theologically-orthodox Anglicanism into endemic crisis. Mainline-liberal Protestantism in the United States continues to abandon doctrinal commitments and hemorrhage members, as it has for decades now. American evangelicalism has bounced back from its embarrassing institutional and cultural losses in the early twentieth century, to have become in recent decades, for better or worse, a major force in US politics and culture—and, increasingly, on the world stage. The Catholic Church has, especially since the Second Vatican Council, transformed its posture toward the modern world and is working out at a global scale the reforms and renovations that the Council launched. And—most significant for present purposes—many of the reasons for Protestantism's historical hostility to Catholicism are now melting away. The very existence of "Evangelicals and Catholics Together"[1] and serious evangelical books with titles like

---

1. See Colson and Neuhaus, *Your Word Is Truth*.

Is the Reformation Over?[2] is simply astonishing, when viewed in broad historical perspective.

We are often too preoccupied by more distracting matters to perceive the colossal religious transformations that are happening in the world today. Too rarely do we recognize the massive changes that have been set in motion before our very eyes. But that does not mean these huge changes are not happening. They most definitely are. In the midst of this big-picture context of dramatic, world-historic change, the personal, existential question that poses itself is this: what, if anything, are you going to do in response?

One option is to ignore it all, keep your eyes focused on intermediate concerns, continue to do what you've always done, and let history and the world go where they may. That is probably what most will do. Is it what you will or should do?

Another option is to "read the signs of the times" and respond accordingly—even if that means making significant changes in your life. This book has suggested that the best response for American evangelicals today, in light of the big picture, is to throw in their lot with the Catholic Church. Catholicism is the Church of Western Christianity's deep past. It is a dynamic Church of the present. And it is the West's and perhaps the world's Church of the future.[3] It is *your* deepest roots. It is where you now belong.

I wrote this book to help show how and why that is the case. The thrust of its argument has been this. You are right for being interested in maybe becoming Catholic. For you as an evangelical to allow God to lead you here, it will help for you first to come to see the many serious problems in and about evangelicalism. Then you need to grasp how Catholicism solves those problems—as well as addresses other ones that evangelicalism was not so bad at handling. That involves learning a lot about Catholicism that you didn't know. That will make you realize that Catholicism does an overall better job than evangelicalism of making sense of Christianity, and potentially of your own faith and life. Seeing that, you then need to adopt and shift into that new paradigm. That

---

2. Noll and Nystrom, *Is the Reformation Over?*

3. If you want your great-grandchildren to be orthodox Christians after you are dead and gone, for example, do not leave them to the instabilities of American evangelicalism. They'll have a much better chance of being faithful Christians if their lives are rooted in Catholicism, its Church and traditions. Think hard about that.

will mean rewiring your brain and altering your behaviors in light of the Catholic paradigm's governing assumptions, outlook, interests, and practices. Finally, you will need to make public and official this change that has begun to take root in you. Then you will be Catholic, ready to continue your voyage into an even fuller life in this new world that is at the same time ancient.

In Thomas Kuhn's terms, which I have used to organize our discussion (though see the appendix for a fuller explanation of Kuhn's theory), to become Catholic you need to collect a lot of anomalies to your evangelical paradigm, reach a point of a paradigm crisis, grasp the promise of a Catholic paradigm shift, experience a Catholic paradigm revolution, and then consolidate and work out the meaning of your life in that new paradigm for the rest of your life. The steps proposed in this book have been offered precisely with the goal of helping set that process of change in motion. While reading this book, you have probably been discerning whether actually becoming Catholic is the right commitment for you to make. I hope God moving you forward with the 95 steps suggested above are convincing you that it indeed is.

In making this life change, you will have to reckon with the question of why more American evangelicals are not also, like you, becoming Catholic. There are many reasons. Some of them are principled and deserve to be honored and respected. But many of them are not so good.

Much of the resistance of evangelicals to Catholicism, I am convinced, stems from a widespread lack of accurate knowledge about post-Vatican II Catholicism. Some of it is also stems from the comfortable familiarity of established Protestant religious habits and traditions, some personal prejudices, and more than a little indefensible emotional baggage projected onto Catholicism through psychological "transference." All of that is reinforced by a huge amount of unreflective historical momentum and social inertia. That may sound harsh. But it is what it is (whatever it is).

Those "reasons" for resisting Catholicism may, as they say, be good enough for government work. But they are not good enough for the kingdom of God. Nobody in that realm—which, in the end, is the only realm that exists—has the option of seeing the truth and not responding. Evangelicals, of all people, surely know this.

The truth that I have proposed in this book, to which I hope you respond with agreement, can be summed up, again, in this simple way:

the Reformation is over. What are the implications? One thing this means is that people who insist on keeping the Reformation going are acting rather foolishly.

Imagine coming home late at night to find your roommate or neighbor partying all by herself—playing loud music, dancing, laughing, and perhaps drinking too much—three hours after her last guest had left her party. What would you say? "Um, Heather . . . the party's over. Give it up." Or imagine finding a football team on the field one hour after they had defeated an opponent, insisting on continuing to play the game against imaginary opponents, just to keep it all going, despite the fact that the other team and the fans had all left. What should you say? "Uh, guys? I think you won already. Go home."

That is something like what evangelical Protestants who today continue to oppose, attack, and remain separated from Catholicism in the name of the Reformation are doing. Somebody needs to give them a clue. To that end, the message of this book is this: "Um, people? The Reformation is over. Go home."

That is the message to you. Go home. Catholicism is your church home, your life's home. You have probably been estranged from your true home for a long time. It is time to be reconciled. Time for a family reunion. Come home.

Appendix

On Paradigm Revolutions—How Change Happens

Few evangelicals become Catholic simply by learning some new biblical, theological, or sociological information to add to their established framework and then changing their mind.[1] The process of change typically involves a much more complicated, outlook-altering transformation. The best way that I can account for what usually happens is to compare it to the kind of changes that happen when scientists develop dramatically new theories, which I describe in this appendix. I know that does not sound very spiritual. And some of the ideas that follow can seem at first to be tricky. But if you can grasp them you'll see how helpful this view is for understanding by analogy the shift from evangelicalism to Catholicism.

The model of scientific change that well depicts the shift from evangelicalism to Catholicism is one described by the famous historian of science, Thomas Kuhn, in his legendary 1962 book, *The Structure of Scientific Revolutions*. I do not subscribe to every detail of Kuhn's analysis. Some of it is too simple. But it is nevertheless a useful tool for making sense of the topic at hand. Many people already know about the argument of Kuhn's book. For them, the following will be review. But many

---

1. Possible exceptions to that may include the occasional evangelicals who marry their Catholic sweethearts and, so as not to be "unequally yoked" and perhaps because love is blind, become Catholic, in solidarity with the ones they love. But there are not many of them. And the "information" that they "learn" usually has less to do with the Bible or doctrine than with hormones and relational bonding.

others do not know Kuhn's argument, nor the model of scientific change he proposed. Since I organize this book around Kuhn's model of change, it is worth describing it here.

How Big Scientific Change Often Happens

As an historian of science, Kuhn was interested in explaining how science has *actually* developed and changed over time—not just how theories said it should change and develop. The received model of scientific development, common up to Kuhn's day, was that science develops and changes over time through the gradual accumulation of new facts. It was assumed that scientists labor at their respective tasks within their shared disciplines. All employ the same unbiased, neutral, and objective scientific method. First comes empirical data collection and analysis, and then comes scientific theory, which describes and explains the facts that the data reveal. Scientists build both empirical findings and theoretical explanations incrementally upon the previous work of earlier scientists, by adding their own new data, findings, and conclusions.

If any scientist makes an important contribution along the way, according to that pre-Kuhnian model, it is only because they are "standing on the shoulders of giants" (famously quoted by Isaac Newton, originally said by Bernard of Chartres)—that is, upon earlier important scientists on whose work they have built. The job of each new scientific investigation is to verify or to discredit tentatively-held hypotheses. In the end, science produces sets of verified theories which describe and explain the lawful workings of the world. Through this progressive process, the more science works, the more scientific knowledge accumulates and the more the larger scientific project succeeds. This process and model—understood to be continuous and cumulative, linear and progressive—was an idea that fit an idealized theory of "positive" knowledge (think Positivism) produced by "scientific progress," an idea that hit its apex in the nineteenth and early-twentieth century.

The only problem, Kuhn observed in his study of real historical scientific development and change, is that this received model did not accurately describe how science has often actually developed and changed. The historical reality, Kuhn pointed out, is messier and more complicated than the received theory suggested. In reality, he wrote, science has lurched forward across different and "incommensurate" frameworks of inquiry and explanation, which he called "paradigms." These usually dominate for a while and then can be overturned by new, upstart paradigms. Scientific development and change, Kuhn argued, are not continuous, cumulative, linear, and progressive. They are rather punctuated, unstable, jarring, and often politically and socially conditioned. All of that will take a bit of unpacking to make clear.

Pre-Paradigmatic Science. Kuhn's model proposed three phases of scientific inquiry and knowledge. The first phase is the "pre-paradigm" phase. That is when a diversity of approaches and theories pursue their various activities without an organizing center or unifying coherence. This phase usually looks pretty "unscientific" in retrospect. During this pre-paradigmatic phase, various assumptions, concepts, focuses, methodologies, theories, and explanations vie for acceptance. As certain ones of these gradually come to seem to best explain the empirical evidence at hand, they become adopted by most scientists, who come to a general consensus about their use and value. At that point, the second phase has begun, which Kuhn calls "normal science."

Paradigmatic Normal Science. Normal science always operates within and is governed by a dominant "paradigm." A paradigm, by Kuhn's account, is an organizing cognitive framework of presuppositions, concepts, and standard explanations. Paradigms are general frameworks of investigation and analysis which govern scientists' work. They are like miniature scientific worldviews that tell scientists what they should assume, on what they should focus their observations, what questions they should ask, how those questions are to be posed, what evidence will count as having answered those questions, and how the answers should be organized as valid findings and conclusions.

Paradigms thus direct, focus, and motivate scientific inquiry—they empower and direct science to do its thing. But paradigms also govern, narrow, and confine scientific activity by posing limits on what science assumes, asks, investigates, recognizes, and explains. In short, paradigms both enable and constrain inquiry.

Scientists conducting normal science are thus people who share a consensus about what they presuppose, what they want to explain, what data will help explain it, and how they should go about explaining it. Scientists may be competing with each other in a race for new findings and breakthroughs. But their competition usually takes place within the shared framework defining what they are even doing and how it is done best. Those same shared frameworks also have the effect of *excluding from view* possible alternative assumptions, interests, questions, evidence, findings, and explanations.

Think, for example, of developments in the science of physics. At the end of the nineteenth century, the well-developed Newtonian-mechanics paradigm dominated physics. It worked with its own assumptions, questions, focuses, explanations, and conclusions about physical reality. In 1900, Lord Kelvin is said to have declared to the British Association for the Advancement of Science that, "There is nothing new to be discovered in physics now. All that remains is more and more precise measurement."

Five years later, Albert Einstein published a paper on "special relativity." It challenged the basic rules of Newtonian mechanics that had explained force and motion for two centuries. Einstein's radically new approach launched a new paradigm in physics that involved things like quantum theory, photon theory, relativistic cosmology, the wave-particle duality, and other theoretical ideas that the Newtonian mechanics paradigm could not have anticipated or absorbed. Quantum physics did not destroy Newtonian mechanics. Nor did Einstein's approach assimilate Newtonian mechanics. They were and are simply two different paradigms that each helps to explain the same reality differently, within the guiding constraints of dissimilar assumptions, concerns, parameters, and explanatory styles.

Paradigm Incommensurability. Kuhn said that many scientific paradigms are "incommensurable." This means that they do not share an independent standard of comparison and evaluation. So they have difficulty persuading each other of their relative merits by appealing to a shared, objective standard. It also means that two paradigms lack a large set of mutually intelligible or readily translatable concepts and vocabularies, so each is often "talking past" the other in something like a different language. This means too that they cannot be easily or perhaps ever reconciled and synthesized into one higher theoretical system.

So, for example, there is no neutral scientific place to stand apart from quantum and Newtonian physics from which to determine which is right. One can only view reality from within the paradigms. And each of them as a paradigm predetermines as a matter of presupposition what, why, how, and when anything matters in the first place. Different scientists have different training and prior experiences and so see and understand the world differently. Different paradigms involve different concepts, vocabularies, sensibilities, and explanations to apply to the same empirical world. And different paradigms propose different problems as priorities to be solved, and different methods and standards by which to solve them.

Another important aspect of incommensurability is the fact that the exact same empirical evidence can be and often is observed, understood, and explained by two different paradigms in two divergent ways. Paradigms do not create intellectual "divisions of labor" in which one explains certain empirical observations and another explains different observations. Paradigms are often rivals in explaining the same empirical observations according to their own particular assumptions, interests, standards, and theories. And often their explanations of the same evidence can be quite different, even incompatible.

Anomalies. Back to Kuhn's three phases in scientific inquiry and knowledge. Here comes a crucial next step. In the course of the conduct of normal science, certain empirical observations that the established paradigm cannot seem to assimilate or explain often arise. These Kuhn calls "anomalies," coming from the Greek wording meaning "not fitting the laws," something like "a-normal." Anomalies are puzzles, observed evidence that simply does not fit the taken-for-granted framework.

The interesting thing about most anomalies is that they rarely discredit the established paradigm. Instead, they are usually set aside or rationalized in some way. Anomalies are often readily dismissed, for instance, as the result of measurement error or the lack of some other information that would make sense of them. When that doesn't work, anomalies are sometimes "resolved" or explained away by the development of new theoretical adjustments, complications, or "work-arounds." However they are dispatched, anomalies rarely cause scientists conducting normal science within their accepted frameworks to lose faith in their working paradigms.

A lot of very troubling anomalies can accumulate, yet still most of those engaged in normal science remain convinced of and loyal to their given paradigms. Most normal-science investigators have far too much personally invested in their careers, which are built upon and within the parameters of their embraced paradigm, to consider abandoning the paradigm and so losing all that they have invested and built upon its presupposed validity. They prefer to adjust away, ignore, discount, or rationalize the anomalies, rather than to face the possibility that the anomalies actually expose fatal flaws in their paradigm—and consequently the revolutionary need to abandon it and shift to a whole new paradigm. Those costs are usually too high.

Revolutionary Science. However, while that is the strategy of most, there sometimes are a small number of "revolutionary" scientists, Kuhn observes, who are prepared to question the taken-for-granted assumptions of reigning paradigms and consider seemingly radical alternatives. Facing the probable paradigm crisis, these bold scientists risk reputation and sometimes livelihood to imagine and propose wildly alternative frameworks of interpretation and explanation. They do so because they believe the alternatives make better sense of all of the available evidence, the regular findings and anomalies alike.

These are the individuals who provoke Kuhn's third phase of "revolutionary science." They are the ones who challenge and potentially overturn the established presuppositions and frameworks of their fields of study. If they succeed, a "paradigm shift" or "paradigm revolution" happens. The majority of scientists—especially the younger, who are less invested in the old paradigm—are persuaded that the new paradigm is superior to the old and "jump ship" to it. The old paradigm is either relativized into lesser status or is abandoned by all but those who then comes to be thought of as "crazy" people (like people today who still believe in a flat earth).

Once a new scientific paradigm ascends to dominance, it solidifies itself and begins to carry out its own work of normal science, governed by its own particular assumptions, concepts, concerns, focuses, and explanations. That project of normal science is then pressed out as far as it can go. In the process, new anomalies often surface with which the new paradigm has to deal. And, Kuhn says, the ongoing cycle of paradigm establishment, normal science, the buildup of anomalies, possible crisis, revolutionary science, paradigm revolution, and a new phase of normal science often continues.

An Illuminating Example. A key historical example in Kuhn's argument helps to illustrate his model. For centuries, astronomers believed that the earth stood still at the center of its planetary system and that the sun, planets, and stars revolved around the earth. This Ptolemaic theory or "geocentric" paradigm was believed by many ancient Greek, Chinese, medieval European philosophers and (proto)scientists alike. A lot of strong evidence seemed to validate it. The earth certainly appeared to be solid, steady, and at rest. And the stars, sun, and planets certainly seemed to revolve around the earth. Plus, the Bible and other sacred texts appeared to presuppose a geocentric view of the universe.

This established geocentric model in astronomy, as a general framework of assumptions and understanding, set the agenda for scientific inquiry of the heavens for many centuries. Astronomers working within that paradigm produced an impressive body of descriptive and explanatory science that operated with great precision and predictive power. They could not explain everything, but they could explain a lot.

However, the invention of the telescope in 1609 began to produce mounting empirical evidence that did not fit the geocentric paradigm. Galileo Galilei, for example, observed that the planet Venus displayed the same "phases" that the earth's moon displayed monthly. That observation was incompatible with the geocentric view, but could be explained by a heliocentric view.

Half a century earlier, in 1543, a Polish astronomer named Nicolaus Copernicus had published an iconoclastic book. In it he proposed the wild theory that the sun, not the earth, stood still at the center of the universe and the earth, other planets, and stars revolved around it. That became known as the "heliocentric" view. In due time, Copernicus' theory sparked controversy. At first, Copernicus' model did not seem able to explain all of the observed facts as well as the established model. That was partly because existing ideas about motion, cycles, and epicycles could not make sense of the new proposal.

But as new evidence accumulated that did not fit the geocentric, but did fit the heliocentric paradigm, and as new concepts and theories of motion and cycles developed, the old normal science was thrown into crisis. Many clung to the established assumptions and explanations. But eventually, the old geocentric consensus disintegrated and its paradigm was overturned by the new sun-centered paradigm. According to Kuhn, a "paradigm shift" or "paradigm revolution" had taken place.

Evidence, Insight, and Change. Important to note in this story is the fact that most of the available empirical evidence was entirely consistent with the outlook of the old paradigm. The geocentric view could make good sense of most of what it observed within the parameters of its assumptions and framework. The geocentric model certainly represented the common-sense experience of ordinary people standing on a planet that was not moving and watching the rest of the universe revolve around it. Some methods of ocean navigation today still rely upon calculations based on geocentric assumptions.

So it was not an incremental accumulation of normal-science findings that led to a progressive development of scientific knowledge. Instead, it was an accumulation of bits of evidence that did not fit the established theory—what Kuhn called "anomalies." They provoked curiosity first, then doubts, then controversy, and then the formulation and advancement of a genuinely rival paradigm based on radically different assumptions. In short, scientific development and change was not gradual, linear, and incremental, but rather lurching, punctuated, and revolutionary.

Furthermore, for the astronomers involved, growing in scientific knowledge did not consist of progressively accumulating new findings that built upon the work of scientific forebears to validate the theories taken to be soundest. It was not a matter of simply adding new scientific findings, bricks-by-brick, so to speak, to the ever rising skyscraper of science's development and progress. Advancing scientific knowledge instead meant realizing in a kind of mind-blowing "ah-ha!" moment that the old paradigm and all of its perception- and inquiry-governing power had gotten things quite wrong. It meant pulling apart the already laid "bricks" of scientific findings and starting over to rebuild a new building based on an entirely different blueprint. Scientific development, in short, meant a revolutionary paradigm overturning a disintegrating paradigm, which it replaces and then launches a new phase of normal science.

Real scientific development, then, according to Kuhn's model, does not involve gradual adjustments here and there to the received understandings. That is only what happens within normal science. *Real* scientific development happens when the normal science of one paradigm is overturned and displaced by the rival outlook and agenda of a competing paradigm. Each paradigm in the conflict seeks to explain as much of the available empirical evidence that it can, given its assumptions, methods, and theories. The paradigm that convinces the largest number of scientists that it offers the greatest explanatory power wins the struggle for dominance and forms a new consensus about and agenda for the proper task of science (within the new paradigm).

In this sense, scientific change is not so much a matter of the inevitable logic of objective research findings as it is a kind of popularity contest seeking to round up supporters. Science is driven by paradigms, and paradigms are sustained by the backing of scientists who believe in them. And those beliefs—and changes in beliefs—can be shaped by social and political considerations. Science thus starts to lose some of the impressive shine of authority it enjoyed when people believed it to be all about objectivity, value-neutrality, and certainty. Kuhn shows us that science is really another human practice, affected by all of the features of every human practice: interests, biases, investments, confusions, judgments, persuasion, emotions, pressures, and sometimes dramatic changes of mind and heart.

Furthermore, if Kuhn is right, then it is not so much the objective empirical evidence that determines which theory is embraced as scientifically validated—at least in the short run. To the contrary, it is the reigning paradigm's theory that determines what is taken to be the relevant data and the important questions to be asked and sorts of explanations to be given about it in the first place. The relevant phrase, which Kuhn helped popularize, is that "All data are theory-laden." There is no such thing as neutral, objective, self-evident data. Different pieces and aspects of potentially relevant empirical evidence are always themselves identified, concentrated upon, understood, and explained by the governing influences of paradigms.

So it is impossible to describe or evaluate "data" independent from theory. Thus, if one is a neo-classical economist, one looks at the world and sees resources, labor, tools, information, scarcity, incentives, opportunities, and economic growth. If one is a Marxist economist, by contrast, one looks at the same world and sees the proletariat, capitalists, contradictions, exploitation, and eventual revolution bringing the destruction of private property. The world observed by both is the same. Over the long run, one theory may prove more capable of explaining how reality works than another. But in the meantime the particular paradigms that different observers bring to understand the world heavily condition what they see, what they do not see, why they see it, how they see it, what it means, and what they want to do with what they see. The data are always "theory-laden."

Becoming Catholic as a Paradigm Revolution

It is important to know that Kuhn's original position is not universally accepted. Some believe an even more radical story. Others argue that Kuhn is too extreme. Kuhn himself modified some of his positions after publishing his book. Why have I described Kuhn's argument about scientific development and progress in such detail in a book about becoming Catholic?

My point is not to say that Kuhn is correct in all of details and implications. I am not trying to convince readers to become purist "Kuhnians" about the history of science. I have some of my own reservations about and disagreements with Kuhn. My point here is rather that Kuhn presents a model of paradigms of inquiry and understanding, and of the nature of shifts between them, that fairly accurately captures how some things in the world do seem to work. Whatever the overstatements and flaws of Kuhn's model may be, it still enables us to see some important aspects of how individual and collective changes of mind and identity sometimes work. I believe for present purposes that grasping Kuhn's model is useful for understanding what it takes to go from being a good evangelical to being Catholic. The more we understand how and why this is so, the more that process—and the conflicts that often accompany it—will be clear and comprehensible. How so?

How Kuhn Helps Us. Understanding the notions of paradigms, incommensurability, anomalies, revolutionary science, and paradigm shifts are helpful, I think, for grasping the process of change between and difficulties in comparing evangelicalism and Catholicism as paradigmatic frameworks of Christianity. Evangelicals operate out of one paradigm. And Catholicism is not simply an incorrect version of that evangelical paradigm (although that is how it looks from within the evangelical paradigm). Catholicism is a quite different paradigm that has its own characteristic assumptions, questions, authorities, dispositions, beliefs, focuses of concern, emotional resonances, and explanations.

No evangelical gets outside of their evangelicalism—especially into Catholicism—on the basis of the assumptions, beliefs, and explanations inherent to the evangelical paradigm. Leaving evangelicalism and becoming Catholic requires a paradigm revolution. It usually entails a gradual buildup of anomalies, a growing realization that the evangelical paradigm cannot explain those anomalies, and an eventual "crisis" in which the old paradigm falters and an alternative paradigm comes to be seen as better making sense of the evidence viewed as a whole. Only then is the "revolutionary science" of conversion to Catholicism seriously examined, embraced, and consolidated. And that change is not gradual, linear, and incremental, but rather, like scientific paradigm shifts, intellectually and spiritually lurching, punctuated, and revolutionary.

Understanding the process in this way explains a few other key points. One has to do with the theory-laden nature of the evidence. In the evangelical paradigm, one set of "data" ordered in a certain way is paramount and decisive. In Catholicism, a combination of some of the same data ordered in a different way, along with a different set of "data," is paramount and decisive. Each paradigm thus helps to define assumptions about which evidence matters, how it is to be understood, and why the rival's alternative data are not convincing or perhaps even visible. Simply placing each set of data side by side for direct comparison does not settle the matter. What is required more fundamentally is to sort out which paradigm's presuppositions, instincts, and focuses are determinative. That then helps to define and order the data in a way that will make sense and commend one side or the other.

This too helps to explain why the idea of becoming Catholic often feels so insane, so incomprehensible to many evangelicals. They do not simply disagree with Catholics on certain points of theology, while otherwise operating in a shared Christian paradigmatic framework. They are actually living and working out of a quite different paradigm. Yet the "normal-science" nature of life operating in paradigms tends to "naturalize" the evangelical paradigm for those operating within it (as it does with all other paradigms). Lacking a Kuhnian perspective, the world as assumed, perceived, and engaged from within the evangelical paradigm simply looks like *reality*. It is just the nature of things, merely "the way things are." And when the world feels that way, it is very difficult for people to gain perspective on the "relative relativity" of their own presupposed outlook and to comprehend the reasons for serious alternatives. The more the presuppositions are invisible, the more alternatives look crazy. The more secure a paradigm is, the more threatening to basic assumptions about reality, truth, and relationships the alternatives are.

Moreover, the more people have invested the living and explaining of their lives in terms of one paradigm, the more costly it is to entertain the possible superiority of a rival paradigm. Scientists who built their personal careers on the geocentric view did not in the early seventeenth century jump for joy over the growing anomalies and increasing evidence that favored the rival heliocentric paradigm. It is hard to admit being wrong, very difficult to retool and start over from the beginning in another, new paradigm. Likewise, it is hard for Protestants to consider the possibility that perhaps Catholics were right after all. The costs of a broken Western Christendom, the shed blood of many martyrs, the religious histories of entire nations, the identities of generations of families, and the educations and careers and practices of whole lifetimes are often at stake in the Protestant-Catholic question. No wonder Protestant conversion to Catholicism often has an air of taboo.

Kuhn's model also helps to explain why the discussions by those involved in conversations and arguments can become so heated and unproductive. Oftentimes the people involved do not share the same basic assumptions and concerns, yet fail to recognize that fact. Because they are operating out of different paradigms—or perhaps because one is committed to a certain paradigm and another is starting to seriously doubt and step outside of it—they are in some sense living in somewhat if not quite different "worlds." So they talk past each other. They fail to "weight" the same evidence by the same "scale" or metric of evaluation. And they often feel that the other side has not been really listening to them, which of course is frustrating.

At least one side in the discussion is in fact "thinking inside of the box," its organizing framework of understanding, often mistakenly assuming that the other is as well. But that box and the space outside of it (or perhaps the two boxes involved) are not connected to some kind of inter-paradigm hot-line that nicely translates the meaning of what each has to say to the other. At least one side often fails to grasp the implications of the incommensurability of paradigms, trying to operate as if the pre-Kuhnian model of change is accurate. At least one side does not understand that "the data" are not neutral, that paradigms set agendas and interests. Only by coming to see the profoundly paradigmatic nature of the issues and process in question—and the deeper challenges of communication which come with that—can the discussing parties hope to understand each other and get anywhere constructive.

Grasping Kuhn's model of change provides a helpful vocabulary for naming and understanding the oftentimes amorphous and elusive intuitions, questions, and problems that most evangelicals recurrently feel or encounter, and which lead some to become Catholic. Kuhn helps us to see that many of those are "anomalies" that just do not fit the established evangelical paradigm, and so are troubling. That explains too why it can be so hard to pinpoint, define, and assess the significance of those anomalies. It is because evangelicals (like everyone else) operate within a particular paradigm that has adaptively evolved. And that means learning to ignore, dismiss, and explain away troubling intuitions, questions, and problems for which it cannot fully account. Hence, the commonly vague and hesitant nature of the doubts, hunches, and troubles that begin the early building up of anomalies for evangelicals.

Kuhn's approach also provides a vocabulary for understanding the change process as it develops. For some evangelicals, anomalies are successfully dispatched and the evangelical world remains happily viable. That explains much of evangelicalism's obvious resilience. But for others, the anomalies do not go away. They build up. They begin to weigh down. Gradually but increasingly the idea suggests itself that the established outlook does not simply need to be adjusted and renewed here and there. Rather, the established outlook is itself part of the problem, the very thing generating the problems. If that kind of thinking continues, then a full-blown "paradigm crisis" is set in motion.

In that context, different options are possible. One might become a radical evangelical critic, seeking to reform or renew from within. One might become a mainline Protestant. One might become non-religious. However, when evangelicals in that context realize that Catholicism not only explains most of what the evangelical paradigm explained but also accounts for the anomalies for which evangelicalism failed to account, then a Catholic "paradigm revolution" is likely to happen. The experience in this case is rarely one of being straightforwardly "convinced." By all accounts, it is more like an "I-can't-believe-I-am-seeing-things-this-way-and-even-considering-this-possibility-but-that-is-*really*-what-makes-the-most-sense-to-me-now" kind of dawning or realization. Most of the same facts that were always there remain on the table. But they are dramatically reordered by another paradigm into a quite different picture that makes more sense than the old picture.

Against Relativism. It is important to note that one of the ways that one might read Kuhn's model of scientific change is wrong, if I have understood Kuhn correctly. That wrong interpretation concludes that scientific relativism is necessary and inevitable. Scientific relativism says that science can never really know what is true, or distinguish better from worse accounts of truth. It is possible to read Kuhn as saying that. But it is a bad reading of Kuhn. It wrongly overemphasizes the incommensurability of paradigms. And that tends to lead to the conclusion that science can never really know anything true about the world. There is no reason to go there.

Paradigms do predetermine understandings of the world and the relevance of data, and they often share few if any independent standards of evaluation by which they can be judged objectively. Therefore, the argument goes, it is never possible to escape the reality-defining nature of paradigms. And it is therefore impossible to know what is true about reality besides whatever your paradigm so happens to tell you—which could be way off. That is the outlook of a radical "social constructionist" reading of Kuhn.

We should not be radical social constructionists, however, nor should we cede Kuhn's insights to that approach. Rather, we should be *critical realists*. That means more than I can possibly explain here.[2] But for present purposes it means that we should believe that a reality independent of our observations and interpretations of it exists, which has the ability to impinge upon us in a way that can shape our observations and interpretations of it. That is why telescopes provided information that led us to believe that the sun and not the earth are at the center of our planetary system—because that is true in reality.

The reality that exists, in other words, has a definite, though not absolute, capacity to inform our understanding of it. That, by the way, is what makes reality so painful sometimes—we don't and can't just make it up just as we wish. There is a certain "brick wall" nature to reality (hence, those pesky anomalies, despite our paradigms). That realization is sometimes hard, but it also spares us from the abyss of scientific relativism. At the same time, reality must always for us be humanly interpreted in order to be understood, is always conceptually and linguistically mediated, and can often be decently explained in more than one way (hence, the inescapability and resilience of paradigms, despite the pesky anomalies).

For present purposes, a critical realist reading of Kuhn gives hope that all of our searching and exploring and reconsiderations are not necessarily useless. They can get somewhere. We *can* sometimes move from a less adequate to a more adequate knowledge of what is true about reality—although that is never guaranteed and our knowledge is never perfect or complete. Sometimes we can discern that the sun and not the earth must be at the center of our planetary system, and we are right!

2. See Smith, *What is a Person?*; Bhaskar, *Critical Realism*; Collier, *Critical Realism*; Danermark et al, *Explaining Society*; Sayer, *Realism and Social Science*; Archer, *Realist Social Theory*, Archer et al, *Critical Realism*.

Getting there is not because our capacities for searching and thinking are so great. It is because a reality really exists independent of our consciousness of it—in which we live and of which we are a part—that can provide objective points of reference toward which to move, at least when we know how to do that well. (Note, however, that it is *reality* that is objective to us, not our human knowledge of it—objectivity in human perception and knowledge was an Enlightenment fable in which we have no good reason to believe.) We are not simply making it all up as we go along without reference to reality, such that the outcome of one story is as relatively valid as any other. But neither do we have direct, perfect, clear, unmediated, and indubitable knowledge of the truth of reality either (despite some wanting to think they do).

All Christians—both Protestants and Catholics—believe that most central to all of the reality that exists independent of our thinking about it are God the Trinity, Father, Son, and Holy Spirit, involving Jesus Christ as the author, redeemer, and Lord of all creation. Christians also believe that God has given his people inspired scriptures as the word of God written, which witness to Jesus Christ and the truth of the gospel. Our paradigms that we use to make sense of the world are always more or less limited and biasing. Yet the reality of God and his Word, in Christ and written, exist outside of the paradigms. They are not dependent for their *being* on our human consciousness of them—even if our proper *understanding* and *interpretation* of them is highly dependent upon our consciousness of them. They therefore can and do help to guide our fallible understandings of them, often knocking us back in better directions when we begin to go too far off course. And that too spares us from the abyss of relativism. So the search for Christian truth can and might really get us somewhere.

At the same time, we should not allow the reasonable insight of this critical realist reading of Kuhn to knock off of the table what is insightful and important in his model of scientific (and often religious) change. Beliefs, evidence, and arguments do not among humans happen in contexts of independent perceptions unmediated by presuppositions that employ objective evidence that leads to universally common-sense conclusions which only the unreasonable and ill-willed resist. The more complicated reality of inescapable paradigms, incommensurability (rightly understood), theory-laden data, anomalies, paradigm crises, revolutionary science, and paradigm revolutions better describe our real condition—especially perhaps when it comes to Protestant-Catholic dis-agreements about the Christian faith.

I have become persuaded after an immense amount of inquiry, reflection, and conversation that Catholicism offers a better account of Christian truth than American evangelicalism does. That is why I became Catholic—despite being raised in an evangelical world. I do not *know indubitably* that Catholicism's account is better. Nobody does about anything. I do not have slam-dunk evidence to "prove" what I have come to believe. No person does about any tradition, religious or otherwise (at least independently of their evidence-ordering paradigms which make it appear to them that they do).

I am well aware of the limitations and frailty and fallibility of my human perceptions and understanding. I know the issues involved are difficult and complex. I could in the end be wrong. But, having worked it through, I see no good reason to believe that I am wrong. And one has to live as best as one can with the best understanding to which one can arrive. Thanks be to God that, in the end, again, it is his gracious loving-kindness and covenant-keeping in Christ, and not the correctness of our human doctrinal understandings, that save us.

Bibliography

Allert, Craig. *A High View of Scripture?: The Authority of the Bible and the Formation of the New Testament Canon*. Grand Rapids: Baker, 2007.

Anderson, Gary. *Sin: A History*. New Haven: Yale University Press, 2009.

Aquinas, Thomas. *Summa Theologia*. 5 vols. Translated by the Fathers of the English Dominican Province. Notre Dame, IN: Christian Classics, 1981.

Archer, Margaret. *Realist Social Theory*. Cambridge: Cambridge University Press, 1995.

Armstrong, David. *The Catholic Verses: 95 Bible Passages That Confound Protestants*. Manchester, NH: Sophia Institute Press, 2004.

Augustine. *City of God Against the Pagans*. Edited by R. W. Dyson. Cambridge: Cambridge University Press, 1998.

Barrett, David, George Kurian, and Todd Johnson. *World Christian Encyclopedia: A Comparative Survey of Churches and Religions in the Modern World*. New York: Oxford University Press, 2001.

Baumgarten, Al. "The Pharisaic *Paradosis*." *Harvard Theological Review* 80 (1987) 63–77.

Berger, Peter, Bridgette Berger, and Hansfried Kellner. *The Homeless Mind: Modernization and Consciousness*. New York: Vintage, 1974.

Bessenecker, Scott. *The New Friars: The Emerging Movement Serving the World's Poor*. Downer's Grove, IL: InterVarsity, 2006.

Bèze, Théodore de. *Epistola I. Clarissimo et Ornatissimo Viro, D. Andreae Dudito*. In *Epistolarum theologicarum Theodori Bezae Vezelii, liber unus. Secunda editio, ab ipso auctore recognita*. Geneva: Apud Eustathium Vignon, 1575.

Bhaskar, Roy, editor. *Critical Realism: Essential Readings*. New York: Routledge, 1998.

Bonnet, Jules. *Letters of John Calvin*. 2 vols. New York: Burt Franklin, 1858.

Cafardi, Nicholas. "Fraternal Correction: Lessons from the Irish Sex-Abuse Crisis," *Commonweal* 137:5 (2010) 9–11

Calvin, John. "Commentary of Luke 11:27." In *Calvini Opera, Corpus Reformatorum*, 45:348–50. Berlin: Braunschweig-Berlin, 1877.

Catholic Church. *Rite of Christian Initiation of Adults, Study Edition*. Washington, DC: International Commission on English in the Liturgy, 1985.

Chadwick, Owen. *The Secularization of the European Mind in the 19th Century*. Cambridge: Cambridge University Press, 1975.

Collier, Andrew. *Critical Realism: An Introduction to Roy Bhaskar's Philosophy*. London: Verso, 1994.

Colson, Charles, and Richard John Neuhaus. *Your Word Is Truth: A Project of Evangelicals and Catholics Together*. Grand Rapids: Eerdmans, 2002.

Condon, Patrick. "Jeff Anderson: One Man's Crusade Against the Catholic Church." *The Huffington Post*, March 29, 2010. Online: http://www.huffingtonpost.com/2010/03/29/jeff-anderson-one-mans-cr_n_516658.html.

Congregation for the Doctrine of the Faith. "*Mysterium Ecclesiae:* Declaration in Defense of the Catholic Doctrine on the Church Against Certain Errors in the Present Day." June 24, 1973. Online: http://www.vatican.va/roman_curia/congregations/cfaith/documents/rc_con_cfaith_doc_19730705_mysterium-ecclesiae_en.html.

Danermark, Berth, Mats Ekstrom, Liselotte Jakobsen, and Jan ch. Karlsson. *Explaining Society: Critical Realism in the Social Sciences*. New York: Routledge, 2002.

Davey, Monica. "A Frenzied Pace for Lawyers Behind Vatican Suits." *The New York Times* April 27, 2010, A14. Online: http://www.nytimes.com/2010/04/28/us/28lawyer.html.

Duffy, Eamon. *Faith of Our Fathers: Reflections on Catholic Tradition*. New York: Continuum, 2004.

Dulles, Avery Cardinal. *Magisterium: Teacher and Guardian of the Faith*. Naples, FL: Sapientia, 2007.

Eire, Carlos. *A Very Brief History of Eternity*. Princeton: Princeton University Press, 2009.

Emerson, Michael O., and Christian Smith. *Divided by Faith: Evangelical Religion and the Problem of Race in America*. New York: Oxford University Press, 2000.

Emerson, Michael O., with Rodney Woo. *People of the Dream: Multiracial Congregations in the United States*. Princeton: Princeton University Press, 2006.

Eusebius. *The History of the Church*. Baltimore: Harmondsworth, 1965.

Gilgoff, Dan. "One Lawyer Behind Many Allegations of Catholic Church Abuse." CNN. April 26, 2010. Online: http://www.cnn.com/2010/US/04/26/church.abuse.victims.lawyer/index.html.

Gregory, Brad S. *The Unintended Reformation: How a Religious Revolution Secularized Society*. Cambridge, MA: Belknap, 2012.

Hahn, Scott. *Signs of Life: 40 Catholic Customs and Their Biblical Roots*. New York: Doubleday, 2009.

Heelas, Paul, Scott Lash, and Paul Morris, editors. *Detraditionalization: Critical Reflections on Authority and Identity*. Malden, MA: Blackwell, 1996.

Heft, James. "Humble Infallibility." In *Learned Ignorance: An Inquiry into Intellectual Humility among Jews, Christians, and Muslims*, edited by James Heft. New York: Oxford University Press, forthcoming.

————. *John XXII (1316–1334) and Papal Teaching Authority*. Lewiston, NY: Edwin Mellen, 1986.

Hildebrand, Dietrich von. *Liturgy and Personality: The Healing Power of Formal Prayer* London: Longman, 1943.

Hunter, James Davidson. *American Evangelicalism: Conservative Religion in the Quandary of Modernity*. New Brunswick: Rutgers University Press, 1983.

Jenkins, Philip. *The Lost History of Christianity: The Thousand-Year Golden Age of the Church in the Middle East, Africa, and Asia—and How it Died*. New York: HarperOne, 2008.

————. *The New Anti-Catholicism: The Last Acceptable Prejudice*. New York: Oxford University Press, 2004.

Kierkegaard, Søren. *Søren Kierkegaard's Journals and Papers, Volume 1*. Edited by Howard Hong and Edna Hong. Bloomington, IN: Indiana University Press, 1967.

Kilpatrick, Joel. *A Field Guide to Evangelicals & Their Natural Habitat.* New York: HarperCollins, 2006.

Lewis, C. S. *Letters to Malcolm: Chiefly on Prayer.* New York: Harcourt Brace, 1964.

Luther, Martin. *The Works of Martin Luther.* 55 vols. St. Louis: Concordia, 1957.

Lutheran World Federation and the Catholic Church. *Joint Declaration on the Doctrine of* Justification. Online: http://www.vatican.va/roman_curia/pontifical_councils/chrstuni/documents/rc_pc_chrstuni_doc_31101999_cath-luth-joint-declaration_en.html.

MacIntyre, Alasdair. *After Virtue: A Study in Moral Theory.* Notre Dame: University of Notre Dame Press, 1984.

McDonald, H. D. "Word, Word of God, Word of the Lord." In *Evangelical Dictionary of Theology,* edited by Walter Elwell, 1185–88. Grand Rapids: Baker, 1984

McDonald, Lee Martin. *The Formation of the Christian Biblical Canon.* Nashville: Parthenon, 1988.

McGowan, Andrew. "Eating People: Accusations of Cannibalism Against Christians in the Second Century." *Journal of Early Christian Studies* 2:4 (1994) 431–42

McKnight, Scot. "From Wheaton to Rome: Why Evangelicals Become Roman Catholic." *Journal of the Evangelical Theological Society* 45:3 (2002) 451–472.

Melanchthon. *Episolarum.* Lib. XI. No. 4142. In *Corpus Reformatorum,* edited by Carolus Gottlieb Bretschneider, Column 801. Halis Saxonum: C.A. Schwetschke et Filium, 1839. Reprint: New York: Johnson Reprint Corporation.

Newman, John Henry Cardinal. *An Essay on the Development of Christian Doctrine.* Notre Dame, IN: University of Notre Dame Press, 1989.

————. *Mary: The Second Eve.* Ney York: Tan, 2009.

Noll, Mark, with Carolyn Nystrom. *Is the Reformation Over?: An Evangelical Assessment of Contemporary Roman Catholicism.* Grand Rapids: Baker, 2005.

O'Connor, Flannery. *Wise Blood.* New York: Farrar Straus & Giroux, 1990.

Paul IV. "Pastoral Constitution on the Church in the Modern World: *Gaudium et Spes.*" December 7, 1965. Online: http://www.vatican.va/archive/hist_councils/ii_vatican_council/documents/vat-ii_cons_19651207_gaudium-et-spes_en.html.

————. "Decree on Religious Liberty: *Dignitas Humanae.*" December 7, 1965. Online: http://www.vatican.va/archive/hist_councils/ii_vatican_council/documents/vat-ii_decl_19651207_dignitatis-humanae_en.html

————. "Apostolic Exhortation: *Quinque iam anni.*" December 8, 1970.

————. "Dogmatic Constitution on the Doctrine of the Church: *Lumen Gentium.*" November 21, 1964. Online: http://www.vatican.va/archive/hist_councils/ii_vatican_council/documents/vat-ii_const_19641121_lumen-gentium_en.html.

Payton, James. *Getting the Reformation Wrong: Correcting Some Misunderstandings.* Downer's Grove, IL: InterVarsity, 2010.

Peters, Joel. *Scripture Alone?: 21 Reasons to Reject Sola Scriptura.* Rockford, IL: Tan, 1999.

Pontifical Council for the Laity. International Associations of the Faithful: Directory. Online: http://www.va/roman_curia/pontifical_councils/laity/documents/rc_pc_laity_doc_20051114_associazioni_en.html#PREFACE.

Rahner, Hugo. *Our Lady and the Church.* Translated by Sebastian Bullough. Bethesda, MD: Zaccheus, 2005.

Rutba House. *School(s) for Conversion: 12 Marks of a New Monasticism.* New Monastic Library. Eugene, OR: Cascade, 2005.

Sayer, R. Andrew. *Realism and Social Science.* New York: Sage, 2000.

Setzer, Claudia. "Tradition of the Elders." In *The Anchor Bible Dictionary*, edited by David Freedman, 6:638–39. New York: Doubleday, 1992.

Smith, Christian. *The Bible Made Impossible: Why Biblicism Is Not a Truly Evangelical Reading of Scripture*. Grand Rapids: Brazos, 2011.

———. "Evangelicals Behaving Badly with Statistics." *Books & Culture* (January/February, 2007) 11

———. *Moral, Believing Animals: Human Personhood and Culture*. New York: Oxford, 2005.

———. *What is a Person?: Rethinking Humanity, Social Life, and the Moral Good from the Person Up*. Chicago: University of Chicago Press, 2010.

Smith, Christian, and Robert Faris. "Socioeconomic Inequality in the American Religious System—An Update and Assessment." *Journal for the Scientific Study of Religion* 44:1 (2005) 95–104.

Smith, Christian, et al. *American Evangelicalism: Embattled and Thriving*. Chicago: University of Chicago Press, 1998.

Stark, Rodney. *The Rise of Christianity: A Sociologist Reconsiders History*. Princeton: Princeton University Press, 1996.

Sullivan, Francis A. *Creative Fidelity: Weighing and Interpreting Documents of the Magisterium*. 1996. Reprint, Eugene, OR: Wipf & Stock, 2003.

Tappert, Theodore. *The Book of Concord*. St. Louis: Concordia Publishing, 1959.

Thompson, M. B. "Tradition." In *Dictionary of Paul and His Letters*, edited by Gerald Hawthorne and Ralph Martin, 943–45. Downer's Grove, IL: InterVarsity, 1993.

Torrance, T. F. "Karl Barth and the Latin Heresy." *Scottish Journal of Theology* 39 (1986) 465–72.

Trueman, Carl. *Minority Report: Unpopular Thoughts on Everything from Ancient Christianity to Zen-Calvinism*. Fearn, UK: Mentor Imprint, 2008.

United States Conference of Catholic Bishops. *Manual of Indulgences*. Washington, DC: USCCB, 2006.

Vatican Council I: *Dogmatic Constitution: Dei Filius*. 1870. Online: http://www.disf.org/en/documentation/11-VaticanCouncilI.asp.

Weigel, George. *Witness to Hope: The Biography of Pope John Paul II*. New York: Harper Collins, 1999.

Wilson-Hartgrove, Jonathan. *New Monasticism: What It Has to Say to Today's Church*. Grand Rapids: Brazos, 2008;

World Census of Religious Activities. New York: U.N. Information Center, 1989.

Index